THE PRESS
AND FOREIGN POLICY

THE PRESS
AND
FOREIGN POLICY

BERNARD C. COHEN

PRINCETON, NEW JERSEY

PRINCETON UNIVERSITY PRESS

Bernard C. Cohen is a Professor of Political
Science at the University of Wisconsin. His
earlier book is *The Political Process and
Foreign Policy: The Making of the Japa-
nese Peace Settlement* (Princeton University
Press, 1957).

🐝

First PRINCETON PAPERBACK Edition 1965
Second Printing, 1967
Third Printing, 1969
Fourth Printing, 1970

Second Hardcover Printing, 1970

Printed in the United States of America
by Princeton University Press, Princeton, New Jersey

TO THE MEMORY OF MY MOTHER

AND MY FATHER

LENA S. COHEN

LOUIS M. COHEN

ACKNOWLEDGMENTS

THIS STUDY had its antecedents in a research seminar directed jointly by Gabriel A. Almond and me in the Graduate Program of the Woodrow Wilson School of Public and International Affairs at Princeton University in 1953-1954. It is a pleasure to record my gratitude to the students in that enterprise, whose interview data started this project going in my mind and were continuously useful throughout my work: Benjamin H. Belknap, George R. Bent, Jr., Donald R. Bowman, J. Woodford Howard, Jr., Henri G. Jacqz, Theodore Kolderie, Demetrios Pentzopoulos, Americo A. Sardo, Joachim Schumacher, and Stanley Weiss. The insights and ideas that Gabriel Almond shared with me during that seminar are only a token of his continuing contribution to my education; my intellectual debt to him over the years is transparent in the pages that follow, and is very gratefully acknowledged.

The real authors of this book are the large number of very cooperative journalists and government officials who gave so much of their time in interviews and informal discussions; I am beholden to them all, and regret the conventions that consign them to anonymity. None of these persons, I hasten to add, are responsible for the picture of the press in foreign affairs that I have drawn; many of them, I suspect, will disown it, claiming that the picture does not look like this to them. I can only respond that after I put together all their individual experiences and attitudes, this is how it looked to me. I hope that the many friendships I made in the course of my preparation of this book can survive the reading of it.

Three beneficent institutions have made this book possible. I began it as part of the research program of the Center of International Studies at Princeton University. Klaus Knorr, Director of the Center, kindly maintained the Center's interest in the study after I had ceased to be a member of that organization, making possible a further period of interviewing and hastening the completion of the manuscript. I am grateful to him for his help and encouragement, and am pleased to have this book published under the sponsorship of the Center, where the plan for the study matured and which supported the empirical enterprise involved.

Secondly, I want to express my thanks to the Research Committee of the Graduate School of the University of Wisconsin, for research support granted from special funds voted by the Wisconsin State Legislature.

Lastly, additional support of a material, intellectual, and inspirational nature came from a Fellowship year at the Center for Advanced Study in the Behavioral Sciences, during which most of the manuscript first saw the light of day. I cannot imagine a better environment for creative enterprise. Conventional expressions of thanks to Ralph W. Tyler, Preston S. Cutler, and Jane Kielsmeier cannot adequately convey my appreciation for the wonders they work.

My thanks go also to the following people: Warren E. Miller, who was a sympathetic and unfailingly useful critic whenever I carried a tangled problem to his door; Milton Rokeach, who read and reacted to a draft of the early chapters; Bryant Kearl, who has always been ready to discuss this subject with me, and who has given me more encouragement than he realizes; Douglass Cater, whose own work on this subject has set a high standard, and who has been generous in sharing his experiences and his comments; John Hightower, who read the manuscript in the aftermath of the Cuban crisis and gave me abundantly of his time, perspective, and criticism; Nelson W. Polsby, who read the whole manuscript with uncommon generosity and care, and planted red warning flags around many peat bogs; and a nameless reader on behalf of Princeton University Press whose insightful comments and criticisms were equally cautionary. While the last three persons especially have forced me to clarify my thoughts at crucial points, all of the people named here have contributed signally to whatever merit this book possesses; few of them would have written it as I have, however, and they may be relieved to be relieved of any responsibility for it.

Mr. E. G. Burrows, Manager of WUOM at the University of Michigan, kindly made available the scripts for the University of Michigan Broadcasting Service's radio series on "News in Twentieth Century America." Marilyn J. Peterson helped with the interviewing for a brief period. Thomas Harding helped to code the interviews, and Kathleen Holbrook performed many small acts of research assistance that lightened my burden. Jean Pearce typed most of the manuscript, and Alice Stapp the remainder. Jean MacLachlan and Mary Lynne Bird at the Center of International Studies edited the manuscript with a fine insistence on clarity of expression. Sheila Rosenthal assisted me in the preparation of the index.

I am grateful to the editors of *World Politics* for permission to use portions of my review article, "The Present and the Press" (XIII, No. 1, October 1960); and to James N. Rosenau and the Free Press of Glencoe, Inc., respectively editor and publisher of *International Politics and Foreign Policy: A Reader in Research and Theory* (New York, 1961), for permission to revise and extend the substance of an article of mine first published there, entitled "Foreign Policy Makers and the Press."

B.C.C.

Madison, Wisconsin
March 4, 1963

CONTENTS

THE PRESS
AND FOREIGN POLICY

CHAPTER I

A SETTING

ONE HARDLY NEEDS to justify or explain
an interest in the relation between the press and
foreign policy in American political life; indeed, there is
scarcely a person alert and sensitive to foreign affairs who
has not at one time or another pondered some aspect of this
problem. It is surprising, therefore, to discover that this concern has never been translated into systematic explorations of
the relationship of the press and foreign policy, either by
journalists or by students of government and policy.[1] Studies
of the press, of which there are many, deal only tangentially
with foreign policy; and in these studies the impact of news-

[1] As between these two groups, the efforts of the journalists have,
on the record, been more profound than those of the political scientists.
It is significant that of the three most perceptive and insightful books
dealing with the press and public (not even primarily "foreign")
policy in the past forty years, two were by practicing journalists—
Public Opinion (New York, Pelican Books edn., 1946), written in
1922 by Walter Lippmann, and *The Fourth Branch of Government*
(Boston, Houghton Mifflin Co., 1959) by Douglass Cater—and one
by a social scientist—*The Washington Correspondents* (New York,
Harcourt, Brace and Co., 1937) by Leo C. Rosten. (A "retake" of
Rosten's book is in preparation by William L. Rivers, as an outgrowth
of his study of "The Washington Correspondents and Government
Information," unpub. Ph.D. diss., American University, 1960.) But
these are landmarks, exceptional works in a generally arid literature.
Journalists as a group are not well equipped by their training to
address themselves to substantive questions about the press and foreign
policy, questions that at bottom concern the political order and the
political system; while political scientists, who should be equipped
to deal with these subjects, have not explored them with comparable
determination. V. O. Key, Jr., has recently drawn together and discussed the literature and the survey data pertaining to the media,
politics, and the public: *Public Opinion and American Democracy*,
New York, Alfred A. Knopf, 1961, chaps. 14-15. See also the comparable efforts of Robert E. Lane: *Political Life*, Glencoe, Ill., The Free
Press of Glencoe, 1959, chaps. 6, 19.

papers on the political system is more often assumed than investigated. Furthermore, that impact is often expressed simply in terms of the potential for political and economic control that publishers and advertisers possess over the communication that flows to the electorate—or even, in popular argument, in terms of the control that the foreign policy establishment exercises over the information that appears in the press. This is but to say that little effort has been made to establish empirically the nature of the behavior that shapes the content of foreign affairs coverage, or the character of the mechanisms by which that coverage has an effect on the political processes of foreign policy-making. This study is an effort to explore this gap, to identify some of the mechanisms that intervene between the press and American foreign policy.

The question to which we shall address ourselves is this: What are the consequences, for the foreign policy-making environment, of the way that the press defines and performs its job, and of the way that its output is assimilated by the participants in the process? The analysis that follows is organized around three major roles the press may be said to play in the foreign policy field—and, indeed, in almost any field of public policy. First, we shall look at some of the determinants of press coverage of foreign affairs that are more or less under the control of elements within the press itself. We shall be concerned, in Chapters II-IV, with the *press as observer*, and shall focus on some salient aspects of the search for, and the presentation of, foreign policy news. Second, we shall look at some of the uses to which this foreign policy coverage is put by official policy makers. We shall be concerned, in Chapters V-VII, with the *press as participant*, concentrating on the impingements of the press on the policy maker—not only on what it gives him, but on what he contributes to it. Third, we shall look at the uses of the press by non-governmental participants in the process. We will be dealing, in Chapter VIII, with the *press as catalyst*, looking at the ways the press is utilized by the public to satisfy its interests in foreign affairs, and at the implications this role has for foreign policy coverage. These three roles, clearly, are not mutually exclusive, but our choice of them is not merely a matter of convenience. Taken together, they define what the press does in the foreign policy-making process, and they help to focus our attention on the systemic consequences of behaviors involving the press of which the press itself is often unaware.

This formulation of the problem differs fundamentally from the way in which the question is customarily put. The standard normative approach to the political processes involved, which pervades the literature of journalism and the private philosophies of most journalists, is well illustrated by the following statement: "Today and every day the American people must make decisions on which their whole survival may depend. To make sound decisions the people must be informed. For this they depend on the nation's free press. How well is the nation's press doing its essential job?"[2] This argument no doubt strikes a responsive chord in most of us, if only because we have heard it so often. It is, indeed, the classic justification in American democratic thought for a free press, and thus one takes issue with it at one's peril. Yet issue has been taken, in a most compelling way. Both Walter Lippmann and, thirty years later, Gabriel Almond have pointed out that "the American people" as a whole do not make foreign policy decisions affecting their survival, in any direct sense; that there are steep gradations of interest and competence in foreign policy within the American public; and that one's relationship to information—both as consumer and producer—is in large part a function of one's position in this policy-making struc-

[2] "Washington and the Press," No. 2 in *The Press and the People*, a series of television programs produced by WGBH-TV, Boston, Mass.; transcript edited and published by The Fund for the Republic, New York, N.Y.

ture.[3] The obvious truths in their criticism require us, rather belatedly, to ask some further questions: If all the people do not have equal need to be informed, then who *does* "need" to be informed, and in what ways? And how do those people who do make decisions in the foreign policy field use the press as an adjunct to their decision-making? It is only through answers to questions like these that one can tackle meaningfully the question, "How well is the nation's press doing its essential job?" Otherwise, since "the people" in an undifferentiated sense are unlikely ever to attain a high over-all level of information about foreign affairs, we would have to conclude that the press will always do a thoroughly miserable job! A useful critique requires a more realistic criterion than this.

In other words, the requirements for "news" about foreign affairs—i.e., information—are established not by any philosophical conception of limitless need, but rather by the nature of the particular process that makes foreign policy decisions at any period in history. Joseph Mathews has pointed out that two hundred years ago war news was brief and technical, since it was written for a small, specialized group of readers whose needs were met by the prevailing style; today, however, a different political and social interest in warfare has meant a corresponding change in the definition of "war news."[4] Similarly, in the foreign policy field, the prevailing political process defines the contemporary requirements for news; the needs for international news in the early modern European period, for instance, were apparently satisfied by having the representatives of the European banking houses serve as foreign news gatherers.[5] Although this notion compels us to pay attention to the foreign policy-making process, it does not

[3] Lippmann, *op.cit.*; Gabriel A. Almond, *The American People and Foreign Policy*, 2nd edn., New York, Frederick A. Praeger, 1961.

[4] Joseph J. Mathews, *Reporting the Wars*, Minneapolis, University of Minnesota Press, 1957.

[5] *Ibid.*, p. 13.

automatically mean a restrictive conception of foreign policy news; what it does signify, however, is a rather different conception of what constitutes adequate or even exceptional performance by the press in any particular sector of the foreign policy-making process.

If one conceives of the over-all role of the press, then, as providing the knowledge on the basis of which the political process can fashion sound foreign policy decisions, the press might be viewed as a sort of intelligence agent to the process; but of course its significance as an intelligence agent is obviously different in different sectors of the process, depending on the existence of alternative sources of knowledge. If this way of conceiving of the subject requires us to pay some attention to that process itself, it also suggests that we think about the requirements of an effective intelligence service. Without getting deeply involved in that subject, it might be pointed out that there is a requirement not only for factual information, but for theoretical premises and contexts that give meaning to "facts," and for subsequent analysis that draws out their consequences and implications.[6] These, too, will be considered later, as criteria to be used in examining the performance of the press.

The very notion of "the press" has different meanings to different people; it may be interpreted in a general way as including all of the media of mass communication, or it may be defined more specifically as the printed media. We have adopted the latter course here; this study is based very largely on the newspaper press. The reasons for this focus were several: (1) Although nearly as many people seem to get their news about foreign affairs from radio and television as from the newspaper, and may even "believe what they see more than what they read,"[7] this communications behavior is

[6] Cf. Roger Hilsman, Jr., *Strategic Intelligence and National Decisions*, Glencoe, Ill., The Free Press of Glencoe, 1956.

[7] John Tebbel, "What News Does the Public Believe?" *Saturday Review*, March 10, 1962, p. 43.

not uniform across the relevant population. The higher one goes in the formal and informal structures of foreign policy-making in the United States, the more time and attention one finds being paid to the newspaper rather than to radio and television as the important source of foreign affairs news and comment. This is due in part to the greater specialization of newspapers in this subject matter, as compared with other media; in part to the preference for the printed word that is characteristic of persons on higher educational and professional levels; in part to the greater accessibility and time-economy of newspapers in the lives of very busy men. (2) The products of the newspaper press are not so ephemeral as those of radio and television; it is possible to collect them, to study them and compare them at leisure, to know their real authors and to query them about particular choices they have made in the course of their work. (3) Newspaper coverage of foreign affairs not only is more lasting than radio or television coverage—i.e., it sits around for longer periods with multiple chances of being read—but is also more extensive and thorough. A serious radio or television news program carries a far smaller number of words devoted to foreign policy items than does a serious newspaper. (4) Apart from the major networks, which maintain their own news-gathering and editorial staffs, most of the news programs that originate in local stations are put together from the wires of the large news agencies, which are treated here as part of the news-paper press. In other words, much of radio and television news is really indistinguishable from newspaper news. (5) Finally, the news-gathering and editing processes in the radio and tele-vision networks seem to proceed on the same bases and in terms of the same assumptions and in response to the same range of attitudes as the news-gathering and editing processes in the newspaper press. In the course of this study, enough attention was paid to radio, television, and also news magazine personnel to indicate that this is the case; and thus the need for economy in research suggested that the newspaper press was a satisfactory representation of the media of communication so far as our present purposes were concerned.

Newspapers as such are not the major subject of study here, however, but rather the people working for them who are responsible for gathering and interpreting foreign policy news in the United States. Given the small number of foreign policy specialists in the American press, there is no important sampling problem involved. Most of the newspapers in this country have no foreign affairs reporters on their staffs; they draw their foreign affairs news from the wire services or from the sources offered by a few of the newspapers with extensive foreign affairs coverage, like the *New York Times*. This is true even of those newspapers that maintain one- or two-man bureaus in Washington, because the job of such a bureau is to cover the full range of public policy as it is presumed to affect the readers of the paper in question; the chances for specialization in any one substantive area like foreign affairs are minimal. The number of American newspapers that maintain staff specialists in the foreign policy field, and that are known for their foreign affairs coverage, is very small indeed— less than two dozen.[8] About six men cover the State Department for each of the major American news agencies. The problem, then, was not so much how to sample these specialists as how to see as many as possible. Seventy interviews were held, with 62 different people, in two series of interviews; these were mostly with newspaper and news agency correspondents and editors, but there was also a scattering of radio, television, and news magazine reporters on the lists, as well as a few correspondents who had only a tangential responsibility for foreign policy. The first of these sets of

[8] Cf. Theodore E. Kruglak's estimate, in 1955, that only 16 newspapers maintained full-time correspondents in all of Western Europe. (*The Foreign Correspondents: A Study of the Men and Women Reporting for the American Information Media in Western Europe*, Geneva, Librairie E. Droz, 1955, p. 72.)

interviews was undertaken in 1953-1954, under the direction of Gabriel A. Almond and the present author, by a team of two students in the graduate research program of the Woodrow Wilson School of Public and International Affairs at Princeton University. The second series was undertaken by the author between 1958 and 1960, with the help of an assistant for a brief period. The number of foreign policy specialists working on papers in the United States may at times be somewhat greater than the number interviewed, but our list includes those with the widest circulations and the highest reputations. Furthermore, since reporters are not reluctant to express themselves in print on the very subjects that interest us, there is an extensive literature that supplements these interviews.

This is a study of the nature and effects of foreign affairs reporting in the United States rather than of foreign correspondence generally, but the connections between the two are so close that we are not wholly constrained from talking about the larger problem. Most of the foreign affairs specialists working in the United States for American newspapers have served abroad as foreign correspondents at some period in their careers; it was possible, therefore, to draw from their experiences abroad the kinds of data that permit comparison of domestic and international reporting in the foreign policy field. And since a large part of what is properly called "foreign news" is not, strictly speaking, "foreign policy news"—i.e., it does not deal directly with foreign policy or international affairs—foreign policy news of domestic origin looms larger in the total flow of foreign affairs news. The essential similarities between these two classes of reporting are underlined—and even shaped—by the actions of news editors, who make little distinction between them when they put their newspapers together; the origin of the news is of less significance to them than its subject matter.

The world of the foreign policy maker is more difficult to investigate than the world of the foreign affairs reporter, both because of problems of access and because there are so many more people involved. Our efforts here were to see as many people with obvious interests and official responsibilities in the foreign policy field as was possible in the time available. Over 150 interviews were held with persons in staff or policy positions throughout the Executive branch, and in the Congress, and also with former holders of these positions. These interviews, too, were conducted in two series, the first in 1953-1954 by teams of students in the same Woodrow Wilson School graduate research program at Princeton, and the second by the author in 1960.

The interviews with both correspondents and policy officials were held at various times, and under various circumstances and conditions. The questions used were designed to open up the taps of practice, experience, and evaluation to the maximum extent, and so the questions themselves were often modified to meet the circumstances of the interview. The second set of interviews was designed to build upon the experience and the findings of the first set, and so they extended into new directions as well as pursued old themes. The result is a distribution of responses that are immensely revealing and suggestive, but that are most appropriately treated in qualitative rather than quantitative terms. Material from these interviews is used freely in the following chapters, but without attribution, reflecting the confidential nature of the interviews. Direct quotations are taken from the texts of the interviews as they were reconstructed from notes made during and after the sessions. In many cases, especially the lengthier quotations and the more colorful ones, the material quoted represents the actual words used by respondents as captured by shorthand notes during the interviews; in the rest, they represent the interviewer's best efforts to recall the words and reconstruct the sentence structure of the respondents. In any case, the extracts from the interviews are used to illustrate the analytical points being made and to enlarge their possible meanings, and not as conclusive proof of their validity.

We should also make explicit here some of the purposes that we hope this study may serve. In the first place, each passing year pushes foreign policy ever closer to the central concerns of American public policy, as the difficulties and the costs of protecting our national values become greater and greater. As the issues become more clearly those of national survival, we can more readily appreciate the great importance that attaches to the foreign policy choices that we make, and, even more fundamentally, to our prior understanding of what the range of choice looks like. It was to this point that Walter Lippmann addressed himself many years ago when he wrote about the importance of "the pictures in our heads," and said: "To traverse the world men must have maps of the world. Their persistent difficulty is to secure maps on which their own need, or someone else's need, has not sketched in the coast of Bohemia."[9] It is here, in the description of the political environment and the suggestion of the policy alternatives that give the best promise of managing that environment, that we shall find the press playing such an important role in current thinking about foreign policy. This "map-making" function of the press is very easy to overlook, because the newspaper is so much a part of our everyday life, like the morning cup of coffee with which it is intimately associated. It is overlooked also because of a general tendency to regard the news as objective or factual and hence to think of the possible impact of the press largely in terms of editorial persuasions. Yet this map-making function is so central to the real impact of the press in the foreign policy field that a few words of elaboration may be appropriate.

It is a truism, but an important one, that none of us has direct experience with the whole range of international affairs, whatever that range may be. We may know very small parts

9 Lippmann, *op.cit.*, p. 11.

of it at first hand, if we are lucky enough to have been participants in or observers of significant events. But generally the
external world, the world of foreign policy, reaches us—or
those of us who are interested and attentive—via the media
of mass communication, and most importantly via the press.
For most of the foreign policy audience, the really effective
political map of the world—that is to say, their *operational*
map of the world—is drawn by the reporter and the editor,
not by the cartographer. (Latin America, for instance, takes
up a lot of space on the cartographer's map, but it scarcely
exists on the political map delineated by most newspapers in
the United States.) And if we do not see a story in the newspapers (or catch it on radio or television), it effectively has
not happened so far as we are concerned.

This is to say, then, that the press is significantly more
than a purveyor of information and opinion. It may not be
successful much of the time in telling people what to think,
but it is stunningly successful in telling its readers what to
think *about*. And it follows from this that the world looks
different to different people, depending not only on their personal interests, but also on the map that is drawn for them
by the writers, editors, and publishers of the papers they read.
Perhaps the notion of a map is too confining, for it does not
suggest the full range of the political phenomena that are
conveyed by the press. It is, more properly, an atlas of places,
personages, situations, and events; and to the extent that the
press even discusses the ideas that men have for coping with
the day's ration of problems, it is an atlas of policy possibilities,
alternatives, choices. The editor may believe he is only printing the things that people want to read, but he is thereby
putting a claim on their attention, powerfully determining
what they will be thinking about, and talking about, until
the next wave laps their shore.

The significance of this may be more patent in the case of
a country like the Soviet Union, where images of reality are

shaped by the careful choices of a government and a ruling party, than in the case of a free society, where reality is thought to have an objective meaning that is simply made manifest by the free choices of a free press. But to say that there may be fewer constraints on our vision of reality than on the Soviets' is not to say that there are no constraints on our side; part of our problem, and one of the purposes of this book, is to gain a better understanding of the substance, the nature, of these constraints. But for the moment it may be enough to repeat that whatever factors help to establish the effective parameters of choice in foreign policy will help also to determine our future as a nation. The very issue of survival, and the instability of power relations in the world, pose such a challenge to our policy ingenuity that constraints of any kind ought at least to be fully understood and, where possible, pushed farther and farther back.

In the daily trial of wits and power that has come to define so much of our foreign policy in recent years, we find another reason for looking more systematically at the press and its policy impact: concern over the asymmetries that the free press in Western countries introduces into the political bargaining processes between East and West. The point is often made that the news-gathering behavior of the press in Western countries gives away the West's diplomatic bargaining positions to the Soviet side, while the Soviets come to such encounters with "a concealed hand of cards."[10] In part this is a structural problem in a democratic society, and it might be argued that the cure for it is very much like the disease—that is, the loss of basic liberties of expression.[11] (On the

[10] A good example, from which this phrase is taken, is James Reston's column in the *New York Times*, September 15, 1961.

[11] Reporters, in fact, are the very first to object on those occasions when American policy makers *do* close up their hand to improve their bargaining posture. *Vide* the action of 13 reporters covering the State Department in formally protesting a Departmental rule, instituted on November 2, 1962, after the Cuban embargo was established, requiring official cognizance of all substantive discussions with reporters. (UPI

other hand, one can argue that, *ceteris paribus*, self-imposed restraints are to be preferred to constraints imposed by others.) But it is also something less fundamental than a problem in the very structure of democratic organization; it is a consequence of the attitudes and customary modes of procedure of the gentlemen of the press in these countries, and here it is possible to investigate causes and suggest alternatives that fall within the limits of our system of political values.

Still another purpose in exploring the problem of the press and foreign policy lies in the hope that it will advance our understanding of the way the American political system operates to produce foreign policy. This may seem, at first glance, to be less spectacular than the public-policy purposes noted above, but in fact they are very closely related, for the impact of the press on the foreign policy choices we make is itself an important dimension of the foreign policy-making process. In a larger sense, the press as a whole is a vital component in this process, and the more we know about that component, the better we can comprehend the whole web of relationships that comprise our system for making foreign policy. And, to the extent that foreign policy is only a partially differentiated variety of public policy, the more we can learn about our more inclusive political system itself.

Almond has speculated in a seminal way on the vital nature of political communication in any political system.[12] Even among modern political systems, it is important to note that the purposes, direction, contents, and even effects of political messages depend greatly on how political power is organized. Where political power is highly centralized, for example, the media of communication tend to become instruments of that

dispatch, dated November 15, published in the *New York Times*, November 16, 1962.)

[12] Gabriel A. Almond, "Introduction: A Functional Approach to Comparative Politics," in Gabriel A. Almond and James S. Coleman, eds., *The Politics of the Developing Areas*, Princeton, Princeton University Press, 1960, esp. pp. 45-52.

centralization; the uses to which the media are put reflect both the needs of the ruling group in maintaining their power and advancing their policies, and also the lines of control that run from the political center out or down to subordinate units. The media, in other words, are important devices in sustaining both the constitutional and political position at the center.

In the United States, however, where political power is widely dispersed, the media serve a different set of purposes. Here the media may be used to sustain the position of any holder of power anywhere in the system; they may be used as effectively against an administration as on behalf of one, as the late Senator McCarthy of Wisconsin demonstrated so clearly. Further, the institutional separation of power in the American political system has to be counterbalanced in some way if national policy is to be made with any vigor; and the media—themselves one of the institutions that are kept separate from the governmental sources of power—are one of the devices that keep the separate parts of the political system in touch with each other, and able to act in response to a more or less common set of political stimuli.

The media of communication are, of course, not the only institutions that perform the communication function in the American political system. Nor are they the only instruments facilitating political accommodation. Indeed, one aspect of the wide sharing of political power in the United States is the wide exercise of the whole range of political functions, however one chooses to define them. Nevertheless, there is specialization in the process; just as it is generally acknowledged by participants that initiative in foreign policy rests chiefly in the Executive, so is foreign policy communication generally regarded as the function chiefly of the media. Thus there is reason to hope that this inquiry into the relation between the press and foreign policy will open up new vistas in our understanding of the communication function in our political system.

CHAPTER II

THE REPORTER AND HIS WORK

———•◦•———

◗   T H E   W E B of interaction that connects the press, the policy maker, and the external environment is very closely woven; one has to cut into it somewhere, and we have chosen to begin by focusing on the press and on the way it gathers and produces foreign policy news. As a first step, we shall look at the foreign affairs reporter himself, being especially interested in how he views the processes of democratic foreign policy-making, and in the way he conceives the function of the press in those processes. We do this because it seems useful to preface our inquiry into what the foreign affairs correspondents *actually* do in the course of their work, with a statement of what they *believe* they are doing, or should be doing. Reporters in this field are keenly aware that there is a social significance to their work, even if they have a difficult time defining it precisely; their image of appropriate behavior may thus be taken as a guide—equally imprecise—to what they try to do in their daily reporting stint.

What is the reporter like who specializes in foreign affairs coverage? If the old image of the reporter as a heavy-drinking, hard-bitten cynic, interested only in sensational scoops, still persists in some realms, it has no place here. The foreign affairs specialist among Washington correspondents is a cosmopolitan among cosmopolitans, a man in gray flannel who ranks very high in the hierarchy of reporters. A close observer of the Washington press corps concludes that State Department reporters, along with Congressional reporters, are "the head groups among the Washington press."

The typical reporter is a college-educated man; though "college" sometimes means a school of journalism, courses in the social science curriculum are nevertheless common in his background. The significance of a college education to reporters in this field is apparent from the sensitivity on the matter of the few who did not attend college. This educational pattern is also found among Washington correspondents as a whole, as well as among American correspondents abroad. A study in the early 1960's reports that about 93 per cent of the Washington correspondents attended college and 81 per cent have college degrees; about 31 per cent did graduate work and nearly 20 per cent earned graduate degrees.[1] In the mid-1950's, a study of foreign correspondents reporting for American media in Western Europe revealed that 73 per cent of the Americans in this corps of correspondents had Bachelor's degrees, "slightly less" than 10 per cent had Master's degrees, and 2 per cent had Ph.D. degrees. Seventeen per cent had done graduate-level work while they were employed as correspondents. "A majority of today's foreign correspondents concentrated their college studies in the fields of political science, economics, history, or international relations. This concentration on the social sciences is even more pronounced in advanced degrees and graduate studies."[2]

The foreign affairs reporter in Washington is also a man of long experience in the field of international affairs. Only a few have been reporting foreign affairs for less than half a dozen years; the mean is closer to 15 or 20 years. And a few of the reporters, including some newcomers, have had governmental experience in the foreign affairs field, which adds to their specialization in the subject matter. In addition, almost all of these reporters have been foreign correspondents at some point in their careers, or have had significant foreign reporting experience while stationed in this country, or have

[1] William L. Rivers, "The Correspondents After Twenty-five Years," *Columbia Journalism Review*, I, No. 1, Spring 1962, p. 6. Cf. also William L. Rivers, "The Washington Correspondents and Government Information."

[2] Theodore E. Kruglak, *The Foreign Correspondents*, pp. 48-49.

lived or worked abroad extensively before they took up foreign affairs reporting. These patterns of education and career specialization reinforce the common description among these reporters that they are, as a group, intensely interested in the subject matter that they write about, and on the whole well-informed with respect to it. By most accounts, furthermore, the working reporter in the foreign affairs field in Washington is conscious of the potential impact of what he writes, and "he does not want to create any more trouble [in foreign policy] than already exists." Many foreign policy officials who deal directly with the press would define "trouble" differently, reflecting their own potful of difficulties, and thus they might not concur with the phrasing of this particular self-evaluation. Nevertheless, in terms of their manifest behavior, they obviously do trust the foreign affairs reporter to behave with substantial discretion as he moves with great freedom in a politically sensitive area. Even though the reporter and the official may not have the same perspective on the functions of the press in reporting foreign affairs, or agree on the nature of desirable policy, the freedom and the trust suggest the stature of the reporter in the political milieu in which he works. It should go without saying, of course, that there are deviations from this norm, and that individual reporters violate the rules of the game from time to time; but the very fact that "violations" can be observed, and described, and even accounted for reinforces the normative code of behavior for reporters who cover foreign affairs.

☉ The Reporter's Conceptions of His Roles

A reporter of public affairs lives a bifurcated professional existence: he is a reporter of the passing scene, yet he is also a part of that scene, in ways that he does not always understand or accept.[3] This duality is evident in almost every phase of his work. He holds two sets of conceptions of the role that

[3] Cf. Douglass Cater, *The Fourth Branch of Government*, p. 7.

the press plays, or should play, in the foreign policy-making process—one set involving him only as a neutral reporter, providing information that enables others to play a part in the fashioning of policy; and another set that defines his active participation in the policy-making process. The first set of role conceptions relates the reporter chiefly toward the public participants in the process; while the second set relates him toward the official policy-making level. These two types of self-images will no doubt be familiar to most readers, since they are both enshrined in our political and constitutional history respecting the nature and the guarantees of a free press in the nascent American democracy.[4] What is significant here is that these two sets of conceptions are not equally reflected in the formal or overt ideology of the reporter (as distinct from that of the editor or the editorial page). The reporter's formal view of the over-all process of foreign policy-making stresses his role as recorder of the passing scene—as servant to the other participants—to the near-exclusion of his role as an active participant in his own right. As a result, his role as a participant more often than not gets "bootlegged" into the reporter's view of the process, accompanied by many of the disadvantages that attend on surreptitious indulgence. Like illicit liquor, the "bootlegged" role is found everywhere, and most reporters know it is there; but political, social, and ideological conventions make it inappropriate to bring it out into the open, where its properties and its impacts can be explicitly discussed and evaluated.

Formal Views of the Process. Each reporter has his own interpretation of the American foreign policy process, and he expresses that interpretation in an individual style. Yet there is a pattern that incorporates the views of most reporters. In this pattern, foreign policy originates in the Executive branch of government, somewhere in the White House, the

[4] Cf. Bernard A. Weisberger, *The American Newspaperman*, Chicago, University of Chicago Press, 1961.

Department of State, or the Department of Defense. From the Executive branch it moves to the press, or is picked up by the press, which has the task of reporting it to the public. After careful deliberation the public makes up its mind on the issues and communicates its preferences to the Congress. The Congress then is in a position to act on the issues, or to react to them by letting the Executive branch know what it thinks. The only significant variation in this pattern excludes the stage of public consideration; in this view the press reports directly to the Congress, which then is in a position to act or react as before. In each of these patterns, the press occupies the strategic center, from which it neutrally transmits the facts about foreign policy from one part of the political system to another.

Some reporters will expressly describe one or the other of these patterns in its entirety; others will describe only a segment, leaving the rest implicit. A few will express alternative conceptions of the process, which incorporate a more active role for the press. Several correspondents, for example, see the flow as moving from the Executive to the press, where there may be a side dialogue with the embassies, and then back to the Executive branch again. But the large majority of correspondents appear to be comfortable with one of the former descriptions of the foreign policy process, finding in it a congenial ideology of the press in American society.

The dominant view of the process, in addition to casting the press as a neutral transmission belt, so to speak, stresses the importance of the Executive branch over the Congress in the making of foreign policy. The Executive is the initiator of policy proposals, and the Congress reacts to them, taking into consideration public feelings as they may have been shaped by press coverage. There is additional evidence that the foreign affairs correspondents assign a special position to the Executive branch in this process. Despite the criticism that is directed toward particular individuals or offices in the State

Department, and the general feeling that the State Department is "always pushing angles" or "selling something," these reporters will defend the Executive's position against an increase in the foreign relations power of Congress, like that contemplated in the Bricker Amendment in the mid-1950's, on the grounds that such a move would cripple American foreign policy.[5] Furthermore, despite his professional interest in storming the walls of secrecy that surround the operations of government, virtually every foreign affairs reporter acknowledges at least in an abstract way the need for secrecy in the conduct of international diplomacy and of national security matters. He is likely to point out that there are some important judgments to be made by the reporter about the relative priorities of secrecy as against the public's "need to know"; yet the Executive's right to conduct some of its operations in private, and to let the press and thus the rest of the political system in "after the event," is freely granted, both in principle and in practice.

Role Conceptions: The Neutral Reporter

The reporter's formal ideology of the press as the neutral link between the active participants in the policy-making process finds expression in a set of roles that have as their aim the more effective performance of the linkage function. In other words, these images of the reporter's role are designed to make the formal process work better, by improving the capacity of the political participants to act constructively in the roles that this view of the process assigns to them.

The Press as Informer. It is impossible to escape the conclusion that most reporters in the foreign affairs field under-

[5] Cf. also the statements by Alexander F. Jones, editor of the *Syracuse Herald-Journal*, at the 1960 meetings of the American Society of Newspaper Editors: "My interest is in having better reporting and better newspaper stories, particularly so that the President of the United States will have a chance to make his views known." (*Problems of Journalism*, Proceedings of the American Society of Newspaper Editors, 1960, p. 219.)

stand their primary role and their chief responsibility to be the providing of factual information about foreign affairs, as it originates abroad and in Washington, to the American people. As a wire service correspondent put it, "The reporter is the eyes and ears of the public, and . . . if he cannot translate what he sees and finds out in popular terms, then the whole purpose of the reportorial process is lost." This is not always the role that most interests the correspondents, or that they spend the most time on, but it comes to the fore consistently and repeatedly as the "fundamental," "essential" job of the press in the foreign policy field.

The most common form in which this function is expressed contains an explicit statement of the significance of information to the public: the press gives factual information so that people can make their own judgments about the issues of foreign policy. This is a restatement of what might be called the classic philosophy or ideology of the free press in the United States, which is built around the notion that it is the people who make decisions in a democratic society. We shall have more to say about this in a later chapter; it is significant here in that it provides the press with its most obvious "responsibility," which is to supply the information on which those popular decisions are based. And, by implication, the better the job that the press does in providing the information, the better the capacity of the people to make intelligent judgments. Here are some of the ways in which this viewpoint is presented. First, by the foreign news editor of a chain of papers: "Think of our postwar programs of foreign aid. Here is a basic policy, the like of which has never existed before. And it receives public support that springs from a generous and wise self-interest. This public enlightenment, this education, is largely received through the communications media, as a result of the day-to-day factual reporting." And by a reporter-columnist: "The Bermuda Conference did not get all the public support it might have because of the restrictions [on the press]. The public has got to have information or its judgment is hurt. . . . Papers give information to help people's judgment."

Notice, also, how the public's judgment, soundly based, is translated to mean public support for foreign policy actions that are made at the governmental level. The implications are several. The correspondents apparently recognize that the public does not "make decisions" in foreign policy matters, but rather reacts in a variety of ways to decisions that are made elsewhere. And secondly, the notion of public support restates the reporter's orientation to the Executive branch as the originator and initiator of foreign policies that—other things being equal, i.e., the reporters themselves having no objections—merit public support as the prerequisite to national support.

The image of the reporter as a supplier of factual information is implicitly an image of the press as an educator. The "education" can have different connotations, here as elsewhere; and one frequently encounters among foreign affairs reporters an explicit extension of this role of the reporter to include informing people on what they *ought* to know.[6] In this view the press's responsibility toward the public does not stop at the "neutral" transmission of factual information about what is going on in the government—we are not asking here whether really "neutral" transmission is humanly achievable, but simply describing the elements of the reporter's ideology—but includes a more active determination of what kinds of factual information, or how much of it, is necessary or desirable for people's judgments to develop in "proper" directions. To say, as one columnist has said, "If it is true that only 40 per cent of the people know who Malenkov is [at a time when Malenkov was Soviet Premier], the press is not doing as good a job as it should," is to insert a standard by which

[6] One finds this outlook among non-media people who are also trying to "inform the public" on foreign affairs. Cf. Bernard C. Cohen, *Citizen Education in World Affairs*, Princeton University, Center of International Studies, 1953.

newsmen themselves can judge whether or not the job of transmitting information constitutes an adequate performance of the educational role. Fred S. Siebert has described this educational imperative in terms of what is called the "social responsibility" philosophy of the press: "The advocates of the theory of social responsibility . . . retain the democratic tradition that the public ultimately makes decisions, and they charge the press with the duty of informing and guiding the public in an intelligent discussion. The press has the duty to keep the public alert and not to divert its attention or its energies to the irrelevant or the meaningless."[7] Clearly, notions such as "to divert," or "irrelevant," or "meaningless" leave no doubt that the conception of the press as educator contains value premises and policy preferences that are not explicit in the conception of the press as informer, and that seem inconsistent with the view of the press as a neutral link between active participants in the process. The inconsistency is but another expression of the dual conception the reporter has of his professional task.

The Press as Interpreter. Next to the purveying of information and education as the basic role of the press in the area of foreign affairs stands interpretation. Notwithstanding that interpretation implies judgments about the significance of events, it is widely held by reporters to be a necessary part of the news dissemination process; it thus fits into a neutral conception of the press. This neutral interpretation of "interpretation" is most apparent in those cases where it is regarded as an essential component of the news itself—for example, where it is even referred to as "interpretive news."[8] But it is

[7] Fred S. Siebert, "The Authoritarian Theory of the Press," in Fred S. Siebert, Theodore Peterson, and Wilbur Schramm, *Four Theories of the Press*, Urbana, Ill., University of Illinois Press, 1956, p. 29.

[8] Cf. Charles Siepmann, Professor of Journalism, N.Y.U.: "News is not, in these days, in this world, it cannot possibly be the mere reporting of facts and of events. It's what these events are fraught with in terms of their implications which brings news into the area of interpre-

also in evidence in the more common distinction between interpretation, or explanation, on the one hand, and editorializing, or the passing of preferential judgments, on the other. A wire service reporter put it as follows: "Most reporters feel that interpretation is part of their job, but they distinguish it from editorializing, which is judging whether it is good or bad. But whether we get a bloody nose in any particular international encounter is a reportable interpretation." In other words, the meaning of particular events is a necessary adjunct of the news about those events and a justifiable function of the news columns of the newspaper, so long as the reporter refrains from expressing his own judgments about whether those events were good or bad, should have taken place, and so forth. Another reporter, highly regarded by his fellow reporters for his output despite his comparative inexperience in the foreign affairs field, said: "My instructions are not to write a story unless I can put into it some analysis and interpretation. The only time I got bawled out was when I stuck to straight news-reporting for once. I have to interpret, explain, advance things. Often after a press conference I will start off with an interpretive lead, about the significance or meaning of events; sometimes I am wrong and sometimes right."

Two sets of reasons emerge from the reporters' discussions of their interpretive role that explain why interpretation is felt to be an integral part of the reporting process (if not of the very notion of news itself). First, there is the nearly universal feeling that the subject matter of foreign affairs has become so complex that most people do not understand the news unless the bare facts about developments are clothed

---

tation. . . . I believe that interpretation of the news is an essential component of any news if it is to be understood and to have meaning for listeners." (The University of Michigan Broadcasting Service, *News in Twentieth Century America*: "The News Media: Competition and Change #4"; this series of broadcasts is cited hereinafter as UMBS series.)

with explicit statements of their significance. "During recent years," said a columnist, "news has gotten so complex that mere reporting isn't good any more. You have to have an analysis." Another reporter-analyst put it almost the same way: "Foreign policy is exceedingly complex. We get the news from all the wire services here . . . and our problem really is, 'what does it all mean?'. . . Our job is to perceive and point out the main directions of policy, or even the failings of policy." This last phrase, incidentally, suggests how close the interpretive role can come, through the making of judgments of significance, to an active conception of the press as a critic of government.

Second, the interpretive role has been "forced" on the press not only by the growing complexity of foreign policy and the leading role of the United States in international affairs, but also by technological developments in the mass communications field in recent decades. Radio and television have taken the newspaper's place as the first purveyor of spot news; once a commonplace, the "extra" edition of the newspaper, bearing tidings that came too late to make the regular edition, has all but disappeared from American journalism. The early announcements of such events are now made through the electronic media, and the newspaper, in the words of a leading columnist, "must now do more in the way of explanation of the process and development of policies, and the meanings of these developments."

We might note, in passing, that it has been relatively easy for reporters to accommodate the interpretive role to what we are calling here the neutral conception of the press's function. The developments we have just observed all came about during the same time period. The importance of foreign policy in American political life, and the complexity of the subject, have become more apparent over the last generation, which is also the period of the technological revolution in the communications media. It is also the period that gave birth to the news magazines, with their explicit interpretation of foreign affairs. In these circumstances, the explanation of the background and the apparent significance of events virtually became part of the newly important signaling of the events themselves, without causing the "objective" journalist any great crisis of conscience over the narrow boundary between interpretation and subjective judgment.

The Press as an Instrument of Government. The more "neutral" the press is—that is, the more it tries faithfully to transmit a record of "what transpires" (including therein the policy statements of officials) and the more constrained it feels about making judgments concerning the meaning or importance of "what transpires"—the more easily it lends itself to the uses of others, and particularly to public officials whom reporters have come to regard as prime sources of news merely by virtue of their positions in government. This is unquestionably the case at the Presidential level; the President is always "news," and his ability to command the media of communication to advance his policy views is obvious. This is equally true, though less apparent, at lower levels in the foreign policy-making structures of the government.[9] But being "used" in this fashion, like being "had," or being "played for a sucker," has undesirable connotations, and one would expect that high-status reporters, conscious and proud of their position in an independent press, would reject any suggestions that they could be so manipulated. Hence the attitudes of reporters toward being used as an instrument of government, or on behalf of a particular political segment within the government, provide a revealing measure of how important the neutral role is to them—how central the informative and explanatory-interpretive functions are in their ideologies.

There is, significantly, a very widespread appreciation on the part of the correspondents of the fact that the Executive branch of the government, and especially the State Depart-

[9] Cf. Cater, *op.cit.*, esp. pp. 106-11.

ment, can, in the words of a reporter who subsequently crossed the line into officialdom, "play on the press as you would on a piano." A writer for a weekly news magazine concluded, "the press hates to be used, but I guess that is the simplest and most honest way of describing what happens." The process is not only understood; it is generally accepted as a fact of the reporter's life. As a syndicated columnist put it, "If you have a policy, you have something to sell that makes a good story for a reporter." The forms of "being used" are widely recognized and freely described by these correspondents. They include the formal as well as the informal and background contacts between press and policy makers, in the course of which stories are "floated," or particular viewpoints stated— such as press conference statements; private background dinners given by a group of correspondents for an official, of the kind that Secretary Dulles used to encourage from time to time; talks at the National Press Club, or the Overseas Writers Club, or luncheon discussions with one of the many informal groups of reporters in Washington that are organized for this very purpose. The news agency men may grumble and call it "propaganda," but they dutifully report as "hard news" most of what the State Department News Officer offers them by way of official Departmental statements at his noon briefings.

These practices are so widespread among foreign policy correspondents in Washington that one may even question the extent to which the press "hates to be used." There are some reporters who go so far as to claim that the press "wants to be used," and the evidence seems on balance to support their argument—the important issue being whether there is "news" to be had, not who is using whom in the process. There are even reporters who describe with pride how the press has been used by the government (sometimes out of an identity or congruence of policy preferences, to be sure, rather than by the policy makers' taking advantage of the press's attachment to neutrality) on behalf of such policies as the Marshall Plan, or the effort to stop the postwar rush to demobilize, or "the great need [in the early postwar months] to correct the American public's wartime delusions about the character and purposes of their former Russian ally. . . ."[10] A small number of the more senior correspondents were the only ones to protest their independence and to announce their refusal to let an administration "play games with us"; but even these correspondents—or, perhaps more accurately, especially these correspondents—are to be found at private background sessions with high officials, or in comparable postures.[11]

In sum, then, the pressure on the correspondent to report "obvious" news seems more compelling to him than the fear of being "used" by policy makers to serve their official or personal ends. This seems to confirm the operational importance to him of the concepts of objectivity and neutrality, and of the particular roles that embody those images. Lest one feel, from this, that the foreign affairs reporter is victimized as a result of his attachment to this portion of his ideology, however, we shall note in the following sections that there is reciprocity in "using" others, and that the reporter can advance some of *his* policy or personal goals, too, by capitalizing on the "newsworthiness" of policy-making officials. Obviously, of course, it all comes to rest on the prevailing understandings—not really definitions—of what constitutes news.

[10] Joseph and Stewart Alsop, *The Reporter's Trade*, New York, Reynal and Co., 1958, p. 15. Max Frankel, writing in the *New York Times* about reporters' unhappiness with the Administration's restrictive news policy during the Cuban crisis in November 1962, observed that "Three weeks ago, while the country stood at the brink of war, the Washington press corps not only cheered the President's clear definition of the issues and objectives, but also acquiesced often in some transparent attempts to manage the news as part of the nation's policy." ("Kennedy vs. the Press," *New York Times*, November 19, 1962.)

[11] Cf. Joseph Kraft's description of how, when "skillfully handled, Reston can be used." ("Washington's Most Powerful Reporter," *Esquire*, November 1958, pp. 123-26.)

○ Role Conceptions: The Reporter as Participant

In the particular roles that define the press as a neutral observer, the press can be said to be a handmaiden to the three branches of our constitutional government, bringing them into closer communication and contact, and facilitating their interaction in the service of policy-making. But in the roles that define the press as itself an active participant in the foreign policy-making process, the press may conveniently be viewed as an extra-constitutional "fourth branch of government."[12] If one needs, at this late date, any excuse for applying this label to the press and not to all of the other manifestations of public participation in foreign policy-making, it can perhaps be found in the continuous and intimate interaction that takes place between the press and the other institutions of government, as distinguished from the intermittent and politically limited or segmented contacts that characterize interest group or individual participation in policy-making.[13] But one suspects that the label, as cultivated by reporters, is meant not simply to describe differences in overt behavior between themselves and other parts of the public, but to assert a higher status for the press than for any other manifestation of public opinion in foreign policy-making. The reporters seem to see themselves as in *competition* with interest groups and other expressions of public opinion. This is suggested by the nature of the participant roles that the reporters distinguish for themselves, which parallel the roles that are commonly ascribed to interest groups in modern political systems;[14] and

[12] Cf. Cater, *op.cit.*

[13] See, in this connection, Gabriel A. Almond, *The American People and Foreign Policy*; and Bernard C. Cohen, *The Political Process and Foreign Policy: The Making of the Japanese Peace Settlement*, Princeton, Princeton University Press, 1957, esp. chaps. 4 and 5.

[14] See David B. Truman, *The Governmental Process: Political Interests and Public Opinion*, New York, Alfred A. Knopf, 1951; and Gabriel A. Almond, rapporteur, "A Comparative Study of Interest Groups in the Political Process," *American Political Science Review*, LII, No. 1, March 1958, pp. 270-82.

by the hostility, laced with contempt, that reporters express toward the interest groups they perceive operating in the foreign policy field—a hostility that is reflected in the omission of interest groups from their descriptions of how the foreign policy process works. There are four participant roles that we can distinguish as important components in the foreign affairs reporter's ideology, although there are, of course, some common elements among them.

The Press as Representative of the Public. A recurrent theme in the statements of correspondents is that the press is the voice of the public in matters like foreign affairs—the people's representative in posing to officers of government the kinds of questions that hold them to account for the exercise of their public trust, and thus their representative in fighting the daily battle to protect democracy. The argument is well stated by Theodore Peterson: "As newsmen became imbued with a sense of responsibility, they contended that the public had a right of access to information, had a basic right to be informed, and that the press was the agent of the public in breaking down barriers to the free flow of news."[15]

The representative role is spelled out in several different ways, reflecting some of the variety of meanings in the concept of representation. Some reporters observe that, so far as the President and many others in the government are concerned, what they hear from newspapermen, or what they read in the newspapers, constitutes the most important element in their universe of public opinion as it bears on foreign policy. In other words, the press *is* public opinion, and thus represents it manifestly or directly. Others state that an important virtue of the press conference is that it provides an institutional means "by which the public gets its questions asked." In this sense, the press speaks for a larger public that does not have the reporters' opportunities to interrogate officials. An editor-

[15] "The Social Responsibility Theory of the Press," in Siebert, Peterson, and Schramm, *op.cit.*, p. 91.

writer elaborated this when he spoke of public opinion as expressing itself directly on election day, and letting the press speak for it "between elections and on specific issues." And a columnist refined the notion still further, claiming that the press "represents the upper 25 per cent, the interested part of the people," thus defining representation in terms of a particular constituency within the general public.

These different conceptions of the press as a representative of the public are of general ideological import, for they add up to a justification of press *activity* and *participation* in the daily round of political discourse on the grounds that it, the press, is performing a political function that is sanctioned by classic democratic philosophy, and by modern interpretations of how democratic participation actually takes shape in the foreign policy field.[16] But it is more than an apologetic justification; it is rather a liberating conception—a Burkean viewpoint that frees newsmen to pursue their own interpretation of the public interest in foreign policy. Since the press speaks for the public, and is even recognized as an expression of public opinion in its own right, then "Where the people are sovereign, the press is king."

The Press as Critic of Government. The critical role of a free press in a free society has a long and honorable history. The press, in what is called the libertarian philosophy, "was charged with the duty of keeping government from overstepping its bounds. In the words of Jefferson, it was to provide that check on government which no other institution could provide."[17] The role has high priority for newsmen of today, despite both the objective and the subjective changes that have taken place in the relation of the press to the political and social system, and that have given rise to a "social responsibility" philosophy of the press. Some current formulations

[16] For example, Walter Lippmann, *Public Opinion*, and Almond, *The American People and Foreign Policy.*

[17] Fred S. Siebert, "The Libertarian Theory of the Press," in Siebert, Peterson, and Schramm, *op.cit.*, p. 51.

of this critical function show an unbroken tie with Jefferson. A leading news agency reporter insisted that "It is one of the tasks of the press to point out what the government does wrong." And a reporter for a midwestern newspaper phrased his "definite philosophy" this way: "We are the fourth estate, and it is our duty to monitor—to watch and interpret—what our government does. We are to have our own definite ideas, and to express our opinions on what the government does."

The role of the press as a critic in the foreign policy field is described and evaluated in positive terms by virtually all of the foreign affairs writers and analysts. There is about as much unanimity with respect to this role as there is concerning the informative role. But while there is consensus that "We are to express our opinions on what the government does," there is ambiguity, as well as some apparent differences in viewpoint, as to *where* such criticism should be expressed. A few reporters try to maintain a rigid distinction between news and views, arguing, a little mechanically it seems, that "Criticism should come only on the editorial page—not in the news columns." Somewhat more common is an identification of "news" and "criticism" that permits the reporter to handle criticism in his news stories with a free conscience. This occurs in two different ways. The reporter can interpret his critical responsibility directly, so that a critique is by definition "news"; for example, "The fundamental job of the newspaper is to check on governmental operations and to report its findings as objectively as possible." Or the reporter can perform the critical task at one remove, by reporting as news the political criticisms of other people—including other newspapers and reporters. Thus, in discussing a series of articles criticizing the Eisenhower Administration's handling of the Point Four program, a reporter commented, "It was not a news story in the conventional sense, but there is nevertheless the *fact* of this discontent [among officials in the program], and the *fact* of the reaction of the church groups, and the *fact* of the decline in importance and the change in character of the Point Four program." Another, and perhaps classic, example is the *New York Times* story, carried on the front page, reporting that a high proportion of the mail coming into the State Department was critical of the Department's handling of the Quemoy issue; although the story itself was apparently meant by the reporter to be a straight news story rather than an essay in criticism, its front-page treatment and the prompt rebuttal given it by the Vice President made the reporter's intentions irrelevant.

"Criticism" is a subtle concept, especially when it travels under the protection of an unassailable democratic philosophy; hence it is important to point out two major sets of meanings that are incorporated in the reporter's understanding of this role. At one level, the reporter defines his critical role in classic terms, as a watchdog against arbitrary positions, procedures, or practices within the governmental foreign policy-making structure. There are a surprising number of correspondents who seem to agree with the Alsops' dictum: "In a democratic society especially, unwatched politicians are always untrustworthy politicians."[18] And what is true of politicians is even more true of appointed officials. A correspondent stated the matter this way: "Who made the country conscious of the implications of the Harry Dexter White case? The FBI chief says this man isn't fit for a high government post—we never know why, or who says so, or what the proof is. Hoover sounds fine to the people—they are inclined to swallow his stuff—but hell, we are talking about America! These implications have got to be made clear [i.e., by the press]." On another level, the reporter defines his role as critic not in respect of arbitrary practices, but rather in respect of wrong policies. As one columnist remarked, "Our job is to perceive and point out the main directions of policy, or even the failings of policy." Reporters, even for the "objective" news agencies, readily

[18] Joseph and Stewart Alsop, *op.cit.*, p. 32.

admit to criticizing policy in their stories, and recount with pride the occasions when the press has "forced a reconsideration of policies" by pointing out "the inconsistencies and errors." A wire service reporter said, in late 1958: "We are always saying that there is no real leadership . . . in our foreign policy, but we say it in the context of particular stories. The press forced a change in our Quemoy policy, and also in our policy with respect to a summit meeting. . . . By asking questions as to whether a policy is soundly based, the press forces a consideration of it. The problem is to find out what a lack of leadership really means; in other words, what is not being done which should be done?"[19] This same agency reporter remarked on the "almost continual conflict of judgment" between the State Department and the press: "The State Department has the tendency always to view itself as out-maneuvering and manipulating the other side . . . but newspapermen may feel differently about it and tell their readers that it was actually the Russians and not Dulles who won the victory."

The Press as Advocate of Policy. Criticism and advocacy, as participant roles of the press, are so intimately related that differentiating them is sometimes arbitrary, for criticism of a particular policy may be merely a preliminary to the recommendation of an alternative course of action. Yet they do proceed independently, and are empirically as well as analytically distinguishable. In either case, they are concrete expressions of the freedom of the newspaper, as representative of the public, to interpret the public interest in foreign policy as it sees fit.

[19] On the Quemoy issue, compare this statement by a columnist who applied the watchdog terminology to policy criticism: "If I go around . . . after the shelling starts, and the Secretary of State makes his statement on the subject of Quemoy and Matsu, and the President then compares the situation here with Munich . . . and all the rest of it, and I find out that in the Embassies people think that this analogy is nonsense, and that they do not believe that the principles that apply essentially to Berlin should be applied to these off-shore islands, and I report this—in so doing, I play a watchdog function."

Policy advocacy is, of course, a recognized and accepted function of a newspaper; the chief locus of the function is the editorial page, and when most reporters talk explicitly about advocacy *as a newspaper function* (rather than as something they themselves might engage in), they will assign it to the editorial page. The apotheosis of the "fighting editor" is a reminder not only that "editorial advocacy" is a redundancy, but that for some people advocacy was the *leading* function of the newspaper. And the experiences of 1898, as well as the isolationist-interventionist controversies preceding World War II, demonstrate that on occasion foreign policy has had pride of place among the things for which editors fought.

But policy advocacy takes place in the news columns of the press, too, which is a much more interesting circumstance—and potentially a more significant one in a political sense, so far as the ordinary reader is concerned. Despite some apparent belief that this practice has been engaged in only by the McCormicks and the Hearsts, it is a more general phenomenon, pursued regularly by the more independent reporters and analysts, and, in times when the issues at stake seem very great, by a majority of the foreign affairs correspondents. In the cautious words of a syndicated columnist, the journalists have an "honest anxiety over policy." The issues that have given rise to this anxiety and conditioned the type of stories that reporters, according to their own accounts, are always out looking for include the major developments in post-World War II American foreign policy. But it is important to note that the anxiety, and thus the advocacy, is aimed as often at the newspaper-reading public as it is at the policy maker. There seem to be as many instances where the correspondents "pushed" issues in cooperation with policy makers—the effort to slow down the post-World War II demobilization was one—as there are instances of policies being urged on the policy-making officials themselves. The Marshall Plan remains, among reporters, a classic case where reporters went out of their way to play up the program in their choice and handling of "news stories"; but even here one finds correspondents claiming with obvious pride that they "were calling attention to the need for more comprehensive aid to Europe before Acheson's Mississippi speech, which was the forerunner of Marshall's Harvard speech."[20]

There are other examples of correspondents' advancing favored policies, directing their efforts sometimes toward the public, sometimes toward the government, depending on where the obstacles to policy progress seemed to lie. A reporter, recalling the displaced-persons bills of 1947, said, "I myself wrote lots of pieces, pushing the relatively unknown Congressmen who were introducing the bills in Congress . . . , a shining example of 'created news.' " The Alsop brothers state that "if we have ever rendered any public service at all, showing up Louis Johnson was our most useful service";[21] and their efforts on behalf of a more substantial posture in national defense are well known. A columnist cited an article he had written at the end of 1953, arguing against the British withdrawal from Suez, and he expressed satisfaction at the response he drew from foreign policy officials. Several reporters termed the press, in both its editorial and its news columns, the most important domestic "lobby" on behalf of Latin American policy.

In the crisis of confidence that washed over the United States in late 1957, in the wake of Soviet missile and satellite successes, Max Freedman, Washington correspondent for the *Manchester Guardian*, wrote a piece of trenchant criticism of the American press's performance during the preceding months. His argument is interesting in that it berates reporters not for straying from the paths of objectivity, but precisely for their *failure* to perform the functions of criticism

[20] For a confirming view from the "inside," see Joseph M. Jones, *The Fifteen Weeks*, New York, Viking Press, 1955, esp. pp. 225-38.

[21] Joseph and Stewart Alsop, *op.cit.*, p. 73.

and advocacy according to the highest standards of American journalism. His criticism itself sheds light on how reporters feel about these two participant roles: "What of the press? One must speak frankly about one's own colleagues and own profession even at the risk of painful misunderstanding. When judged by the austere standards which glorify the American press, the present record must be accounted an inglorious and disappointing one. Did the American press raise its voice in constant warning over Russia's alarming growth in military and scientific power? It did not: it left that unpopular task to the prophetic wisdom of the Alsop brothers. And now, without a touch of the admirable self-restraint which has kept the Alsops from pointing a finger of scorn, all too many papers are engaged in a loudmouthed campaign as if their record were a model of infallible wisdom and a triumph of stainless courage."[22]

The Press as Policy Maker. The last of the participant roles that the foreign affairs correspondents define for themselves—perhaps it would be more accurate to call it the culmination of those roles—brings the press very close to the stream and the structure of policy-making, even to the point of actual participation in both the political processes and the decision-making processes involved. In this role, foreign affairs reporters are actors in the process, trying to influence the opinions of both the public and the government official.[23] This is by no means a minority viewpoint; foreign affairs correspondents generally perceive and accept this role for the press, even when they do not define their own efforts in these terms. But we should note that influence vis-à-vis the government

[22] *Manchester Guardian Weekly*, December 19, 1957, p. 3.

[23] See, e.g., the role of E. W. Kenworthy of the *New York Times* in urging Senator Monroney to introduce his resolution calling for an International Development Association. (James A. Robinson, *The Monroney Resolution: Congressional Initiative in Foreign Policy Making*, Eagleton Foundation Case Studies in Practical Politics, New York, Henry Holt and Co., 1959, p. 3.)

official—i.e., influence *within* Washington rather than outside of it—is not always influence on matters of substantive policy. Sometimes, when the reporter speaks of his participation in the inner councils of government, what he has in mind is consultation on what might be called "public relations" questions—i.e., the best modes of presenting issues or positions via the press in order to get desired reactions from a particular audience. The particular audience, however, may consist of *other* government officials in Washington, as well as some element in the larger population. Specifically, for example, reporters may participate in decisions within Executive agencies on how best to handle a problem in the context of Executive-Congressional competition. Thus a reporter stated, during Eisenhower's first administration, "I spent three hours recently with a White House staff member who was telling me what they were going to do with the Congressional leaders. He asked my advice, and I said I thought the thing to do was to steal a march on —— and —— [in Congress], and capture the headlines away from them."

The reporters see the policy influence of the press in many guises. Some of the correspondents have expressed their understanding that they are participating as actors in the policy-making process when they are only supplying objective, factual, information. One reporter, formerly a foreign correspondent, observed that the press affects the foreign policy process "by supplying the raw material; the policy makers get more information from the press than they get from their diplomatic sources, and they generally get it quicker. . . . It is hard [within the State Department] to get the attention of the Secretary of State on questions of land reform in Laos, even though it may be terribly important to do so. The top people are just much too concerned with the pressing matters of the day. However, they are likely to read such a story in the newspaper. . . ." A wire service reporter-analyst made the same point even as he tried to disavow its implications: "Writing in order to try to influence policy is much more true of the specials [i.e., correspondents writing for a particular newspaper] than it is of the wire services; we have to write for the increasing number of people who want to know what is going on in the world. If there is a gap—for instance, a development or area about which the United States government is doing nothing—you may have some influence on policy simply by reporting the fact of the gap. But you write it because it is newsworthy. . . ." The Alsops have argued the same way, in their portrayal of the excitement and rewards of the "reporter's trade": ". . . sheer force of circumstance has made the American press almost the only forum in which our national debate is carried on. . . . It is mainly carried on in the news columns (or, as we hope, by columnists dealing in facts), by the publication and counterpublication of barrages of information on all sides of every major issue."[24]

Beyond these insights into the political significance of "objective reporting," there is a less well-defined but palpable assumption of the press's influence, on the part of the vast majority of the foreign affairs reporters and columnists. Sometimes this is credited to the newspapers' editorial power, but more often to the nationally syndicated columnists, who, in the words of one of them, "have a show window in Washington, and they have access to policy makers which is better than the access that all the newspapers had twenty years ago."[25] Foreign policy influence of a personal kind is also attributed to the major columnists, as a by-product of their reputations

[24] Joseph and Stewart Alsop, *op.cit.*, p. 12; Robert Barton, editor of the *Lima* (Ohio) *Citizen*, has described the same process of participation-by-reporting on the local level, involving local political issues. (UMBS series: "Objective Reporting.")

[25] These beliefs about the policy influence of the work of columnists are not without foundation: e.g., in his memoir of the weeks leading up to the Marshall Plan proposal, Joseph M. Jones observed that Walter Lippmann "had a powerful impact upon policy thinking. His proposal that the European countries be asked to get together and agree upon a common recovery program and present us with a consolidated deficit was, so far as this writer can discover, original." (*Op.cit.*, p. 232.)

as columnists. The columnists themselves sometimes document a modest claim to significant political participation by citing examples; for instance, "In 1945, Byrnes, then Secretary of State, called me one day to ask me for some advice about the OWI [Office of War Information] and the Voice of America. . . ." Another reported an occasion when the Secretary of State had asked his opinion on political sentiments in a Far Eastern city, after the columnist had returned from there. Equally illuminating is the circumstance reported by a correspondent to a friend, and quoted by Douglass Cater: "I have had one very important experience in this town. I knew Arthur Vandenberg when I thought he was the most pompous and prejudiced man in the United States Senate. I saw him change partly by the processes of mellowing old age, but mainly by accident and particularly as a result of public reaction to his famous speech of January 10, 1945. I happen to know that that speech, or rather the main parts of it, were largely accidental. I can say to you privately that I was, myself, quite by chance responsible for that change in the speech. But my point is that what changed Vandenberg was not the speech itself, but the press of public reaction to the speech, and from then on, as you know, he played an important and perhaps a decisive role in winning bipartisan support for the concept of collective security."[26]

Another good measure of the salience of the policy-making role among foreign affairs correspondents is the frequency with which the reporters expressed a positive desire to influence policy. Unequivocal expressions of this type are more abundant than comparably unequivocal denials of any personal intention or desire to make or influence the making of policy. On the affirmative side, one of the best statements is that of the Alsop brothers: "Above all reporting offers the sense of being *engagé* in the political process of one's own time. The reporter who is not consciously *engagé* is in fact

[26] Cater, *op.cit.*, p. 12.

likely to be a very bad and unsuccessful reporter. . . . [H]e must . . . be *engagé*, if only because he himself is a most necessary part of the political process."[27] Two other remarks by correspondents will delineate the values they find in the policy-making role: "Ideas *have* to come from the outside; if it weren't for Lippmann, the Alsops, and the like, there would be no meaningful public discussion of foreign policy. . . ." "The bigger work of the newspapermen . . . is not their actual job. A younger ambitious man rushes to the typewriter with everything he learns. Once he learns and really understands about privacy, a newspaperman can become really influential."

On the other side, there are some reporters who would echo the views of one who said, "You can't run a government from a newspaper column." They make the explicit claim that they themselves "never write to influence policy"—but they nonetheless talk freely about the impacts that the press, as a result of the work of others, can make on policy. And some of them will acknowledge the effort of their colleagues to be men of influence, even while they express their doubts that in practice these reporters "exercise much influence over what the State Department does." But one can only conclude that for this body of correspondents, generally, one of the attractions of foreign affairs reporting is its proximity to the seats of power, and that the reporter, by and large, gets personal satisfaction from his contribution to the political processes of foreign policy-making. "We can have an impact on policy, just like

[27] Joseph and Stewart Alsop, *op.cit.*, pp. 9-10. Cf. also the remarks of Iverach McDonald, foreign editor of *The Times* (London), in a *Festschrift* to Walter Lippmann: ". . . all of us know the misgivings and frustration while waiting for even a faint sign that some of our work has landed anywhere. . . . [A]s for influencing action, it is like dropping a stone down a well and waiting in vain for a splash or rattle at the bottom. . . ." ("The Logic of Allied Unity," in Marquis Childs and James Reston, eds., *Walter Lippmann and His Times*, New York, Harcourt, Brace and Co., 1959, p. 126.) Mr. McDonald's disappointment at this state of affairs reflects his preferred relationship to the political process.

the *New York Times.* . . . We all can have an influence on policy sometimes."

A variation on this policy-making role contemplates press participation directly in international relations. A number of correspondents, including the most prominent, made remarks that suggested their great sensitivity to the role they play, as newspapermen, in international affairs. This is expressed in various ways, from the caution of the wire service reporter who stated that "The average reporter in this country covering foreign affairs . . . doesn't want to create any more trouble than already exists," to the enterprise of the columnist who seeks out the reactions of foreign embassy personnel in Washington to Executive policy and its legislative impact, and "reflects and reports their views without mentioning who they are, in a way that maybe even the Secretary of State hadn't thought about because he and they are not in contact." And, of course, there is the personal interaction of diplomatic personnel and foreign affairs correspondents growing out of the latter's reputation for being well informed; for example, "Some of the ambassadors spend half their time clipping newspapers, and they call me asking if something is true if they cannot get a straight answer from the State Department."

The now-legendary story of the American press and the rise of Fidel Castro to power in Cuba provides an excellent illustration of press participation in international affairs that is no doubt familiar to all American reporters in the foreign affairs field. Whether true or not, an unequivocal statement of the press's responsibility was made by the former United States Ambassador to Cuba, Andrew Gardner, in testimony before the Senate Internal Security Subcommittee, and reported in the *New York Times*:

"Three front-page articles in the New York Times in early 1957, written my [sic; should be "by"] the editorialist Herbert Matthews, served to inflate Castro to world stature and world recognition. Until that time, Castro had been just another bandit in the Oriente Mountains of Cuba, with a handful of followers who had terrorized the campesinos, that is the peasants, through-out the countryside."

"After the Matthews articles," he added, "which followed an exclusive interview by the Times editorial writer in Castro's moun-tain hide-out and which likened him to Abraham Lincoln, he was able to get followers and funds in Cuban [sic] and in the United States. From that time on, money and soldiers of fortune abounded. Much of the American press began to picture Castro as a political Robin Hood."[28]

The Cuban episode is by no means an isolated occurrence; the press itself is so often an issue in foreign affairs that ex-amples abound. For instance, a column by C. L. Sulzberger in the *New York Times* of November 24, 1958, criticizing developments in Italy concerning NATO, provoked a reply from the Italian Premier[29] and some press conference question-ing of Secretary of State Dulles.[30] The *New York Times*'s capacity to affect foreign chancelleries may be dispropor-tionate among American newspapers, but it is hardly singular. When Soviet Premier Khrushchev, in one of his letters to President Kennedy at the very peak of the Cuban crisis, tem-porarily veered from a near-accommodation and suggested the exchange of Soviet missile bases in Cuba for Western missile bases in Turkey, he was widely believed to be respond-ing to a similar suggestion that Walter Lippmann had made the previous day (October 27, 1962) in his syndicated column, "Today and Tomorrow."

Conclusion. These four roles add up to substantial freedom

[28] *New York Times*, September 11, 1960. Nearly two years before this statement (in December 1958), a Washington reporter made the same point: "Matthews of the *New York Times* put over Castro as a force for good and enlightenment; but he is just a bum, with no government and no program."

[29] *Ibid.*, November 26, 1958.

[30] *Ibid.*, November 27, 1958. These events seem to confirm the semi-jest reported by Joseph Kraft: "'If the [*New York*] *Times* ran a piece about American policy toward Costa Rica,' a State Department press officer once hypothesized, 'and it was all cockeyed and came from a postal clerk, it would still take at least an assistant secretary to con-vince the Costa Ricans it wasn't true.'" (*Op.cit.*, p. 126.)

of the press in the political sphere—a justification for extensive, on occasion even massive, participation "by right" in the processes of foreign policy-making in the American democracy. We might repeat, however, that the farther we move away from the neutral conception of the American reporter, the more we are dealing with roles that are not a part of his articulated views of the process and are not ascribed to him by democratic political philosophy. The representative and critical roles, perhaps even the advocate's role, might be said to be part of a traditional American ideology of the press (even when they are not incorporated into the reporter's description of how the press fits into the foreign policy-making process), if one confines the discussion to the *editorial* function of the newspaper. But these roles, and the policy-making role, *when exercised by reporters*, are legitimated essentially by practice, and not by a well-understood body of "theory." The argument here, and in the following chapters, is not that it is wrong for the reporter to do these things, but that the implicit and unexamined character of much of the participant behavior, and especially of its relation to the more obvious (though still not well-understood) neutral roles, tends to obscure its significance for foreign policy-making. If the newspaper were really only a mechanical purveyor of factual information, then its omission from theories of foreign policy-making would make little difference. But if foreign policy news is itself a product of all these roles, then any dependence on such news for an understanding of the larger world means that the correspondents are authentic participants in the politics of foreign policy-making, and thus the newspaper in all its aspects needs to be brought into our theories concerning foreign policy.[31]

[31] V. O. Key, Jr., has recently written some insightful pages on the press's impact on the political system, discussing the problem in many of the same general ways as we do here, and looking at many of the same phenomena. Yet his analysis and this one head in quite different directions. In the present context, for example, Key distinguishes different types of roles for the press, but he treats the non-neutral roles

The reporter, of course, is not likely to be conscious of all these varying, and sometimes inconsistent, claims on his performance. In fact, he would most likely regard the above discussion as an artificial and an unnecessarily elaborate breakdown of an essentially simple function: "reporting the news." But we can see these roles reflected in various contexts, and they will help us explain—in the remainder of this chapter—some dilemmas in the reporter's orientation to himself and his work, as well as to understand—in the next chapter—what the pursuit of news is like.

◓ The Competence Dilemma

As the foreign policy reporter contemplates the range of behavior available to him in the everyday practice of his profession, he quite apparently makes certain choices—consciously or otherwise—as to which ones he would prefer to specialize in, or as to how he orders his preferences among them. Competence in different types of roles, however, seems to call for different kinds of skills; the neutral roles would appear to demand of a man that he be a "good reporter"—a faithful observer with an understanding of what is news and a capacity to write, whereas the participant roles call for a greater substantive knowledge and analytical ability. Consequently, the way that foreign affairs correspondents define the requirements for competence in their field tells us a great deal about the roles that they as individuals find important and congenial.

For present purposes we can distinguish three general classes of attitudes toward competence requirements: there

---

chiefly as expressions of editorial judgment. He also argues that the press is in fact becoming a "common carrier" rather than a "cuegiver"—a reporter of "objective news" rather than a political interpreter or guide. He is thus led to see different orders of political significance in the daily operations of the press than we do here. But this may be due in part to his concentration on national politics, and to ours on foreign affairs. See his *Public Opinion and American Democracy*, chaps. 14 and 15, and esp. pp. 388-95.

are those who believe that a good reporter, like Gertrude Stein's rose, is a good reporter is a good reporter; those who believe that foreign experience is a prerequisite to foreign affairs reporting; and those who think that some kind of special training and *expertise* is necessary for a good foreign policy reporter. There is a slight (and natural) tendency for reporters to value the backgrounds that they themselves possess, but a lack of comparable data on the background of many of the correspondents keeps us from having much confidence in this proposition.

Of the foreign affairs correspondents interviewed for this study, more subscribed to the third point of view—the need for specialized training—than to the other two combined. If we consider the educational level of these men and their past opportunity for specialization, this finding should not be a surprise; yet it suggests the importance that these correspondents attach to the participant roles that require a detailed knowledge of complex subject matters. "A reporter cannot know too much. Look at all this science that is thrown at us nowadays. I have to know what it is all about, basically, but my child knows more about apogees and perigees than I do. An understanding of strategy and tactics is necessary; but history and political science are the main things. . . . You have to read everything you possibly can. . . ." The social sciences generally stand out among the subjects familiarity with which is thought to be necessary or desirable—especially history, economics, and political science, in that order. But the list ranges widely, including languages and literature as well as technology.[32]

The second ranking point of view was that foreign affairs reporting was not substantially different from any other kind

[32] This suggests the continuing validity of Leo Rosten's observation in the 1930's that a "majority of the [Washington] correspondents often feel inadequate to cope with the bewildering complexity of the news they are assigned to cover." (*The Washington Correspondents*, p. 162.)

of reporting, and hence that any "good" reporter would make a good foreign affairs reporter. "I think the practical experience of covering stories when they happen is by far the most important thing. You get a feeling of the various forces that are involved. We can draw on others for the history when we need it. But sheer newspaper experience—how to write a simple sentence, for example—is very important." This seems to be a widespread attitude among reporters at large in the United States, one that is encouraged by the fact that both the recruitment and training of journalists today favor generalization rather than specialization.[33] This attitude is reflected in the assignment of foreign correspondents: "Covering Europe or Asia or the Far East is basically still a good reporting job."[34] It also recurs in the history of war correspondence: ". . . the idea that a war correspondent is simply a reporter with a different title has been applicable from the beginning. . . . The importance of this lies in the fact that for the past century or so the great bulk of available information on wars, through which public concepts have been formed, has been a typical newspaper product. . . ."[35] In view of the prevalence of the attitude, one may legitimately be surprised to find so little explicit adherence to it among the foreign affairs reporters. But since a great deal of the actual foreign affairs reporting in the American press *is* "a typical newspaper product," or, in our own terms, aims at a neutral, transmission-belt conception of the press, we might be safe in concluding that many of the correspondents thought it so obvious that a "good reporter is a good reporter" that they failed to make the point explicit.

The same thing may also be true for the third ranking

[33] As V. O. Key, Jr., puts it, ". . . a substantial strain of belief remains in the newspaper world that ignorance of the lore of economics, of political science, and of history constitutes a positive advantage for an entrant into the reporting trade." (*Op.cit.*, p. 395, fn. 8.)

[34] Robert Serling, Radio News Manager, UPI, Washington, in UMBS series: "The Foreign Correspondent."

[35] Joseph J. Mathews, *Reporting the Wars*, p. 244.

requirement: foreign experience. Only a handful of reporters gave prominence to the view that "you have to be where things happen. . . . Going abroad every year is essential for anyone who talks about foreign policy." Yet most foreign affairs reporters in Washington have been foreign correspondents at some point in their careers, or have had significant foreign reporting experience (including, for example, a number of important and extensive international conferences), or have lived and worked abroad extensively. And the frequence of their travels today suggests that foreign experience is generally regarded as a necessary part of one's background and continuous preparation, as part of the wider perspective that makes one a better reporter, a better interpreter, a better critic, and so forth.

These views on the requirements for competence are not mutually exclusive. Many reporters subscribe to more than one of them, attaching different orders of importance to them. But on occasion a reporter will display some inconsistency, suggesting either that he has not given the matter much thought before, or that there may be some conflict within him as to the roles in which he should be competent. Pierre Huss, covering the United Nations for UPI, gave this reply to a question whether there were specific qualifications a UN reporter must bring to his job: "Well, I would say that experience stands as the most important quality and qualification. In that experience, I would say first of all, experience as a newspaper man at any time. . . . The longer the experience the better. I should think the most important quality is a good background of knowledge of world history and world economics, and of course world politics."[36] And the Alsop brothers

[36] UMBS series: "The United Nations Reporter." In the program on "The Foreign Correspondent" in the same series, Eric Sevareid replied in a similar vein when asked whether he believed that languages and the study of culture were more important than a news sense: "No, I don't. You've got to have people who've got the knack of knowing what news is, how to find it, and how to write it. That doesn't mean that

argue that their brand of political reporting requires hard work and study in complex subject matters, but they also claim that being a Washington correspondent is "very much like being a reporter anywhere else."[37]

⊖ The Objectivity Dilemma

Earlier in this chapter we said that the political reporter has a bifurcated professional existence, as he accommodates himself to two different conceptions of the role of the press. The duality in his approach to his work may be summed up, and restated, in his attitudes toward objectivity.

Anyone who has been reared in the American political tradition, or who has observed it carefully from outside, will recognize the bright thread of preference for objectivity of the press in the fabric of our political philosophy—even though we cannot formulate a discriminating definition of the phrase. The closest we can come to such a definition is to say that an objective press does not "slant" the news or otherwise manipulate it for personal or partisan or policy ends; but since the real content is missing from such a definition, it is not a serviceable instrument. The preference for objective reporting is as deep and as real on the reporter's side of the printing press as on the reader's side; it is the base line from which the correspondent's discussion and analysis of news tend to start, even though they rarely end there. "The reporter . . . just records happenings accurately." "I report as factually and objectively as I can." "The people want to hear the facts, and then make up their own minds." "My task is to report as objectively as I can."

In part this preference reflects the practical experiences of the American press as it worked out its present structure. The large telegraphic news agencies numbered among their cus-

---

they have to be somebody off a police beat somewhere who's never studied any language and not studied much history. They mustn't be."
[37] Joseph and Stewart Alsop, op.cit., p. 5.

tomers newspapers with a diversity of audiences and political preferences, and antiseptically objective reporting became the means of maximizing customer satisfaction. But Theodore Peterson adds both a "growing sense of professionalism" and a "philosophical foundation" to the economic reasons for the development of objectivity in reporting, and he asserts that by 1947, when the Commission on the Freedom of the Press issued its report, "objectivity was no longer a goal of the press; it was a fetish."[38] And the reporters' repeated assertions that the news should be reported objectively have a counterpart in their belief—which we shall look at more closely in the next chapter—that news has an independent, objective existence.

But since there is no definition of objectivity that will carry all correspondents through all the difficult moments of choice—notice, for instance, that reporters say they write "as objectively as I can"—it is obviously necessary for each reporter to interpret the concept for himself. Almost every newsman will readily acknowledge the need to be selective, to make choices as between the stories he will write and those he will not write, between the events he will report in those stories and the events he will not report, between the things he thinks need to be said and those that do not. Each man will phrase it differently, but this formulation, by a Washington correspondent for a south-central newspaper, expresses fairly typically the common sentiment: "There is no such thing as completely objective news-reporting. The mere fact of selecting news is your exercise of editorial judg-

[38] Theodore Peterson, "The Social Responsibility Theory of the Press," in Siebert, Peterson, and Schramm, op.cit., p. 88. See also Fred Siebert, "The Libertarian Theory of the Press," ibid., p. 60: "The news agencies instructed reporters and writers to remember that their writings were being distributed to both Democratic and Republican clients and had to be acceptable to both. Writers became adept at constructing nonpartisan accounts, and from this practice grew the concept of objective reporting which has permeated American journalism to the present."

ment. . . . All you can be is honest according to your standards. As a human being you have to tell people the truth as you see it."[39] The reporter frequently defends his exercise of selectivity with the argument that "This business of purely objective reporting is a fine thing, except that the reader may not get the full story that way. You just have to get into some interpretative writing so long as it is reasonably honest."[40] The suggestion here, that subjective honesty is the factor that reconciles selectivity and objectivity, is also a common one; it solves the dilemma as it salves the conscience: "It always concerns us when we select, and thus pass judgment. We know we are doing this. But what matters is what we are aiming at. If we aim at unbiased news, we are all right. If we in fact achieved unbiased news, it would be sterile indeed. But if we aim at it, then one gets a feeling of fairness."

The important question, then, is what it means, in practice, to be "honest according to your standards." What is "truth" as the reporter sees it? What is the everyday meaning of news in the foreign policy field? Just as we can distinguish two conceptions of the role of the press, and two attitudes toward objectivity, and two notions of competence, we can also observe two different patterns in the gathering of news.

[39] Cf. Lippmann, *op.cit.*, pp. 271-72: "There is a very small body of exact knowledge, which it requires no outstanding ability or training to deal with. The rest is in the journalist's own discretion. . . . There is no discipline in applied psychology, as there is a discipline in medicine, engineering, or even law, which has authority to direct the journalist's mind when he passes from the news to the vague realm of truth. . . . His version of the truth is only his version. How can he demonstrate the truth as he sees it? He cannot demonstrate it. . . . And the more he understands his own weakness, the more ready he is to admit that where there is no objective test, his opinion is in some vital measure constructed out of his own stereotypes, according to his own code, and by the urgency of his own interest. He knows that he is seeing the world through subjective lenses."

[40] Cf. also Theodore Peterson's discussion of the Commission on the Freedom of the Press, in "The Social Responsibility Theory of the Press," in Siebert, Peterson, and Schramm, *op.cit.*, pp. 87-89.

CHAPTER III

GETTING THE NEWS

———— •◦• ————

● B E F O R E we discuss the actual behavior of foreign affairs correspondents in the processes of news-gathering, it is important to spell out in a preliminary way what "news" seems to mean to them. For the approaches to news-gathering that prevail among these reporters reflect the fact that there are no precise definitions and understandings of what constitutes news.

Perhaps the most significant general characteristic of news, as the term is commonly employed, is that its substantive connotations are usually implicit. Reporters have great difficulty in putting into words just what they are hunting for each day. The successful foreign affairs reporter has antennae, so to speak, that have become sensitive to what the trade regards as news, but he cannot describe it in terms that are discriminating and non-tautological. He can point to particular classes of phenomena, such as outbreaks of war or violence, changes of governmental personnel in the foreign policy field, foreign policy pronouncements by high government officials, and so forth—events on which there is a convergence of judgment among newspapermen that they have some importance in foreign affairs. But where the particular events are not so distinctive, and are less well endowed with a past history of judgment,[1] there is no convergence and the reporter is hard-pressed to define what he means by news. The implicit nature of conceptions of news may be expressed by references to "the news-values inherent in the stories,"[2] or

[1] The significance of prior newspaper treatment of events may be discerned in the general practice of handling all air accidents, no matter how small the plane or the number of persons involved, as "obviously" news.

[2] Leo C. Rosten, *The Washington Correspondents*, p. 226.

in the tautology that "a story is what is interesting, what is important." "There are no hard and fast rules about how news is selected. It is a spontaneous thing; things happen and they are reported."

There are some widely used classifications of news that appear on the surface to be explicit and discriminating, but even these turn out to have very large implicit components. The most common of these classifications among the foreign policy correspondents is that "big names" make news. For example, "The President is always news." "Adenauer is clearly significant." So, apparently, is Harry Truman: "Truman spoke here last week [late in 1958] at the National Press Club; the wire services had already killed the news aspect of his talk, so in the search for something different I chose to write about his language." (Note here that Truman is news even though the "news aspect"—the substance?—of his talk had already been reported.) Where the names are those of top-level foreign policy officials, there are grounds for accepting the classification that may not need to be made explicit; but even here it is apparent that not *everything* associated with these same officials is equally relevant, and hence that there are implicit criteria being employed to winnow the news from the irrelevancies concerning these people. When one considers public figures who do not hold official positions, however, the classification becomes even less discriminating, since it reflects unarticulated and not necessarily widely shared assumptions about what is either important or interesting.[3]

The observable nature of news is another misleadingly "explicit" classification; while most reporters seem to agree that "something has to happen" before there can be news, there is no agreement on what the something is. For example,

[3] Cf. Malcolm Muggeridge's musings about the publicity on such occasions as Churchill's golden wedding or Montgomery's retirement from NATO: "I can never make up my mind whether the publicity creates the occasion or the occasion creates the publicity." ("London Diary," *New Statesman*, October 4, 1958.)

the news value in the fact that somebody *said* something—i.e., something observable happened—is properly due to the fact that somebody *significant* (according to some unspoken criteria) said something *significant* (also according to some unspoken criteria) and not simply that some words were uttered. Furthermore, the "observable nature of news" criterion is often contradicted implicitly by reporters when they argue that foreign policy news is also found in ideas, trends, developments, even in lacunae—i.e., in things that have *not* happened, or not yet happened. Human interest as a classification is also without explicit foundation, but it does not show up very often in the news typologies of foreign affairs correspondents.

There is one classification of news, however, that is a little more explicit than most; it includes conflict, controversy, crisis. It is also the definition of news that is most often cited by the foreign affairs correspondents. Theodore Kruglak, for instance, quotes a news agency bureau chief: "When it's quiet [in Trieste], there isn't any news."[4] Another expression of this point of view: "Take Dulles' press conference two days ago. Everybody knew it was going to be important. It had drama. It was anti-McCarthy. It came out as a head-on clash, giving the view of the State Department and the White House in the matter. So there was a general agreement on the newsworthiness." Or this statement by a wire service reporter: "The major story in the foreign policy field is like the major story in any field—the principal ingredient is conflict." The relative unambiguity of contention as a source of news may even be the reason for its prominence, both in the reporters' minds and in the news columns.

There are reporters who claim that disagreements in American national politics are exacerbated by the reporters' penchant for controversy; the same point is made in the field of international politics. One newspaperman, for example, claimed that the Lebanese civil war in 1958 was "created by the UP,

[4] Theodore Kruglak, *The Foreign Correspondents*, p. 81.

first by its constant use of oversimplification . . . and second by the creation of a sense of crisis beyond real significance." And the fear of some correspondents lest they create more trouble in the world than already exists, which we took note of earlier in a different connection, is also evidence of concern on the part of the reporters about the consequences of employing such an easy criterion of news.

With some slight exception in regard to this last criterion, these definitions are not useful; they do not make reliable distinctions between what is indisputably news, and what is equally indisputably not news. News, in other words, does not spring full-blown from the head of Jove, already labeled. It is helpful to think of patterns of news-gathering as, *inter alia*, different ways of coping with the equivocal character of something (i.e., news) that is thought to be objective, hence easily identifiable. We can distinguish two patterns, two different approaches, toward news-gathering. The first is simply "reporting the news"; this corresponds in a very general way to the neutral conceptions of the role of the press in American democracy. The second is "making the news"; this is a more consciously creative act, one that corresponds, again in a general way, to at least some of the participant roles of the press. The distinction between these two patterns is not simply analytical; it is real in the sense that the reporters themselves are in some measure responsive to the different requirements and values of each. One example may illustrate this awareness: "A good part of the news, I'd say about 75 per cent, is of this kind—a reporting of developments that are of international significance or foreign policy significance. Then there are a lot of stories that are not generated by events, but rather by the curiosity of the reporter. These are the unanswered questions that we feel should be reported on. This is non-spontaneous news, news that is not pegged to an announcement of particular statesmen or officials, but prompted by the reporter himself or his editors." Let us look more closely at each of these patterns, and then at the way they interact in the daily pursuit of a news story.

● Reporting the News

The reporter, it will be recalled, views his chief responsibility as providing information, and he translates this into a mandate that he report the news in an objective way. Indeed, the very phrase suggests the objective, independent existence of the news, and the mechanical nature of the reporter's job. But vague and implicit definitions do not permit an unequivocal identification of news. How, then, is it identified? Where, in practice, do congruent judgments about foreign policy news come from?

They come, in the main, from the newspapers themselves, both current and past; for what we call experience, and might more accurately call the development of implicit theories, is a product of repeated exposures to *prior* judgments about news, as those judgments are revealed in the daily newspaper. The significance of the newspaper as a definer of news, as a boundary maker for the correspondent, is manifest in his behavior as well as in his words. The foreign affairs reporter typically begins his day by a careful reading of the newspapers; he begins his daily search for news by reading the news that was collected the day before by correspondents who started *their* daily search for news by reading the news that was collected the day before that, and so on. Before he can begin to order his day, he soaks himself thoroughly in the news—that is, in the output of other journalists as it has made its way through the editorial processes involved in newspaper publication. Because it is, by definition, news, this daily immersal in it is one of the important ways that a correspondent develops and refines his news sense.

This behavior is characteristic of foreign affairs correspondents no matter what kind of writing they do, and no matter what kind of journal they do it for; thus each of them is shaping both his news sense and his working day by examining the output of his professional colleagues, all of whom are simultaneously doing the same thing. A reporter for a paper with a large staff of foreign affairs reporters described the process this way: "The first thing that a newspaperman has to do is study the press. This has to be done if you are looking for leads for further stories." The correspondent for a smaller paper, on the other hand, said the same thing in a different way: "We are not like the *New York Times*, which has a large staff and covers all the news of the day [sic]. We have to decide, is it *really* news? We use the wire services and the *Times* as a springboard." A reporter from the Midwest pointed out that "You shape your day on the basis of the loose ends [in other stories] that you want to look into." Even columnists may work this way: "I have total free choice in what I write. . . . I don't go off to the side lines just to make sure that I am writing about something on which no one else is writing at that particular moment. I go for the heart of the biggest news."

All this means that the foreign policy reporter approaches his task largely within the frame of reference of prior judgments about what is important, knowing that he cannot stray too far from that range and still be regarded as a man with a good nose for news.[5] What is reported, then, becomes news; it takes on a new quality, like a successful candidate who is suddenly vested with the mystique of his freshly won office. It exists, almost independently of the myriad of choices that made it exist. In this sense, news takes on a kind of objective reality: what was reported is news; what was not reported— for whatever reasons—is not news. And once it *is* news, it exercises a powerful claim on the attention of reporters.[6]

[5] Cf. the remarks of a reporter who was struck by the plight of American correspondents abroad: "Except in places like Britain and France," he said, "US correspondents abroad operate in a vacuum; they do not know what the news is."

[6] As Leo Rosten put it: "News is highly imitative. And because news

What Newspapers Do They Read? How do these correspondents steep themselves in the news? What are the bounds to this process? What newspapers do they read? Almost without exception, they read the *New York Times* and the *Washington Post*; they will also keep up with the wire service teletype machines in the course of the day. The *New York Times* is the only newspaper to be mentioned explicitly by all correspondents; it is accorded all the verbal priority that one would expect, and it is generally read first, too, although it has strong competition from the *Washington Post*, the local morning newspaper. Beyond these sources there is greater variation in exposure, but the other newspapers that are most often read by the foreign affairs reporters are the *New York Herald Tribune*, the *Wall Street Journal*, the *Washington Evening Star*, the *Baltimore Sun*, and the *Christian Science Monitor*. And to these, of course, each correspondent will add a few others that satisfy some personal preferences. For example, the government publication, the *Foreign Broadcast Information Service*, a monitoring of foreign news broadcasts, is rather widely read by the correspondents, although many of them think of it as their own private discovery: "the best newspaper in the world," one called it. Except for the last-named item, this pattern of newspaper reading is extremely close to that which Leo Rosten discovered twenty-five years ago in his study of the Washington press corps, and which William Rivers has reported to be still true for the run of Washington reporters.[7] All of these newspapers, it should be noted, are eastern metropolitan papers that can be obtained easily in

---

in the last analysis is what newspapers choose to print, a correspondent may be forced into writing a story for which he has no particular taste simply because his competitor has brought it into the focus of public attention." (*Op.cit.*, p. 261.)

[7] *Ibid.*, pp. 170-71; William L. Rivers, in *Columbia Journalism Review*, I, No. 1, Spring 1962, pp. 7-8. See also George V. Underwood, Jr., "The Washington Military Correspondents," unpub. M.A. thesis, School of Journalism, University of Wisconsin, 1960, for comparable habits among this branch of the Washington correspondents.

Washington shortly after their publication, when the information they contain is still fresh. It would have to be so, or else they could not be used for the purposes being considered here. If the monopoly that proximity has granted to this eastern metropolitan press may turn out to be a wasting asset in the jet age, it has not wasted away yet. The ecology of newspaper readership and the economics of newspaper publishing still combine to give most newspapers a local or at best only a regional circulation. Certain eastern newspapers, like the *New York Times*, the *Christian Science Monitor*, and the *Wall Street Journal*, circulate nationally, but on a small scale and not always on the day of issue;[8] similarly, a great many newspapers from the central and western parts of the country come to Washington, but not in large numbers and not as large-scale purveyors of fresh news.

By reading chiefly these few newspapers, reporters can cover most of the new material on foreign affairs that appears in the American press on any one day. For these newspapers, together with the wire services, are the major producers of foreign and foreign policy news for American readers. Other newspapers have relatively extensive foreign affairs coverage, but it comes mostly from the wire services, syndicated columnists, or from other newspapers through a syndicated service; sometimes they will have one or two correspondents located abroad, generally in one of the so-called news capitals of the world, but most of their coverage is bought from other sources. It is thus possible for a foreign affairs correspondent in Washington to keep reasonably "on top of the news" as it flows from abroad and from Washington through these major channels of foreign policy communication. The special role that these papers exercise in keeping reporters informed and in shaping their understandings of and conceptions of the news might be said to constitute them an elite among the

[8] Since this was written, the *New York Times* has begun to publish a West Coast edition.

press. They perform a comparable function among policy makers, too, as we shall see in a later chapter, which extends the significance of this elite press within the foreign policy-making process.

The Continuing Big Story. News being defined as that which appears in the newspaper, there is a structural reason for the leading news item to tarry a while. Since it becomes the frame of reference for reporters the following day—providing them with their initial perceptions of the range of possible stories—it tends to persist in the headlines in changing form, as an event that is obviously more important than all those events that never made the newspaper in the first place. Here, then, are both cause and consequence of one of the significant phenomena of the press, "the continuing big story." As a wire service reporter put it, "My job is to stay with the major story for the day . . . and over the weekend to put it in focus." A reporter-columnist who has "virtually free choice" of what he wants to write said, "I stick with an important story while it's going on."

There are two aspects to the continuing big story that reveal much about the work habits of the foreign affairs reporters. The first, which is implicit in the phrase itself, is that one set of events, one news story, is the major one at any particular point in time, standing clearly above the other things that are happening in the world at that same time. Whether the reason for this is the reporter's belief that the American newspaper reader "can digest only one big news story at a time,"[9] or whether it represents the reporter's need to nurture and to demonstrate his news sense—that is, his capacity to discriminate what is "really important"—in practice the effect is much the same. When two or more major developments take place simultaneously, the newspaperman's view of the news is subject to strain; an obvious way to lift

[9] James Reston, "The Number One Voice," in Lester Markel, ed., *Public Opinion and Foreign Policy*, New York, Harper and Bros., 1949, p. 74.

the strain is to reimpose the hierarchy of importance, treating one of the developments as if it were qualitatively different—more important, more interesting—than the others. The press treatment of the Suez and Hungarian affairs in 1956 may be instructive in this regard.[10]

Secondly, there is a belief that "things stay important for a long time." In other words, the "continuing" part of a continuing big story, the persistence of particular items, is due not simply to the attraction of reporters to what has become the news, but in a related way to a conviction that major stories have an inherently long life (thus making it convenient as well as sensible for reporters to turn their attention to them). A column writer for a midwestern paper put his view of the matter this way: "Unless stories are intrinsically violent, it takes several days for a story to build up; then it dies out slowly, even if it is intrinsically important. You can't sustain a story more than two or three weeks. The Congo is an exception. . . ." Notice how, in this view, the life cycle of a news story is seen as relatively independent of what reporters *do*—a further encouragement to the reporter to ride the wave while it is high, without perceiving that this is how the waves are made even higher. The notion that stories last for some time, and hence that there is considerable mileage to be had from them, is applied to run-of-the-mine stories as well as to cosmic ones; at least its effects are apparent in the ordinary reluctance of reporters to drop a subject, even if it means a desperate and losing battle to find a fresh angle that has any substance to it. Stories are thus dragged out, and space consumed, by reporting yesterday's events with no essential changes or additions.[11]

[10] Cf. Wilbur Schramm, ed., *One Day in the World's Press: Fourteen Great Newspapers on a Day of Crisis*, Stanford, Stanford University Press, 1959; and Bernard C. Cohen, "The Present and the Press," *World Politics*, XIII, No. 1, October 1960, pp. 165-74.

[11] For some examples of this, see John B. Junius's perceptive and amusing essay on the "today angle" in "The Morning After," *The Reporter*, XX, April 30, 1959.

When the big story seems likely to continue for more than just a week or two, the resources of the press are mobilized to cover it—a self-fulfilling prophecy at work. Additional correspondents are flown to the spot—recall Suez, the Congo, Berlin, Quemoy, in recent years—with an obligation to file at least a story a day. The resulting flood of material keeps the situation "in the news," which means that it continues to affect the priorities of the reporters and analysts who cover foreign affairs in this country and in others, too.

Reaction Stories. Both the identification of news as that which is in the newspaper, and its persistence as news over a period of time, are made manifest in the foreign affairs reporter's interest in the "reaction story." One of the basic choices open to him, as he begins his daily quest for a subject to write about, is the reaction of officials in Washington to developments elsewhere in the world as reported in the latest editions and broadcasts. There are some clear advantages to stories of this type. They are unquestionably news, by definition; they minimize the effort needed to locate an acceptable story as well as the problem of choice in selecting one; and they provide the comfortable reassurance that if other possible stories do not work out in time, the correspondent will still have something to write up. The emphasis that reporters give to this type of story varies, of course; for some it is merely "one type of news here in Washington," while for others it represents a more regular orientation to the news day. Thus a correspondent for an afternoon paper discussed his choice of stories this way: "This morning it is obviously the reaction to the latest Soviet note. . . . I start to call people in the State Department. . . . After I have done my writing, I read the rest of the papers. After that I begin to follow certain leads. Today the obvious story is the reaction here in Washington to Macmillan's visit to Moscow. The important things are what really went on there, and what people here think about it."

It is difficult to be more precise than this about the priority that reaction stories have for the larger community of foreign affairs reporters in Washington. It quite apparently is a common element in their experience, yet a rather fine line separates the explicit reaction story from the ordinary direction that the latest news gives to the reporter's search for a fresh story. Hence it is often impossible for the correspondent himself or for the observer to separate stories *about* reactions to . . . from stories *in* reaction to. . . .

● Making the News

The second pattern of news-gathering is a more challenging and creative enterprise than the first, in that it requires the newsman to leave the warmth of already established news and venture out into the cold world of independent and private constructions and valuations of events. Here he is dealing not with events that have already been in the newspapers, but rather with items that in his opinion *should be* in the newspaper. In the words of a correspondent, "I might then track this [casual suggestion] down regardless of the day's news"— a mode of expression which incidentally suggests that the act of publication is like the laying-on of hands, transforming something of possible importance into news. The degree to which a newspaper varies from day to day is a measure of the extent to which hitherto unreported items have managed to break into the winner's circle. We are interested here in the criteria that help a correspondent to recognize a new item as one that should be in the news, or to reject a new item as not newsworthy—or even, since the processes are the same, to choose among two or more competing subjects that are already in the news and therefore should continue to be reported. These criteria comprise the antennae with which the correspondents scan the world of news each day; they include a diversity of phenomena, from those that grow out of the commercial nature of their enterprise, to those that inhere in the reporters' own theories, conceptions, and preferences in respect of the world around them. We shall be concerned here more with the character of these criteria than with their distribution; in most cases they are not mutually exclusive criteria, and not much can be said at the present time as to which ones might be commanding at particular times or in particular types of circumstances.

Commercial Criteria. The unending discussion about the political and social consequences and responsibilities of the press in American life can never quite obscure the fact that every newspaper—even the best—is a business enterprise. From the publisher's viewpoint, newspapers have to sell or he cannot stay in business; if no one buys copies of his paper, no one will advertise in it. Even though the advertising revenues may be more significant to the publisher than the subscription revenues, the "unseen audience" that spends its money both on the newspaper and on the products advertised therein is the key figure. From this develops a conviction, widely reflected among the working reporters, that to stay in business a newspaper has to "give people what they will read." A long-time reporter from the Midwest argued that, "In the first place, a paper has to make money. If it doesn't make money, then it can't do all the other things it is supposed to do." Another held up the *San Francisco Chronicle* as "an example of the sad fate of a newspaper that tries to be more internationalist in its coverage than its readers want. The guy who is buying the paper has the right to read what he wants." Others acknowledge the circumstance, but with less tolerance or equanimity: "Too many American newspapers are run by men who would be running filling stations if they could make more money doing so. They have no publishing instinct or tradition. Their papers are strictly commercial enterprises."

But what is it that the people want? What do they read?— and what do the newsmen think that they read? Not surprisingly, there is consistent evidence that foreign affairs news is not one of the main attractions in the newspaper so far as

the public as a whole is concerned. The volume of foreign
and foreign policy news in American newspapers is low, relative to other types of news, to begin with, and the amount of
it that gets read is lower still.[12] Very few correspondents can
cite specific figures on readership of foreign affairs news, but
their existence is legendary; a typical example: "It's a well-
known fact that surveys show foreign news to be down at the
bottom as far as public interest goes." Furthermore, these
foreign affairs correspondents operate with offhand impressions about reader interest that influence their selection of
news. One of these impressions is that the non-coastal population in the United States has a much more limited interest in
foreign affairs than have the residents of the two seaboards;
another is that interest in foreign affairs is low everywhere
in the United States, and that reader interest—sometimes
expressed even as public demand—precludes a market for
serious discussion of matters like the United Nations or the
Rapacki Plan, to use examples offered by newsmen themselves.
Merely to mention these attitudes or viewpoints is to leave a
number of interesting questions unanswered, for consideration
at a later and more appropriate point; for example, while reporters believe that readers will not buy serious discussions of
foreign affairs material, they nevertheless write such material—but for whom? And what is the larger significance
for the policy-making system itself of the way reporters, editors, and publishers view the public audience for foreign
affairs news?

The more immediate impact of this conception of the newspaper as a business is speculation about how to satisfy the
customer while informing or educating him. This line of
thought leads newsmen (none of whom wants to see his newspaper collapse beneath him) to the view that foreign affairs
news has to be popularized—that is, that it should be assimilated to the standards that govern the entertainment value of

[12] See Chapter VIII for data relevant to these points.

a newspaper in order to increase its readership, or at least maintain it. In other words, the same news values that are attached to other classifications of news are attached to foreign policy news. To say, as a columnist does, that there is a "distortion of emphasis in the interests of mass circulation" is to imply that there is an accepted norm somewhere in the absence of mass circulation; we do not need to accept that implication in order to understand that there may be *different* emphases in the selection and interpretation of information concerning foreign affairs when mass circulation is an issue than when it is not.

How events are chosen and handled to make them popular and appealing is no doubt familiar, in terms of our prior discussion of what news is, if not in terms of our everyday experience. One mode is to stress the conflict and controversy that inhere in political situations. Edwin Kretzmann, formerly a Public Affairs Adviser in the State Department and then Deputy Assistant Secretary of State for Public Affairs, once said that "Newspapermen are frank to tell me that stories written in terms of sharp conflict increase the sale of newspapers."[13] We might note in passing that we are not judging the validity of this proposition, but simply pointing out that reporters believe it to be true, which may be consequential enough. Another way of making this subject matter more attractive is by casting it in terms of the involvement of major public figures who have some news value in themselves. A third way of popularizing foreign affairs is to simplify its presentation, as regards both the structure of the issues themselves and the language in which they are cast; reporters repeatedly mentioned the art of simple writing as one of the major assets of a successful correspondent. It may be a moot point whether the process has been carried too far, or not far

[13] Edwin M. J. Kretzmann, "New Perspectives in Foreign Relations," a lecture delivered under the auspices of the Walter J. Shepard Foundation at the Ohio State University, April 4, 1959, p. 13.

enough. Lester Markel, editor of the Sunday *New York Times*, has argued that the lack of reader interest in foreign news is a direct function of the difficulties of learning, and that reporters should work harder at the writing aspects of their craft: "Surely the writing of international reports can be simplified and made more graphic. Certainly more background, more interpretation can and should be supplied. The reporting should be done largely in the language of the average reader."[14] But it can also be argued that if the reporting of developments in terms of conflict exacerbates conflict, then, *mutatis mutandis*, the simplification of foreign affairs reporting exacerbates the dangers of simplification in the approach to complex issues.

These standards are not evenly distributed among newspapers or correspondents, to be sure; there are singularities as well as regularities among the objective financial situations of newspapers, and among the subjective appraisals of these situations. In any case, these commercial criteria of selection do not stand alone, for any correspondent. Rather, they should be viewed as constituent or underlying criteria, for they are overlaid with, and continuously interact with, a variety of what might be called *Weltanschauung* criteria—those that reflect the correspondent's own theories and preferences about the substantive and procedural aspects of foreign policy, and about the role of the press in relation to it.

Criteria Developing from Substantive Theories. In a talk to the American Newspaper Publishers Association in April 1961, shortly after the failure of the Cuban invasion effort, President Kennedy was moved to ask newsmen and their employers to reconsider some of their criteria of selection. "Every newspaper," he said, "now asks itself, with respect to every story: 'Is it news?' All I suggest is that you add the question:

[14] Lester Markel, "The Flow of the News to Marilyn Monroe," *Problems of Journalism*, Proceedings of the American Society of Newspaper Editors, 1960, p. 77. See also International Press Institute, *The Flow of the News*, Zurich, 1953, pp. 67ff.

'Is it in the national interest?' "[15] On the face of it, the President's suggestion looks like an appeal for an explicit, easily defined, criterion of news; but on closer inspection it, too, turns out to be implicit and non-guiding. The unending debate on all foreign policy in this country may be expressed as divergent attempts to answer the President's second question, and decisions about the publishability of foreign policy events are subject to the same kinds of divergent evaluations. But the negative response of newspapermen to the President's suggestion underlines the fact that foreign affairs correspondents, like other close observers of and participants in the foreign policy debate, have theories of their own that they bring to events, and that give them some guidance as to the importance and the newsworthiness of those events. The word "theory" in this connection should perhaps be used with caution; correspondents are more or less alert to the subject matter that they deal with every day, but they are not scholars in that subject matter. To say that they have theories is not to say that they tend to be theoretical in their approach to the subject. Nevertheless, some of them do have notions about the interrelations among at least a few political variables, and about cause and effect in the foreign policy arena, that have the power to alert them to particular developments and to endow those developments with significance.

Some further cautionary remarks about the nature of these theories may be in order, before we look at their manifestations. They are, in general, highly individualized, and their components, in the fragmentary form in which we can see them, are generally unintegrated in the mind of the correspondent. And even these fragments, more often than not, do not stand out clearly but rather must be pieced together, often by working backward from actual choices of news to the judgments that lay beneath them. Furthermore, it is not possible on the basis of this kind of evidence to say that the

[15] *New York Times*, April 28, 1961.

theories or hypotheses that are detectable are central enough or comprehensive enough to be determinants of the news-gathering behavior of correspondents; all we can say is that they seem to be influential. To discover *how* influential, and under what circumstances, would constitute a major study in itself.

What can we say about reporters' theories of international relations and foreign policy? In the first place, it is important to note that while most of the prevailing hypotheses about international political affairs are political in character, a few of them are not. For example, a United Nations reporter for a radio network specified an understanding of human relations as a qualification for UN reporting, "because my pet thesis is that international relations are human relations. And in order to interpret what the United Nations is trying to do, one has to get down to the basic human problems."[16] Secondly, much of the time, and possibly more often than not, the relevant theoretical propositions are implicit rather than explicit; circumstances are judged important to correspondents for reasons that they are unable to articulate—or because they have had no experience articulating them. Some typical remarks: "In 1955 I went to the Persian Gulf, Saudi Arabia, and the oil islands, on the theory that the Middle East was going to be more important." "I get onto my stories in different ways. . . . I might have had dinner last night with an official or a diplomat who casually suggests to me some things of importance which have not been reported before." Sometimes implicitness looks like the total absence of theoretical propositions; for example, "Reporters need an instinct for knowing what is about to become important." The implicit character of their propositions is most easily seen, perhaps, in the observations of many correspondents that certain subjects or areas of the world are underplayed in the press, while others are

[16] Pauline Frederick, in UMBS series: "The United Nations Reporter."

getting too much attention. In the late 1950's, for example, a number of correspondents felt that the United States press was not paying enough attention to Latin America. The reasoning behind these judgments was likely to be tautological: Latin America "is going to be far more important than we now think."

Thirdly, and despite all these qualifications, many foreign affairs correspondents do possess a stock of explicit hypotheses of a political nature concerning the world of foreign policy that are apparently reflected in their choice of news stories. A number of examples may clarify the character of these theories. Several reporter-analysts have expressed their conviction over the years that the new economic position of the United States in the world makes the tariff and the economic development problem the most important issues in foreign affairs. In the words of one of them, "I happen to believe that the hearings that Hale Boggs is now holding on the Hill, on how you get the capitalist system to use its capital development funds overseas to compete against this new technique of the Communists in the underdeveloped areas of the world, is a story of fundamental importance to the security of our country." A wire service reporter remarked on the continuity of foreign policy development: "Regardless of what happens in political campaigns, the political choices open to the government that it can pursue in order to fulfill American interests are relatively few. The necessity of holding together diverse alliances narrows these choices down." A reporter for a mountain-state newspaper listed "three basic aspects" of American foreign policy, in terms of which every individual policy had to be justified: "(1) Strengthen yourself; (2) consider your allies; (3) don't lose sight of the fact that a world system is to be created." Another columnist justified his attention to foreign reactions this way: "People who say that anti-Americanism in Europe is not important may be right in the short run. Over a long period of time, however, such a development would, by the very functioning of democratic processes, be reflected by an increasing number of anti-Americans in the various governments. This we cannot afford." A final example, from a wire service reporter, involves the testing of two contradictory hypotheses to see which one might be correct or most relevant: "I'd like to get some sound opinions in town as to what the Tibetan situation means for the long-run position of communism in Asia. Nehru is disenchanted; the Indonesians are taking a 'plague on both your houses' line. I'd like to see if Tibet is having an impact on them that is a good thing from our long-run viewpoint in this part of the world, or whether it is a bad thing in the sense that 'everyone likes a winner' and China won!"

While we may not always be able to describe and locate accurately the relevant intellectual baggage that foreign affairs correspondents carry with them, or even to say with any sense of confidence what its impact on foreign affairs coverage is, what we fondly call our common sense tells us that there *is* an impact, and that it is discoverable. The influence of theories, implicit as well as explicit, can be detected in the appearance in the newspapers from time to time of stories about trends in international affairs or in policy areas—like the progressive weakening of the Diem regime in South Vietnam, or the decay of democratic government in Ghana, or the prospects for foreign aid programs within the American government. Such stories differ from ordinary news in the sense that what is happening is detectable not by everyday commercial news values, or by yesterday's headlines, or by an intuitive sense of big and exciting developments, but rather by some hypotheses that lead a particular reporter to the conclusion that these small and "unimportant" individual developments have a collective policy meaning that commands attention.

There is one major noticeable pattern in the theories shared by a large number of reporters, but since it is related also to their policy preferences, we can best look at it in that context.

Criteria Developing from Policy Preferences. In the last chapter, it was pointed out that foreign affairs reporters find job satisfaction through their sense of participation in the policy-making process. The various participant roles acquire their substance and their direction not only from the theories that foreign affairs correspondents entertain, but also from their personal policy preferences. It is not merely that a correspondent's theory of foreign policy tells him that something is important because of its impact on other variables; he is also concerned about its impact on particular *values*. A correspondent, in other words, actively prefers some policy outcomes, and dislikes others, for reasons that may have little to do with cognitive theories. "Scratch a journalist," wrote Leo Rosten, "and you find a reformer."[17]

It is hard to find a reporter who carries the myth of objectivity to the point of erasing or denying his own policy preferences; on the other hand, one often comes across correspondents who are conscious of the influence that personal preferences exert on the stories that they and their colleagues choose to write, and on the emphasis given to facts in those stories. Sometimes the preferences are those of editors, but mostly they are the property of the reporter himself.[18] (They may, of course, be shared by editors, either by accident or by various modes of selection; for example, "My preferences happen to coincide with those of the management.") Some common expressions of the reporter's pursuit of his preferences: "I look for stories . . . that interest me personally." "I write more on what I am personally interested in." "You write it because it is newsworthy, because the United States is overlooking something that in an honest reporter's opinion ought to have something done about it."

[17] Rosten, *op.cit.*, p. 157.

[18] Rivers confirms that few Washington correspondents feel the pressure of editorial preferences. (*Op.cit.*, p. 5.) Underwood also found this to be true among the Washington military correspondents. (*Op.cit.*)

The most common pattern of policy preference among these foreign affairs reporters—one that provides them with a theory that is normative rather than empirical—may be summarized as an attachment to a liberal internationalist position on foreign affairs, if such a phrase still has distinctive meaning. Most of these reporters favor policies of heavy United States involvement and commitment in international affairs and international institutions; they support liberal trade policies;[19] they share a sense of the urgency of responsible participation and inspired purpose as against a narrow parochialism in international affairs; they are committed to the defense of American values and institutions in the face of the Soviet challenge. A reporter for a magazine discussed his own experience and his observation of his friends and colleagues: "I would say that my having an international liberal outlook on foreign affairs conditions the type of stories I am always out looking for and going for. I would say that most reporters—including a large number of those who are covering the State Department—have a broad basic agreement with certain international policies that can be reflected in their writing." Many reporters have pointed to the Marshall Plan, and to the effort to slow down the rush toward demobilization after World War II, as outstanding illustrations of how the press rallies behind policies that fall within their broad policy consensus. To say so may do violence to some cherished popular illusions about the press—in intellectual circles at least—but it is not only the so-called irresponsible newspapers that mix preferences with news on the front page. For example, many of the "best" papers have run stories calling attention to the contributions of the foreign aid program when its future seemed to be in doubt, or stories on the American image abroad when the USIA budget was imperiled. These are, in fact, common

[19] Some interesting supportive data: in a survey of the policy views of foreign correspondents in Western Europe, Kruglak found that 80 per cent of the correspondents polled were in favor of further liberalization of tariffs. (*Op.cit.*, p. 92.)

occurrences; if they receive little attention, it is because they are muffled by the policy consensus among reporters (and among the articulate critics of the press), and by the prevailing judgments that so long as these stories were published in major newspapers they must have been news after all.

No attempt was made in this study to establish the political preferences of the foreign affairs reporters. It is often said, however, that while the large majority of their employers support the Republican party, the body of the "working press" (the phrase itself conveys the ideological distinction) is Democratic.[20] The fragmentary evidence on this point in the data at hand—including the observations of reporters on the political preferences of their colleagues, as well as the known or reported political predispositions of individual correspondents—tends to support this conclusion, although the situation is not so simple as the "working press" notion implies. Some of these men are among the highest-paid journalists in the newspaper business;[21] both their social and their professional milieus are in many ways closer to those of their editors and publishers than to the circles in which the ordinary reporter is presumed to move. Kruglak's data on the Presidential preferences of foreign correspondents in Western Europe are rather ambiguous; he interprets them as a demonstration of the independent political status of these correspondents, although he could as easily have claimed a slight advantage for the Democrats.[22]

Finally, there are noticeable signs among the foreign affairs reporters of interest or disinterest in particular areas of the world, preferences that are heavily shaped by the personal

[20] For corroborative though incomplete data on the political preferences of Washington newspaper correspondents, cf. Rivers, *op.cit.*, p. 5.

[21] Rivers reports the median salary for all Washington correspondents as $11,579, which is $4,500 higher than the national average for reporters. (*Ibid.*, p. 6.)

[22] Kruglak, *op.cit.*, pp. 87-89.

experiences, including travel experiences, of the correspondents. The wire service reporter who wanted to test his conflicting theories about the effects of the Chinese suppression of the Tibetan revolt prefaced that statement with this remark: "Before the week is over, we will back off and look at Tibet. I'm very interested in this myself, maybe because I lived in Southeast Asia for several years." A columnist said, "I don't like to write on areas or subjects I do not know anything about. I have been to France and studied about it, so I like to write about France. Some people have no great compunctions on this score, but this limits me a great deal." Another column writer, not located in Washington, pointed out how his writing had been directly influenced by his travels, but added that since he had now been about everywhere in the world, his special area interests were blending into a general global interest. Disinterest, too, plays a part in shaping news stories, although it is not so readily confessed; for example, "Latin America as a subject area bores me. . . . It is hard to screw yourself up to the subject, but it has to be done once in a while." These highly individual expressions of interest and disinterest, however, do not form any particular pattern that affects the selection of news in substantively predictable ways, whereas the value and policy preferences of correspondents do tend to shape news coverage in directions that one can anticipate.

Criteria Developing from Attitudes Toward the Political Process. Another set of criteria grows out of correspondents' observations and attitudes concerning the way foreign policy is made in this country; in other words, they are sometimes led to news by hypotheses about the makers of foreign policy. The most common hypothesis involves a substantial measure of distrust of foreign policy officials when these officials take the initiative in disseminating information. This distrust is most strongly expressed in the statement, heard more than once, that truth is the opposite of what the State Department says. Other reporters put their disbelief more cautiously, but no less firmly: "A healthy skepticism is a necessary attitude toward the process of policy-making." "Always remember that the State Department is selling something; a good newspaper-man must take the wrapping off." "A good reporter always checks the other side of the story anyway." "A responsible newsman questions what his sources tell him." These are different formulations of the same basic notion, that the policy makers are not telling the important stories—i.e., the features of contemporary developments that the reporters think are the most relevant—and that the correspondent has to probe on his own to get some glimpse of the things that are "really" going on beneath the surface of the State Department and of the government generally, out of the sight of the press and the public. These attitudes, in other words, lead reporters to seek out their own interpretations of events; the policy makers may initiate the news dissemination process, but the reporter, who is looking for the fire that has given rise to the smoke (or the smokescreen), goes after his own rather different conception of the story—of what the news is.

The assumption that the State Department habitually con-ceals the most relevant information has a pervasive impact on the reporter; it reduces easily and often to a handy series of operational questions, such as: "What are they trying to conceal?" "Why are they trying to conceal it?" "What game are they playing?" These questions, if pursued assiduously, can frequently net the reporter a good story, in the sense that he turns up something new about the processes of foreign policy development that was not being publicized. Concomitantly, however, they may earn him the institutional suspicion of those in the State Department and elsewhere in the government who believe that foreign policies bloom better in quiet confer-ence rooms than on busy street corners. This mutual distrust frames enough of the discourse between press and foreign policy makers (as we shall see in more detail in Chapter V) for it to become a factor in the policy-making process that must be taken into account.

Reporters' attitudes toward foreign policy-making are not all compounded of distrust and hostility, however. There are other notions, too—perhaps the most important of which is one articulated frequently by James Reston of the *New York Times* and shared by a growing number of journalists. Reston has long been concerned about the progressive hardening of policy positions and the progressive reduction of maneuverability as a policy moves along its institutional path, and he has stressed the responsibility of the press to illuminate the arena of policy choice before decisions are made that are for all practical purposes irreversible. "What reporters have to do now is to move in much earlier in the development of policy. . . . Never before has there been such a need for aggressive reporting during the drafting process so that there can be debate before it is too late."[23] Reston and others who share this view are thus inspired to look for news in those institutions and among those people who stand near the beginning of the foreign policy-making process, in positions where they can exercise policy initiative and early veto. This requires very good sources, needless to say, and thus it probably comes most easily to reporters with high standing in the fraternity. To the extent that they succeed, of course, they write about a policy-making circumstance before it is news in the common meaning of the word; that is to say, they "make" news.

It should be added that this attitude toward foreign policy-making may sometimes stir up the suspicion and distrust of the official, because it intrudes the press into the sensitive exploratory phases of the political process. The problem posed here by the conflicting "requirements" for some airing of

[23] Quoted by Joseph Kraft, in *Esquire*, November 1958, p. 126. There is a further justification cited for this new "responsibility" for the press: radio and TV have pre-empted the "spot news" field, requiring the newspaper to carve out for itself a new and distinctive contribution in the field of public affairs.

important issues to whatever publics are interested before policy positions become fixed, and for privacy in the early discussion, planning, and bargaining stages of the formulation of foreign policy, is one of the central issues in the press-government relationship. We shall come back to this question at a later point, after we have explored more fully the political impacts of press coverage of issues.

Criteria Developing from Role Conceptions. Lastly, and briefly, we can look back to the conceptions that correspondents have of the appropriate roles for the press as a further source of criteria for identifying news. The participant roles are more fertile in this respect than the neutral roles. The neutral roles tend to put the burden of creating news onto others, and to favor reporting it instead—that is to say, judgments about what is newsworthy are likely to reflect the prior judgments of other colleagues, of editors, of government officials who disseminate information. The participant roles, on the other hand, offer more independent criteria by which to determine newsworthiness. Those who believe in the critical role of the press, for example, are likely to be sensitive to possibilities of writing articles of policy criticism; those newsmen who feel that the press has a responsibility to bring its influence to bear in favor of the policies that seem to them to make the most sense will no doubt be sensitive to opportunities in the ordinary course of duty to advocate their preferences or to try to shape the trends of policy. To say this is to repeat the essence of our prior discussion of the different roles of the press; but it seems useful to make the point explicitly that in their creative moments or creative aspects or opportunities (and nearly all of them have these moments), the foreign affairs reporters may deem important the kinds of news stories that reflect their dominant images of what the press ought to be contributing to the foreign policy-making process. Each of these participant role conceptions will generate criteria for selecting news that are more or less distinctive; taken together, however, it seems that they would lead in the direction of more elaborate, differentiated coverage of foreign affairs, since the relevant conceptions of what is newsworthy lie less in the parade on on-going events than in some notions about what the larger society *requires* by way of foreign policy intelligence.

◑ The Pursuit of a Story

These two patterns of news-gathering—the creative and the reportorial—are in daily competition with each other, as the foreign affairs correspondent makes his daily rounds in pursuit of story possibilities. By following this process to its culmination in the choice of the particular story or stories to be written up and handed in, we can see some of the influences that bear on the reporter and shape his final news product.

A veteran foreign affairs correspondent described the general problem this way: "There is constant pressure to keep abreast of developments. At the same time you have to see things that are not in the news, things that occupy nobody's attention." The reporter is caught between these two competing professional requirements, in a way that is not commonly appreciated. On the one hand, he is pressed by the ideology of the scoop—in the most general sense, by the notion that he can distinguish himself by "doing a job that needs doing, and that no one else is doing." A major accomplishment for a reporter is to get an exclusive story that his colleagues would like to have gotten, or to get a desirable but more generally available story somewhat earlier than his colleagues, or even to write a good story that other reporters have overlooked for one reason or another. Many reputations, as well as prizes, have been secured by journalism of this kind. On the other hand, and perhaps more importantly, the reporter is haunted by the professional necessity to validate his news sense—to demonstrate that his antennae are as good as the next man's—by making the same judgments about news as his professional colleagues make. The pursuit of the scoop or the exclusive or different story is obviously hobbled when the reporter can also make a secure reputation by "doing a job that needs doing" which *everyone else* is doing—namely, reporting the news. There are further inhibitions to intellectual independence even in the search for an exclusive story, because it must be one that other reporters would like to have gotten or written. The correspondent fears being caught out on a limb by having written a story that is not admired or picked up by other reporters—that is, followed by a rush of validation. He is also constrained to keep his eyes and his ears on his fellow correspondents by a fear that he in turn may be scooped by someone else. This fear is circumscribed by the area of competition that a reporter thinks is meaningful—for example, the AP *vs.* the UPI, or the *New York Times vs.* the *New York Herald Tribune*, though not the *Atlanta Constitution vs.* the *Los Angeles Times*—but within that area it is a powerful constraint.

The ever-present need to validate one's news sense forces the foreign affairs correspondent to keep in close contact with his colleagues—not really a novel pattern of social behavior, to be sure, but a substantively significant one nonetheless. The reporter maintains this contact by reading his colleagues' output, as we have already seen, and also by continuous personal interaction and cooperation. The correspondents work together in the State Department Press Room, in the National Press Building, and in several other downtown Washington office buildings; they organize clubs for the purpose of eating together and inviting "news sources" (including even the Secretary of State) to lunch or dinner, where information is transmitted to the whole group at once, and a collective interview takes place; they share conviviality and information at the Press Club restaurant and bar; and, although ostensibly bored with the communal character of the formal press conference in Washington, they invariably attend those with a foreign affairs content, and they reproduce the communal features of the press conference when they invite officials to address the Press Club.[24]

In short, the foreign affairs correspondents go hand in hand in quest of news, looking everywhere together, yet each one also looking on his own and hoping that his narrow channel of the broad front will yield a different, or an original, or the first, discovery. He may leave the collective framework of the news in response to leads tossed out, wittingly or not, by persons in government, or he may follow his own curiosity and pursue stories he thinks are important according to his own criteria. Yet he is never so free of the need to validate his news sense that he can fail to keep a close eye on the prevailing market for news, like a general guarding his flanks.

Every foreign affairs reporter cherishes the opportunity to do something different, something on his own. Almost without exception these correspondents find the prevailing standards confining, if only to their creative sense, and they take particular enjoyment in their more individualized writings. They also have a positive need for some leads to stories for quiet days when it is not so clear what the news is. Each correspondent has his own favorite sources of ideas for stories that are not "in the news" at the moment, but which might be or, in their opinion, should be. The sources for these stories or leads include government publications, historical records, foreign affairs journals, as well as people with good inside information. A correspondent for a Washington newspaper put it this way: "In a slack period, reporters go off in all directions; then personality determines what a guy writes." This might be restated to read that when the constraints of the news are lifted, a process of creative disintegration sets in, in which each correspondent pursues his own leads, or follows his own conceptions or theories of what is important, and why.

These alternative possibilities present themselves to the

[24] In other words, things have not changed much since Leo Rosten's day. (*Op.cit.*, p. 88.)

reporter in the context of the daily choices he makes; and he tries to create as favorable an environment of choice as he can by pursuing a number of different possible stories at once. He may not settle on one of them until late in his working day, and until the point of choice he tries to keep several possibilities alive by exploring them simultaneously, comparing them against a conception of the day's news and a conception of "intrinsic importance." A correspondent for a New York newspaper described this aspect of his day in considerable detail: "Today . . . I lunched with someone from the State Department. I will look into several stories, such as our reply to the Soviet note on Berlin (maybe I can get the substance of it), or an agreement between the United States and the Soviet Union on an exchange of exhibits is being signed, or I will check in at the —— desk [in the State Department] as I always do. . . . At lunch today I heard that there has been a working group on the question of Berlin for some time now, composed of United States, French, British, and German representatives, and so I will ask the German ambassador about it, since he was a member of it. One little thing seems to lead to another. I heard that the president of the World Bank is in London and is going to go to the Middle East to mediate between Britain and Egypt on the release of blocked Egyptian funds in Britain. I can ask about this in six or eight different places around town, and when you ask about things like this, you get ideas as to other stories." Another correspondent said: "I have to keep my finger on all trends. If the Associated Press happens to get four or five leads all at once, they are likely to use them all at once; but we do not shoot all our wad at once, especially if part of it will last until the next day or so without anyone else using it."

The limits to this procedure are obviously set more by the capacities of the correspondents than by the amount of foreign affairs activity in any particular day; and of course the whole business is subject to upset by the intrusion of events that all reporters intuitively recognize as superseding in importance *all* of the possibilities they individually have been juggling. Apart from this last contingency, however, the area of choice that the reporter has managed to carve out for himself in the course of his day also represents a constraint in the sense that it establishes the range from which the particular choice of tomorrow's news will be made: the correspondent cannot move very far beyond the circle of these few stories in which he has invested his working day. The investment is long-term as well as short-term, too, because the correspondent has picked up and stored items of information that may make up future stories in addition to present ones.

The notion that the correspondent chases his stories conveys some sense of the pressure he is under to keep up with the news and additionally to turn up something fresh that will become news. Walter Lippmann, who writes from a study in his home,[25] and who can get officials to come to *him*, is singular. The prevailing habit is precisely the opposite; the Alsops have designated it as the first rule of the reporting craft: "His feet . . . are a much more important part of a reporter's body than his head."[26] This theme is repeated by other correspondents: "The real secret is to keep moving and keep asking." "Mobility is the key." "You try to get in touch with as many people as you can."

The suggestion that movement is more important than cerebration is not wholly accurate; the Alsops' second rule, for example, is that the reporter has to have "some general idea of the right questions to ask."[27] And there are other purposes in the continuous movement and probing: "The reporter has to talk to enough people so that he can reduce the degree to which he may be misled." And he has to talk to enough people

[25] Lippmann's working habits are described by James Reston, "Conclusion: The Mockingbird and the Taxicab," in James Reston and Marquis Childs, eds., *Walter Lippmann and His Times*.
[26] Joseph and Stewart Alsop, *The Reporter's Trade*, p. 5.
[27] *Ibid.*, p. 7.

so that his sources cannot be easily identified. Yet it is hard to avoid the implication that when the reporter is deliberately looking for something new, the production of news is less an act of limited creativity on his part than a process of accidental discovery as he stumbles across something that looks good to him and has not been published before.

Where a story gets pursued is not without significance. If reporters keep on the move all day long, the paths they trod will show up in the stories they write. A member of a small Washington bureau who covers the whole capital scene for his newspaper, or a "stringer" who writes for a number of newspapers, or a syndicated columnist or high-status reporter can follow the thread of a story wherever it appears throughout the government. But the foreign affairs specialists among the Washington correspondents are found mostly in the larger bureaus and in the wire services, and the division of labor in these institutions is shaped by the political structure of the government. The foreign policy "beat"—or area of assignment—in Washington is substantially circumscribed by the State Department and the foreign embassies. A good number of these reporters maintain their desks in the State Department Press Room, and spend the greater part of their day within the building. Other reporters for these same newspapers and news agencies have the chief responsibility for covering Congress, the White House, the independent agencies, and the like. There are sound bureaucratic reasons for dividing the pie in this fashion; and there are additional practical reasons that inhere in the desirability of the reporter's getting on good terms with a large number of officials in his substantive area. So, rather than overlapping dispersions of effort, small plots are farmed intensively. "I cover foreign affairs, that is, the State Department and the embassies generally. I do not cover the Hill; we have another man for that." "I go mainly to the State Department." "I spend all my official work time at the State Department."

The size of the network of sources that a reporter has in the State Department varies, of course, with the individual, but only rarely are these lines of access limited to the formal public affairs channels in the State Department. One reporter estimated that each of his colleagues had a good working relationship with at least six persons in each of the major divisions of the State Department, there being six such divisions at the time the estimate was made. Some of these Departmental sources were the same for a number of reporters, because each reporter's list no doubt included the Public Affairs Adviser, or press officer, in each Bureau—no matter what he may have thought of him; one reporter called the Public Affairs Advisers "the gateway to the obvious"—and some of the officials in very responsible positions rather near the top. Reporters who cover all of Washington for their papers cannot establish so extensive a network of relationships in any one Department. These reporters, who are not foreign affairs specialists in the sense that we are using the term here, turn to a much smaller number of people, perhaps a half a dozen, who can speak more or less authoritatively in particular fields. Beyond this, the cultivation of contacts in the foreign embassies in Washington follows more individualized paths, depending on the amount of foreign affairs specialization and the personal interests of the correspondent, the status of the correspondent and his newspaper in the eyes of the separate embassies, the "importance" of the embassy, and even the size of the embassy staff.

This core of the foreign policy beat may be extended in two directions by those reporters whose newspapers grant them a measure of personal freedom and by those with less of a specialization in foreign affairs. The beat may be stretched to include other Executive agencies or even Departments that have foreign affairs responsibilities, such as the Atomic Energy Commission, the United States Information Agency, and the foreign aid agency, or it may cover Capitol Hill, especially the foreign affairs committees of the Congress. It is a rare reporter who moves freely among all these institutions, but even those correspondents who dwell in the State Department will make occasional forays in some of these directions as the questions of the day seem to suggest. Equally rare, on the other side, is the reporter who said, "The first rule is to avoid the State Department. There are other relevant people and committees . . . also embassies and government agencies . . . as well as organizations like the International Bank."

The prevailing definition of the foreign policy beat as largely bounded by the State Department and Embassy Row has a constraining influence on the choices open to the reporter, and hence on the conception of foreign policy that he presents to his readers.[28] It is a commonplace today that foreign policy has outgrown its proprietary home in foreign offices, moving into almost every phase, as well as institutional manifestation, of government. It is repeatedly said that about fifty separate agencies in the Executive branch of the government are involved in foreign policy, and its invasion of the legislative process is equally apparent.[29] The division of foreign policy into segments corresponding to institutional reportorial assignments, so that the White House correspondent treats of the President's involvement in a foreign policy matter, and the Congressional (or perhaps just the Senate or House) correspondent reports its Congressional aspects, and the Defense Department reporter or military analyst covers other dimen-

[28] Cf. the prediction of Frederick W. Collins, formerly Bureau Chief of the *Providence Journal* and the *Evening Bulletin*, on what would happen to the US foreign trade story in 1962: "When the story moves from the State Department and the White House to Congress, the men covering the State Department and the White House who have steeped themselves in the subject, read all the texts, following developments for years, will be kept downtown, and the story will be covered by men who know Congressmen and politics." (Quoted in *Columbia Journalism Review*, I, No. 1, Spring 1962, p. 13.) Note, too, the strong Executive orientation in these remarks.

[29] See Holbert N. Carroll, *The House of Representatives and Foreign Affairs*, Pittsburgh, University of Pittsburgh Press, 1959; and James A. Robinson, *Congress and Foreign Policy-Making*, Homewood, Ill., The Dorsey Press, 1962.

sions of it, thus seems to interfere with an integrated conception of the foreign policy universe. And to the extent that this is true, it may make more difficult an integrated approach to the use of foreign policy instrumentalities among those who rely on the newspaper for their conceptual framework and their substantive information concerning the world at large.

The Choice of a Story

At some point in his day, the foreign affairs correspondent has to select from the basket he has been carrying the story or stories that he wants to write up and submit to his editors. What makes a story stand out in his mind?

In the reporter's final choice, whatever elements of the competition between reporting the news and making the news still linger are most commonly resolved in favor of the former. Reporting the news takes priority over the possible contributions that a correspondent might make to the flow of information on foreign affairs. The inherent possibilities of anguish in making this choice are dissipated by the authoritative claims of the news. As one correspondent put it, "The stories that come to the top are the things that claim the headlines"—an apparent tautology but to the reporter a meaningful description of the sequence of events. His choice, in other words, is profoundly influenced by the choices of his professional colleagues—by the circular reasoning that news is what is in the newspaper, and especially in the headlines, and hence that a reporter must stay within its ambit. Another reporter described his process of choosing a story as "a question of determining what is the main story at that moment." Another said, "The one story I write is at the top of the news, or near the top. And it is something that the wire services may have left cloudy or undone."

Even the columnists, who are more or less freed from the tyranny of the headlines, feel their pressure. We earlier quoted a good statement of this position: "I have total free choice in what I write. What I choose to write depends upon the flow of events. . . . I don't go off to the side lines just to make sure that I am writing about something on which no one else is writing at that particular moment. I go for the heart of the biggest news." Another columnist dismissed the problem with the explanation, "I stick with the important story." Those columnists or analysts who do exercise freedom of choice tend to justify their behavior as an explicit reaction to the common practice of staying with the headlines, rather than in terms of their own conceptions of what constitutes important information. James Reston is reported to have explained his choices this way: "I try to ask myself: What's not getting reported? What's not on the agenda? What's the big story we're all missing? That way I lean against the wind."[30] Another columnist said, "I hate to write on what everyone else is writing on."

We have noted earlier, and repeatedly, that the foreign affairs reporter defines the news and refines his news sense by constant exposure to the output of his colleagues. It is important to add here that editors, his own and others, are also instrumental in determining what is at the "top of the news," and thus in shaping the reporter's final choice. The influence of editors may be indirect, in the sense that, as one reporter-columnist phrased it, "I am influenced by the selections or judgments of the people who decide what goes on page one." This would be true not only for a reporter's own editors, but equally for the editors of newspapers that compete with his, and for other bellwether editors, such as those who determine the news budget of the news services. Or editors may exercise a direct influence on a reporter's final choice of a story for the day; they may ask him to investigate a particular problem, or the reporter and his editors may together decide what the big news is that he should write on. To be sure, the editors themselves do not work in a vacuum; they in turn are influ-

[30] Quoted in Kraft, *op.cit.*, p. 125.

enced by the output of the reporters, which gives them the universe from which they make their own selections, and by the judgments of the editors of whatever other newspapers or news services they use to help develop their conceptions of significance. The "flow of the news" may indeed be an inappropriate metaphor; the "circle of the news" is a more apt description.

The dominance of this pattern of reporting quite obviously does not exclude other kinds of material from the news columns; but it often compels the reporter to come to terms with it in order to get his more creative stories into prominent positions in the newspaper. These stories are often introduced by explicitly connecting them to other stories that are unquestionably "in the news." This is known as "hanging a story on a news peg," and is a venerable practice even in the foreign affairs field, where reporters are conscious of the limited space given to foreign affairs news and of the attendant difficulties in securing prominent display space in the newspaper for material that, standing alone, might not be regarded as especially newsworthy. If the reporter thinks that his story will hold up without immediate publication, and if he has satisfactory alternative stories, he will quietly gather the material for the story and wait for a development in the news that will serve him as an appropriate peg. For example: "For a rainy day I am saving a trend story on Japan's trade with Communist China. I have been accumulating material for about a week now, waiting for a news peg on which to hang the story." And another: "If a Congressman were to make a major statement about Tibet, I could hang what I want to say on a 'today' peg." But if the correspondent is hard-pressed for a suitable story on a subject that is already in the headlines, or if he is impressed with the immediate relevance of his story and wants to secure a favorable reception for it, he will fabricate a news lead. The time-honored way of constructing such a news peg is to ask an important official a leading question.[31] For instance, "I asked what had become of the project [a particular cultural exchange between the United States and the Soviet Union]. I got a rather inconclusive answer, to the effect that somebody had studied the problem and nothing had happened to it and nothing more was heard from it. But it doesn't really matter what I got for an answer; I know already what I want to write . . . and all I wanted was a peg to hang my story on, and I got it by asking my question."

This is not to say that reporters have to stamp out the vestiges of independent thought and of wide-ranging conceptions of what is important in the foreign affairs field, or must always smuggle them in in the guise of fresh news. Even though "reporting" takes precedence over other kinds of writing, it does not exclude the latter; while it may constrain the reporter's imagination and narrow his sense of what is potentially significant in foreign policy, it still permits him to evaluate new developments as obviously important. He runs the risk, of course, that his editors may not see these developments in the same light as he does, but he has past experience to guide him in his understanding of the kinds of stories that will sell, and he also has a reputation as a good reporter, which helps to surround his writings with the aura of news. If there is any question in his mind as to the reactions of his editors, he may need to work up a substitute for the "news peg" out of the more standard variety of news values—controversy, conflict, drama, and so forth. This is easy to do, most of the time, and with practice it becomes such a commonplace in the life of the reporter that he begins to see and evaluate importance in a mixture of these terms and whatever implicit or

[31] Cf. Rosten, *op.cit.*, p. 61. Donald Matthews quotes a correspondent as saying: "When we find some newsworthy item, we take it and 'bounce it off' some news source. Then it becomes news." (*U.S. Senators and their World*, Chapel Hill, University of North Carolina Press, 1961, p. 205.)

explicit theories he may have brought with him as original equipment.

There are other modes of choosing the day's ration of news that bear mention. In the simplest case, the problem of choice is resolved by the collapse of the juggling act. That is to say, all but one of the possibilities that the correspondent has been entertaining all day may turn out to be manifestly unripe or worthless from his point of view; either nothing has "happened," or what has happened does not strike him as interesting or significant. This is an extreme case of the more general situation wherein the reporter, given his own understanding of what news is, sees a qualitative difference between one possible story and all the others. When his alternatives melt away like this, the reporter is more or less obliged to use the story that is left to him, whether he takes satisfaction in it or not. The import of a news story that is chosen this way may be just as great, however, as that of a story selected on more deliberate or purposive grounds. One story that exercised official Washington for several days in the fall of 1958 had been submitted only because the reporter's other leads had evaporated in the course of the day, and the reporter was greatly surprised when his editors gave the story a front-page display.

An equally painless resolution of the problem of choice is that which is practiced by the wire services. Unlike their colleagues who write a daily column, or who file one story or occasionally two a day, the news agency correspondents in the State Department send in a steady flow of stories. Thus there is no need for them to winnow the less significant from the more; anything that looks like news gets phoned in. In the words of one of the news agency correspondents, "We are running another Safeway Store here." This is not to say, however, that the agency correspondents automatically transmit every item that comes their way, without applying any standards of judgment. The problem of what is news is still relevant;

but, with a larger canvas to work with, the agency correspondent does not have to worry greatly about the possibility that he may have chosen to paint the wrong aspect of the foreign policy scene.

The news agency reporters consciously pay most attention to transmission of factual stories that are already "in the news," or in a standard way are generally regarded as news. But their agency machines have insatiable maws, and as the ordinary news begins to run short in the course of the working day, the wire reporters have an opportunity to send in stories that are more speculative, tentative, peripheral, or long-range in character. "For the most part you go at it with the firehouse technique, staying on top of the current breaks; this is our primary responsibility. Further along in the day we will try to take up some further issues that are out of the public spotlight, and try to bring the picture into focus."

⊖   A Note on the Foreign Correspondent

Although our focus in this book is on the foreign affairs reporter in the United States, it is important at this point to look abroad, at the orientations toward the process of getting the news on the part of American correspondents stationed in other countries. (We shall consider some other aspects of foreign correspondence in a later chapter.) For if the patterns that obtain among the correspondents at home are repeated by those abroad—and they seem to be—then we can speak with greater confidence about the impacts of those particular patterns, in the expectation that they are reinforced rather than contradicted by the remaining sources of foreign affairs news. (Remember, too, that this news from abroad is an important part of the well of news into which the correspondents at home collectively dip, so the impact of the patterns of foreign correspondence come to the reader both directly and indirectly.)

The foreign correspondent has a different responsibility

than the typical foreign affairs reporter in the United States; where the latter specializes in foreign affairs, often in a very narrow sense, the correspondent abroad has to cover a particular country or area rather than a particular subject matter. A reporter who had just returned from several major foreign assignments said, "The job is to describe what is going on in a country, to make it more understandable to the average American." Thus he has to cover sports and drama, fashion and society, as well as politics and foreign policy. In this respect the foreign correspondent is more like a member of a one- or two-man bureau in Washington who has to cover the full span of governmental activity, including foreign affairs, as he looks for things of interest to his readers back home, than he is like a member of a large and specialized news staff. And the foreign correspondent faces difficulties in the course of his work that the foreign affairs reporter in this country does not face; while the latter is in the midst of a familiar political environment, the former is in a strange one where the problems of understanding and reflecting "reality" are considerably greater.[32]

Both these special problems of foreign correspondence make it harder for the reporter to be confident that he knows what is going on—what "the story" is. It is not surprising, then, that in these circumstances the correspondents follow the same routine as the reporter at home in order to sharpen and validate their news sense. In fact, the similarity in the reporting routine is sometimes extended into an argument that foreign correspondence, like foreign affairs reporting, does not require any special preparation or training, although area and language competence are generally acknowledged to be useful.

[32] Cf. Joseph and Stewart Alsop, *op.cit.*, pp. 45-46: "Except for a few who spend years on end in their chosen countries, reporters abroad cannot know of their own knowledge, or understand with their own understanding. They can describe what they see with their own eyes, whether it is a street fight or a coronation. But they cannot themselves instinctively trace the complex interplay of forces in a foreign land that may produce the street fight, or cause one ruler to abdicate and another to be crowned."

"Covering Europe or Asia or the Far East is basically still a good reporting job. . . . Language is badly needed. But I've seen many UPI men go overseas on assignments and do a very terrific job without any particular training *per se* in foreign correspondence."[33] In a similar vein, Kruglak quotes from a letter to him from an American editor: "Basically there's no difference between the European assignment and the local courthouse beat in Podunk."[34]

Like the reporters back home, the foreign correspondents walk through their day arm-in-arm with "the news"; the newspapers are repeatedly described as their first and most important source, which is then followed up—where necessary and possible—by the ordinary procedures of filling out, or checking, or advancing a story. A Washington column-writer said, "My observation is that US foreign correspondents abroad spend a great deal of their time reading the local press." In the Soviet Union, where newsmen's access to government officials is restricted, the newspapers have been described as "virtually your only source for stories."[35] In a recent broadcast interview, Leland Stowe, a veteran foreign correspondent who is now a Professor of Journalism, replied to a question on how the foreign correspondent goes about gathering news: "First he must read up to a dozen or more newspapers, of many different political opinions—just to keep posted on what's going on. Then comes his absolutely indispensable 'leg-work.' . . . [He must see many different types of people] not all in one day, but many every day, according to what news is breaking, or what vital developments demand probing for more information or for interpretation."[36] Finally, Kruglak notes that the foreign correspondent is also sensitive to the requirements for getting

[33] Robert Serling, Radio News Manager, UPI, Washington, in UMBS series: "The Foreign Correspondent."
[34] Kruglak, *op.cit.*, p. 102.
[35] International Press Institute, *The News from Russia*, Zurich, 1952, p. 11.
[36] UMBS series: "The Foreign Correspondent."

his stories on page one, and that he will write on those subjects that are demonstrably news rather than on more specialized topics that may end up, for example, "on the financial page, or in the waste basket."[37]

In brief, it appears that the reporter who covers foreign affairs abroad operates with the same professional standards and norms as the foreign affairs correspondent at home, even though the environment of his reporting task is different in many other important respects. He starts his quest for news under the guidance of the news that is already published, and from then until he ends the daily chase he is subject to the same general patterns of choice-possibilities and choice-constraints as his home-based brethren.

● Some Implications

The *modus operandi* of the foreign affairs reporter, the understandings and customary procedures that define how he gets the news, have a noticeable impact on the shape and content of the daily segment of reality that is served with breakfast and again at dinner in this country.

For one thing, the prevailing conceptions of news tend to attract and to focus the dispersed policy attentions of various foreign policy audiences at any particular time on some particular issues, alternatives, and even on modes of policy thinking, at the expense of others. When the correspondents themselves flock to the "big story," they are helping to create and maintain a hierarchy of importance that finally reaches the reader via the make-up of his newspaper. Where space is limited and the make-up of a paper communicates judgments about the relative importance of developments, the pursuit of the big story unavoidably muffles other phenomena; rich news items get richer, while poor ones, with less prominence or even no space at all, get forgotten. Furthermore, the fact that the big story is almost by definition a continuing one—anywhere

[37] Kruglak, *op.cit.*, p. 101.

from a few days to a number of months, as in the cases of Berlin and the Congo in 1958 and 1959—helps to secure its position at the forefront of attention for an extended period, again at the expense, at least temporarily, of things that are simmering in the foreign policy pot.

Whether this focusing of attention is to be regarded as desirable or undesirable, as positive or negative in its effects, depends on many things—on the particular choices of news in a particular context, on the particular foreign policy theories in the eye of the beholder, even on the foreign policy interests and activities of the beholder, and on the particular audience he has in mind. One could argue, for example, that heavy concentration on a few news items is undesirable precisely because it pushes other items out of the readers' sight and thus creates a "distorted" environment of articulate interest and opinion to which the policy official is obliged to respond. Or one can make a case that focusing the attention of the attentive public onto a few policy issues is better than not focusing it—that patterns of press behavior that structure public thinking and hence give some form and content to the elusive dialogue between government and governed are to be preferred to patterns (if one can imagine them) that impose little or no order on a very large range of possibilities. In particular circumstances, too, one can argue for or against the concentration of newspaper space on some items rather than on others, depending on the interests, preferences, and causal relationships that percolate in the mind of the critic. The point being made here is not that the narrowing of attention is inherently or necessarily undesirable, but rather that it is a reality, and that it has variable consequences that need to be spelled out and studied in detail before their significance can be assessed.

These attitudes and procedures of the press not only focus attention on selected parts of reality, but they do this in disconnected and unrelated ways, which perhaps raises more serious problems as far as foreign policy-making is concerned. Correspondents hover around the major foreign policy story like moths around the brightest light; and, like moths, they drift away when the light fades or is surpassed by another. A discerning official with many years of foreign policy experience in Washington observed that reporters "don't bother you unless there is something urgent going on." To follow the "big story" is to "stick with the news that comes to the top," and the outcome of this practice is a moving picture of the world that skips from crisis to crisis, each one in a different locale, with a different cast, a different script, and so on. This coverage might be charted not as a series of discrete jagged peaks and valleys but rather as a sequence of overlapping arcs, each one representing the rise and decline of press coverage of a particular story; as one story begins to wane, the arc of the next crisis begins to rise, and the lines cross. (It becomes a peak-and-valley chart, however, in the hands of those editors who print only the news at the top of each arc.) This pattern is partly due, also, to criteria of selection that emphasize the attractions of conflict and controversy; the correspondents are not only drawn to the "big story," but their predilection is to make the arenas of conflict and controversy the subject of these big stories. But quite apart from the particular news values in any particular conflict—quite apart even from the substantive content of the big stories—the very process of focusing attention on one problem area after another, seriatim, makes for discontinuities in the points of information that comprise one's picture of the foreign policy world. It is like a very slow radar scanner, or one that does not keep scanning the same area; the information it yields comes in so slowly and in such unrelated segments that a sense of the whole cannot be gleaned. Walter Lippmann used another analogy: "It is like the beam of a search light that moves restlessly about, bringing one episode and then another out of darkness into vision."[38] For those many people who depend substantially on the mass media for their basic and continuing picture of the international environment of foreign policy, even a careful reading of foreign policy news may convey an image of an endless succession of problems having little systematic relationship to each other or to some corpus of American values and American political choices. As Lippmann correctly noted, "Men cannot do the work of the world by this light alone."[39] But even though there may be other lights playing on foreign policy problems, this beam is one of the most powerful in the battery, and it impinges on foreign policy-making in ways that we shall have further occasion to explore.

The reporter feels a pressure to write about the biggest news, but he is equally compelled to say something different about it than others have said. "I try to pick a story that I can add some new things to." "What they were saying on Tuesday didn't advance things any, and all I could do was hash over old stuff, not adding anything, so I didn't write." The reaction story commends itself to the correspondent precisely because it allows him to add something new to the big story. But political reactions to political events do more than just "advance the story." They are themselves part of the interplay of politics, and by leading or urging others to react publicly, or just by putting different points of view or fragments of ideas in juxtaposition perhaps for the first time, reporters are contributing new ingredients to the foreign policy stew, which in turn become the frame of reference for other reporters the following day. This process might be likened to a duel that is pressed on a pair of reluctant gallants by their eager seconds. It is commonly said that the press overstates the disagreements and understates the accommodations in international relations, by virtue of its special attraction to controversy. But quite apart from the news values involved in controversy as against

[38] Walter Lippmann, *Public Opinion*, p. 275.
[39] *Ibid.*

agreement, the procedure of prying reactions out of officials in order to add something to the news itself adds to the impression that contention is the mainstay of all international political life.

The persistence of a big foreign policy story "at the top of the news" for some days at a time, embellished and extended by the reactions and the reactions-to-reactions of other policy makers, imposes on the uncertainties and approximations of these foreign policy actors an ordering of importance with respect to particular issues, and a necessity to respond to them, that may differ significantly from the priorities as they earlier presented themselves to the policy makers. Again, this process may be either negative or positive in its impact, depending on the same kinds of considerations that were discussed above; and here, too, the consequences merit further exploration.

Finally, the steady obeisance to what is incontrovertibly the news results in the pages of the press being filled with observable events that have already happened—that is, with the "past." By its own canons, the press does an unsystematic, haphazard job of stimulating or structuring discussion of ideas or possibilities in advance of issues, crises, or events. Diligent exploration of the political universe is regarded as part of the general background that the press provides; but it provides it generally either *after* the event, in the train of public interest, or when "things are dull" and the reporter is thereby free to use the story he has been working on but which is not in the news. But, as we noted earlier, this latter kind of exploration explicitly covers terrain that no one else is covering, so that the task of stimulating political foresight is performed in response to no uniform or explicit theory about what kinds of foresight may be either necessary or useful to particular individuals or groups.

It is relevant at this point to recall that democratic ideology argues the need for a free press on the grounds that the people have to be informed with respect to the decisions they will be called upon to make—a doctrine that the philosophers of the press have adopted as the preamble to their own constitution. The fact is, however, that the press itself violates this norm as a matter of course when it stresses what *has* happened at the expense of what *might* happen under varying contingencies, and when it discusses the future in haphazard, unsystematic ways.[40] Whatever else one may wish to say about how people make up their minds on foreign policy issues, it is still clear that more or less rational calculation in this area requires information about future possibilities as well as past certainties; it is also obvious that responsible political participation requires foreknowledge of the patterns and procedures of political choice. The press fails to provide these kinds of knowledge with the abundance or regularity that would make its contribution meaningful.[41] A few foreign affairs analysts in the press are aware of this problem, but they are a small minority and they too are caught up in the daily whirl of the press. Even James Reston, who has often expressed the responsibility of the press to break into the policy-making process before issues are already decided, is of two minds about the practical possibilities of doing this successfully for the average newspaper reader. On the one hand, as we have already seen, he has argued the need for more aggressive reporting during

[40] The norm is also violated when reporters adopt commercial criteria of news selection that work on the emotions sooner than the intellect. The kind of news that results from the application of these criteria—conflict, drama, personalities, etc.—skews the cognitive perceptions of the foreign policy world in the direction of simplistic, personalized, and polarized constructions. Their contribution to either the art or the science of policy appraisal is negligible.

[41] Cf., in this connection, Lewis A. Dexter's remarks on political communications to Congressmen: "Congressman Amiable says, commenting on his wide experience in a state legislature and in Congress, 'You always hear from business too late.' And this is true *in general* because businessmen and their representatives respond to the news. . . ." ("What Do Congressmen Hear: The Mail," *Public Opinion Quarterly*, xx, No. 1, Spring 1956, p. 26; emphasis in original.)

the drafting stages, making possible a timely debate on the policy issues involved. But he is also motivated by his belief that "A distracted people, busy with the fierce competitions of modern life, must be addressed while they are paying attention, which is usually at the moment of some great national or international event."[42] The discrepancy between these competing "truths," and also between the prevailing norms and prevailing practices, will compel us at a later point to reconsider our body of empirical and normative theory concerning this aspect of the role of the press in a democratic polity.

The attitudes and modes of procedure among leading foreign affairs correspondents that contribute to these effects are learned early and well—so well, indeed, that it is often said of an able reporter that he has an "instinctive" sense of news. But it should be clear that the attitudes and modes of procedure themselves are *not* instinctive, nor are they inevitable; they are the product of professional and social group norms. The reporter believes, in essence, that there is an independent flow of news that is beyond his reach—a condition of nearly perfect competition wherein he is unable to affect the market in news in any major way by his own individual choices or decisions. So his major effort is to "keep up with the news," or to "stay on top" of it, rather than to try to reshape it by exercising his independent judgment. But it is a curious sense of the order of things that denies the effects of individual decisions by particular correspondents. By denying his freedom to do as he likes in the face of the flow of the news, the reporter displays his sense of a lack of mastery; but he does not alter his individual share of responsibility for the end product. The few foreign affairs reporters and analysts who do follow their own stars stand apart from, and above, the rest of their colleagues, demonstrating not only that it is *possible* to make independent choices about what is worth writing, but that

[42] Quoted in Kraft, *op.cit.*, p. 125.

there is a large and important market that values their products. One might argue that there are also qualitative differences between the writings of these men and the writings of the bulk of their professional colleagues; but this argument relates to the competence of individuals, which is a much more crucial and relevant concept than the alleged immutability of the "flow of the news."

CHAPTER IV

FROM NEWS TO NEWSPAPER

———•••———

⊖   F R O M the reporter's selection of a story to the final shape of the news in the newspaper, there are additional sequences of choice. The process from news to newspaper may be visualized as funnel-shaped. Each stage in the process slightly narrows the dimensions of the news that the next stage has to work with. At the end, in the newsrooms, the final and severe choices are made as the news runs through the small neck of the funnel into the newspaper. The temptation to say that either the early or the late stages in this process are the more significant must be resisted. The news-gathering stages have the importance that comes with defining the outer boundaries of choice; the editorial stages are important because, despite the peculiar constraints that hedge the gathering of foreign affairs news, the amount of available news exceeds the space that any newspaper is willing to give it, and thus the editors are ultimately responsible for the particular shape that reality takes for its readership each day. Before we look at these editorial judgments, however, we should have a brief look at the last reportorial act, which links the correspondent with his audience: the writing-up of his story.

⊖   The Writing of Foreign Policy News

By the writing of foreign policy news is meant the way in which the subject matter is handled in its presentation to the newspaper-reading audience. In one sense the writing may be indistinguishable from the story itself, for the way that policy issues and events are presented may be the very thing that constitutes them as news. But because almost any subject can be presented in more than one way, and because there is this intimate relationship between the mode of presentation and the perception of reality itself, the factors that bear on the manner of writing deserve some scrutiny.

Writing as Affected by the News Medium. It perhaps does not even need to be said that a correspondent writes his stories according to the way he visualizes the requirements of his own publication. In large part it is the audience of the publication he has in mind; and we will take this factor up in a moment. But the medium itself has an independent existence of a sort, which seems to set some requirements for the reporters that do not consciously run as far as the ultimate readership. In the foreign affairs news field, there are two significant types of media: the wire services and the large newspapers that can afford their own staffs of foreign affairs specialists.

The wire services dominate the foreign affairs news field simply by virtue of the fact that the overwhelming majority of the daily newspapers in the country depend on them exclusively for their foreign and foreign policy news. Special correspondents—even when they are only stringers who supply a number of papers—are expensive items; and in quantities large enough to present any serious alternative to the coverage that the news agencies offer, foreign affairs correspondents are prohibitively expensive for the vast majority of newspapers. Many papers have special correspondents who cover foreign affairs along with everything else in Washington, but these are not meant to be competitors with the wire services for the daily run of international news.

The news agencies have to serve—and satisfy—all sizes, shapes, and political colorations of newspapers. A United Press International reporter graphically likened a news agency to "a man with a thousand mothers-in-law." The need to tread a neutral, innocuous political path in these circumstances has led to an orientation toward "hard news": the new and indisputable fact, the observable event. Having evolved in this direction, the two major American wire services, the AP and UPI, are caught up in competition with each other in the supply of hard news even in the foreign affairs field. Hard news thus must be fast news, fed in a continuous stream to the news tickers; this is not the sole product of the wire services, to be sure, but it takes precedence over other kinds of reporting and over background material. Non-agency reporters who are critical of the wire services point to the haste of their operation—to the "snap judgments" about the meaning of complicated events, documents, and so forth, and to the disorganized, bits-and-pieces product—and to the distortions and exaggerations of their writing style. "Their only urgent interest in news is to get it on the wires. Usually this means that news are not digested, pulled together, or organized, but are rather presented as a mad surge of stuff." And another: "The UP, for example, has a jazzy approach to news; they are always trying to make snappy front-page stories, using hyperbole and the rhetoric of crisis." A wire service reporter himself pointed out, more moderately, that the UP grew up with an international clientele, and so it "writes from the viewpoint of international detachment . . . as if we were from Mars. . . . The man on the desk makes sure we don't get too enthusiastic about anything we are writing on."

The special correspondents for the large newspapers write about foreign policy in the shadow, so to speak, of the wire services. They cover the same beats as the wire reporters, yet they do not try to compete with them at their own game. Instead, they view their job as doing something that the wire services have not done, or have not done well. And since wire service reporting is regarded by other reporters as being committed to rapid-fire hard news distribution, the "specials" (as they are called) deliberately aim at a more interpretive, hopefully more reflective, conception of news. That their reach exceeds their grasp may be due chiefly to the fact that these reporters often end up substituting for, rather than complementing, wire service coverage in their own newspapers, and thus they have to do both jobs at once;[1] hence the more or less common role conceptions and conceptions of news that were discussed in previous chapters. For example, "I can't duplicate the wire services, and so I write in greater depth. . . . But the one story I write is at the top of the news, or near the top." Despite these aspects of the craft that are widely shared by reporters of all kinds, the particular medium for which a reporter writes does pose a certain standard in the writing of foreign policy news, one that makes a noticeable difference even if it is not a dominant pattern.

Writing as Affected by the Audience. More significant than the type of news outlet in its impact on the writing of foreign policy news is the conception of the audience that any particular news outlet reaches.[2] Two basic images of the audience prevail among the foreign affairs reporters. One view regards the audience as intelligent and deeply interested in foreign affairs, while the other sees it as made up of ordinary people, of medium to low interest, and non-expert in foreign policy matters.

The image of the audience as especially interested in foreign affairs incorporates both the view that the readers are the foreign policy elite,[3] and the feeling that they are in unspecified ways unusual or distinguished though perhaps not expertly knowledgeable. The elite image is found chiefly among—but it is not wholly coextensive with—reporters for New York and Washington newspapers, and some columnists. They see their newspapers, and thus their own stories, as read by government people all the way up to the top levels, by editors of other newspapers around the country, by university pro-

---

[1] Cf. International Press Institute, *The Flow of the News*, pp. 16-18.

[2] Cf. Ithiel de Sola Pool and Irwin Shulman, "Newsmen's Fantasies, Audiences, and Newswriting," *Public Opinion Quarterly*, XXIII, No. 2, Summer 1959, pp. 145-58.

[3] In Gabriel Almond's sense; see his *American People and Foreign Policy*.

fessors, by the clergy—by the molders of policy and of opinion in the foreign policy field. The foreign policy audience of the *New York Times*, for example, is often described this way, by reporters who do not work for it as well as by some who do. More commonly, this audience, both in Washington and nationally, is described in more general terms as "fairly literate," and "unusual"—even as "the 5-to-10 per cent" of the population who are presumed to be interested and reasonably well informed on foreign affairs, who have ideas and who want answers. "You should go on the assumption that only 10 per cent of the best-informed people in the country are going to read foreign affairs anyway, and do your writing for them. They are not fooled by gimmicks. A straightforward presentation is the best way to handle this."

Some of the reporters who point explicitly to the small attentive public in the foreign affairs field, however, do not write explicitly for that part of the audience. One correspondent said, "You must think of this element that wants the answers. At the same time, you must write so the other 90 per cent can understand you." Another talked about "the 5 per cent" as a special audience that had to be served by the newspaper, just as those readers interested in comics had to be served. These reporters, in effect, represent the second viewpoint, that the audience is mostly an ordinary one, undistinguished by any special interest, intelligence, or competence. This point of view is in general more characteristic of wire service reporters and correspondents for newspapers away from the East Coast, and is shared by some columnists who see their national audience in these same non-discriminating terms. It is widely believed by foreign affairs correspondents that once one leaves the eastern metropolitan foreign-news market one enters a different world; for example, "My stories go out for the papers in the Midwest. It's rather elementary reporting. Most reporting in this area [i.e., Washington and New York] is over people's heads there. I don't mean to say that people there are less intelligent or less knowledgeable, but they don't have the same interest." While the *New York Times* might be said to conceive of its foreign affairs audience as including the diplomats and policy makers, the United Press International believes that it writes about foreign affairs (and other subjects) for the milkman in Omaha, Nebraska. And like the widespread belief in the elite character of the *New York Times'* audience, the stereotype of the provincial audience between the Appalachians and the Sierra Nevada is shared by those who do not write for it as well as by those who do. For example, a reporter for a New York paper remarked, "The general public will not read interpretive articles on foreign affairs; that is why John Hightower [an Associated Press foreign affairs analyst] is not carried on the AP wires out to Minnesota"—an incorrect but revealing statement.

How does this image of the ordinary reader affect the writing of foreign policy news? "We try to make the facts about remote or complex things as understandable as possible." "We use a lot of similes in order to get people to understand the complexities of foreign affairs." "We sometimes slip into a little sensationalism to make a story more readable, so long as we don't tamper with fundamental facts." The differences on this score as between this group of reporters and those who think of their audience as particularly interested in foreign affairs are sometimes less than one might expect; correspondents of both groups wade together through the bogs of journalistic style. Even the *New York Times* finds it necessary to identify the Secretary of State by his full name and title in every news story in which he appears, and to write successive daily installments of the "continuing big story" by repetitious recapitulation, as if assuming that its readers had not been reading the "big news" or could not remember the salient details from yesterday's account.

These definitions of how to make a foreign policy story interesting and understandable raise some troublesome questions. The issues of international affairs are admittedly complex, and their details are difficult to follow; but are these issues and events more realistically understood, or are they so oversimplified or personalized or sensationalized as to be distorted, when they are brought down, in the words of a wire service reporter, "into the language that can be understood by someone with a lower high-school education"? Obviously there can be no simple or easily agreed-upon answer to the question whether a larger readership of foreign-affairs-made-simple is to be preferred to a smaller readership of material that more accurately reflects the crucial complexities of the subject matter. But even this formulation of the question assumes that more simplified writing of international affairs will result in wider readership[4]—a proposition that is not at all self-evident. We shall consider this whole problem more directly in Chapter VIII; at the moment it may be enough just to state it.

There are other conceptions of the audience for foreign affairs news that are worth passing mention. Some reporters see their audience in geographical terms, claiming that they write for a midwestern audience, for example, or for a sophisticated New York or Washington audience; but in each case these geographical definitions turn out to be restatements of the two basic images presented above. Those reporters who mentioned eastern metropolitan areas were thinking about an attentive and elite audience, while those who spoke about other areas had in mind an undifferentiated audience, a general public. Finally, one correspondent stated flatly that "Every newspaperman writes for other newspapermen; this is the common law. He writes for his peers who are competent to judge him." When one considers how much time correspondents spend reading each other's stories, and how much use they make of them in shaping their understanding and pursuit

[4] For a forceful statement of this position, see Lester Markel, "The Flow of the News to Marilyn Monroe," *Problems of Journalism*, 1960.

of news, the only unusual thing about this statement is that it was not echoed by more of the foreign affairs reporters.

Writing Affected by Effects Sought. Finally, and for the sake of completeness, it should be repeated that the way foreign policy stories are written up may be strongly influenced by the personal preferences of the correspondent, and by the effects he seeks in the policy and opinion markets. Reporters, be it said once more, want to capture the attention of the Secretary of State with their latest bit of information gleaned from sources not readily available to him, or with the wisdom of their unencumbered opinions; they also want to see their stories on page one rather than page ten or twenty, not only because that is the mark of the successful reporter but because capturing prime space and capturing people's policy attention are part of the same process. There are enough illustrations of this in preceding chapters not to have to repeat them here; it should be understood that the participant roles are worked out not only in the choice of stories, but in the choice of audience and in the manner of presentation as well. This may not be the dominant force in foreign policy reporting, but it is by no means irrelevant or insignificant, particularly for correspondents in the eastern metropolitan region who know, to begin with, that through their newspaper they have a foot in the policy maker's door.

The Newspaper as the Determinant of News

The daily newspaper is more than just the end product in the transmission of information; it is the starting point for news. For unless a story is actually printed, and printed relatively prominently, it is not regarded as "in the news," and thus it exerts little claim on the attention of the reader and the reporter alike. When the correspondent combs the newspapers every day, he is looking for the authoritative measure of the news, for only in this way can he acquire a secure line to the immediate future. The news process, as we stated earlier, is not linear, but circular. It runs from news to newspaper to news, in a chicken-and-egg-like progression. In other words, the editors and their newsroom staffs have an important, though not always apparent, influence on the shape of reality as it is perceived by the producers of news as well as by the consumers; and we are interested here in the decisions they make that help to define what that shape will be. We tend, as a rule, to take the newspaper for granted—to regard it as the bearer of objectively determined news, even though we might wish in particular circumstances that our newspaper had more news of one kind or another. We rarely think of the human processes of decision-making that create every newspaper; we think of the reporters and feature writers and editorial writers who have fashioned the building blocks, but we are less often aware of the architects and construction workers who trim and combine the blocks into a particular structure. "Every newspaper when it reaches the reader is the result of a whole series of selections as to what items shall be printed, in what position they shall be printed, how much space each shall occupy, what emphasis each shall have. There are no objective standards here. There are conventions."[5]

Competition for Scarce Space. The starting point for any discussion of newspaper coverage of public affairs must be an understanding that there are practical limits—variable, to be sure, but still limits—to the space in a newspaper and thus to the amount of news it can publish. What those limits are for any particular newspaper is the result of a complex of economic calculations involving size of market, number and kind of advertisers, profit margins, and so on. Even the *New York Times*, despite its favorable economic structure and its awesome motto, prints only about 15 per cent of the million or so words that come in to its editors in any one day. In other words, no newspaper anywhere is able to shovel out to

[5] Walter Lippmann, *Public Opinion*, p. 268.

its readers as news the total stock of information and stories that it receives; severe selection processes are universal.

Within the limitations established by the size of any newspaper, and by the amount of advertising it runs, there must be further decisions allocating the available space among the various possible claimants. The foreign affairs specialist, or the politically interested layman, may argue that national and international news dealing with foreign affairs is the most pressing item on the public agenda, and thus deserves top priority in the allotment of newspaper space; and in this argument they would be supported by a considerable number of editors who regard foreign affairs as the "top story" on a continuing basis. But even these editors, and these readers, are talking about priorities and not absolutes. The most fundamental circumstance affecting the publication of foreign policy news is that it is, in the minds of all the people who put out newspapers, only one category of newspaper content out of many, and that it has to compete with all kinds of news and features for the limited space available. The editors and publishers argue that there are readers to be satisfied as well as an ill-defined "public interest" to be served, and so most editors and publishers divide up their space on the basis of their intuitive understanding of what their readers like—or what will sell papers.

These space allocations are not made inflexibly, nor are they made and remade daily, or even frequently. They are matters of fundamental policy in a newspaper, and are subject to considerable inertia; once made they tend to persist until changes in top personnel or in the fortunes of the paper suggest new ones. At any point in time, then, both the editors and the reporters have to work within the confines of the rules-of-thumb that constitute the blueprint for the newspaper. The correspondent has to write his stories on foreign affairs in the knowledge that, in the words of a wire service reporter, ". . . American newspapers are interested in City Hall, county government, the State House; and the room that is left over from this and from the most recent murder they devote to international affairs. . . ." In the process of competing for this limited space—and we shall see in the following section just how limited it is—reporters develop the explicit definitions of news that they hope will give their output a better-than-even chance: conflict, drama, and the like. The editors, in turn, have to fill up the space allotted to international affairs; they are the judges of the competition, and they choose in a manner that is consistent with prior decisions on what their readers will buy.

The Foreign Policy Allocation. How much of the "news hole"—the newspaper space available for general news of all kinds—is assigned, on the average, to foreign affairs? What is the general configuration of this competition for news space? It is exceedingly difficult to get consistent measurements here, because of different interpretations of what should be measured, and because of the great variation in foreign policy coverage among different newspapers. (For example, large metropolitan newspapers contain proportionately more foreign news than non-metropolitan papers.)[6] The data available are in agreement, however, on the order of magnitude, which is small.

The International Press Institute's study of 93 US newspapers during four separate weeks between October 1952 and January 1953 (during the Korean War) concluded that "the average proportion of *foreign material* to text space . . . is a little more than 8 per cent. . . ."[7] Another study of this same

---

[6] Cf. Ralph D. Casey and Thomas H. Copeland, Jr., "Use of Foreign News by 19 Minnesota Dailies," *Journalism Quarterly*, xxxv, No. 1, Winter 1958, pp. 87, 89.

[7] *The Flow of the News*, p. 219; emphasis in the original. This may be regarded as a generous estimate, since "foreign material" was defined as "foreign dateline news, foreign news pictures, editorials, columns and editorial cartoons dealing with current foreign developments. . . ." For some of the problems that were involved in arriving at these and the following percentages of foreign affairs news, see Robert L. Jones and Roy E. Carter, Jr., "Some Procedures for Esti-

sample of American newspapers in the first half of 1956 found that "an average of 3 to 5 per cent of general newsspace was devoted to items on foreign affairs."[8] In a study of six newspapers in three cities on two dates in 1958 and 1959, the space "devoted to foreign items of every description" averaged 12.5 per cent of total editorial space. Restricting the measure to "substantive" foreign affairs topics brought the figure down to 7.7 per cent of total editorial space.[9]

Translating these percentages into absolute figures does not change the impression that the volume of coverage is low. For the 93 newspapers in the International Press Institute's study, the average space given to foreign dateline news including headlines (foreign dateline news comprised about 75 per cent of the larger category of foreign material) was 4.4 columns a day; the range was between 32 columns a day for the *New York Times* and .7 columns for the *Yreka* (California) *Siskiyou News*.[10] A readership survey of 51 newspapers, conducted by the American Institute of Public Opinion for the International Press Institute, put the daily average of column inches of international news of both foreign *and domestic*

---

mating 'News Hole' in Content Analysis," *Public Opinion Quarterly*, XXIII, No. 3, Fall 1959, pp. 399-403.

[8] Carnegie Endowment for International Peace, *The United States Public and the United Nations: Report on a Study of American Attitudes on the U.N. and the Communication of Information to the U.S. Public*, New York, 1958, p. 28. This may be regarded as a narrow estimate, since "general news" was defined in this study as all non-advertising, non-pictorial matter in the newspaper, and "foreign affairs news" did not include foreign news of a "trivial" nature, nor did it include news of internal political affairs in foreign countries.

[9] Edward W. Barrett and Penn T. Kimball, "The Role of the Press and Communications," in American Assembly, *The United States and Latin America*, Columbia University, 1959, pp. 90-102. The six papers were chosen because their foreign news content was "closely comparable" to the coverage in the 93 newspapers that were the subject of the prior studies mentioned. " 'Substantive' refers to topics dealing with politics, economics, social affairs, diplomacy, etc., as opposed to crime, disaster, entertainment, sports and trivia." (*Ibid.*, p. 100.)

[10] *The Flow of the News*, pp. 22, 219-20.

origin at 106, which is about 5 columns.[11] Barrett and Kimball, however, measured the average column inches of all foreign items in their 6 papers at about 275, or between 12 and 13 columns, and the average column inches of "substantive" foreign items at 167, or about 8 columns.[12] Finally, a study of the foreign news available during the course of one week in April 1960, in 5 newspapers that circulate in Madison, Wisconsin, produced the results shown in Table 1, which were cumulative for the week.[13]

TABLE 1

Newspaper	Total News Space (in col. inches)	Total Foreign News[a] (in col. inches)	Total Foreign News (in cols.)	Foreign News in per cent of Total News Space
Capital Times[b]	17,248	438	20	2.6
Wis. State Journal	21,472	744	34	3.5
Chicago Tribune	29,472	1,744	80	5.8
Milwaukee Journal	32,472	1,940	88	6.0
New York Times	40,476	4,081	185	10.0

[a] "Foreign news" excludes foreign travel, religious, and sports news, and includes headlines and pictures.
[b] The *Madison Capital Times* has no Sunday edition.

How does this volume of foreign affairs material published in American newspapers compare with the volume of such material that is available to them for daily use? Perhaps the best measure is a comparison of the news agency flow with the amount of foreign affairs news published. Since there is considerable duplication of news in the material supplied each day by the major wire services available to American newspapers, we can take as a minimum working figure the approximately 22,000 words per day supplied (in 1952-1953)

[11] *Ibid.*, pp. 62-63.   [12] Barrett and Kimball, *op.cit.*
[13] This material was drawn from tables by James F. Scotton, in "Foreign News Presented to Newspaper Readers in Madison, Wisconsin," unpub. MS., University of Wisconsin, 1960.

by the "agency used most extensively by American newspapers"[14]—the Associated Press. This translates roughly into 27 columns of foreign news a day; how much more should be added to this figure for a more realistic estimate of available news is a function of the non-repetitive content of the other agencies, and the number of agencies to which a particular newspaper subscribes. The average of approximately 5 columns of foreign news published daily in American newspapers works out to between one-fifth and one-sixth of the total supplied from this one source, and of course to a much smaller fraction of the total supplied by all the major wire services each day. So the small volume that is published, and its small fraction of the total news on any one day, are due much more to the decisions of the editors than to the sources of supply.[15] A foreign affairs reporter who once ran a small newspaper recalled what it was like: "You throw in a few international pieces as a gesture to international affairs, then you fill the rest with the stuff that sells papers." A significant point in all this is that the severe limitation of space allocated to foreign policy news, permitting the publication of only a handful of stories each day, lends especial importance to those few items that are printed. They become the chief elements in the portrayal of the foreign policy world, and thus build up for their readers a comparably limited picture of the scope and character of international political relations.

It should be borne in mind that some of the above figures include foreign policy news originating in Washington, while others exclude such material, treating it as "national news." It is doubtful that the systematic inclusion of this news would substantially alter the picture presented here: with the excep-

[14] *The Flow of the News*, p. 19. The figure of 22,000 words per day still seemed to be a good approximation of the situation as of 1962.

[15] Cf. Scott M. Cutlip, "Content and Flow of AP News—From Trunk to TTS to Reader," *Journalism Quarterly*, xxxi, No. 4, Fall 1954, pp. 434-44. Cutlip points out that foreign news is cut in greater amounts throughout its transmission sequence than any other category of news.

tion of a very few newspapers, the daily stream of information of relevance to American foreign affairs is thin indeed. Lest some hasty conclusions be drawn at this point, we might anticipate a later discussion and note that if the volume of foreign affairs news that is published seems low, the amount that is habitually read is, again on the average, lower still.

The "Play" of Foreign Policy News. The men who run newspapers determine what is "news" by the location and space they give to particular items, as well as by the number and kind of items they choose to print in the first place. There are conventions involved here, too, which are of course subject to individual interpretation, but in general the largest headlines, the front and early pages, and especially the right-hand and left-hand columns of the front page are the places and signs of the "most important" news of the day.[16] As a general rule, also, reporters aim for front-page treatment of their stories, and regard back-page treatment as being only barely "in the news." The editor's task may be defined as the ordering of the day's stream of stories of all kinds in all areas—the attachment of relative significances by the decisions as to where to publish particular items, how much space to assign to them, how big a headline to write, and so forth. In this sense, "the news" is made on the editor's desk (and how it is done will be discussed in the next section). What this can mean may be illustrated by a small example. American foreign aid legislation has long stipulated that a fixed percentage—usually 50 per cent—of American goods shipped abroad under such programs should be sent in American ships. The protectionist implications of this provision were particularly significant in the early post-World War II years because it deprived recipient countries with their own merchant marine of an opportunity to earn dollars. At the time of the original legislation

---

[16] For evidence on the "effect of position" of articles in the newspaper, cf. Ralph O. Nafziger, "The Reading Audience," in Wilbur Schramm, ed., *Communication in Modern Society*, Urbana, University of Illinois Press, 1948, esp. pp. 105-6.

on the European Recovery Program, however, the *New York Times* with few exceptions carried stories about the shipping lobby and its political activity in Washington on the shipping page, which is the second from the last page in the paper,[17] where they were likely to be read chiefly by people with shipping interests rather than by those with broader foreign policy interests. (Most papers, no doubt, ignored the matter completely.)

To say that editors attach relative significance to particular foreign policy stories—indeed, to all stories—and thus tell their readers what to think about, is to say also that the reader adapts to his newspaper, so that he knows how to receive signals about importance or salience, and how to interpret them. He learns both the general conventions of the newspaper business and how particular editors and publishers modify them. He learns that an editor, by using the various ways of conveying orders of significance, is saying, "This is the most important thing that happened today; this is second; this is third," and so on down the line. The reader thus becomes familiar with the priorities held by those who put out the newspapers he regularly reads.

The significance of the reader-editor relationship may be appreciated when a person picks up an unfamiliar newspaper in a strange town. Applying his customary measures of significance, he may flounder immediately, for the signals are likely to be different. Sometimes he can reorder events so that they correspond to the familiar priorities; it takes no great sophistication, for example, to know that a local housing-authority scandal is less important in a foreign policy sense than a political revolution somewhere in the world which it may have squeezed off the front page. But then he may begin to wonder what else has happened in the last twenty-four hours that got

[17] Holsey G. Handyside, "The European Recovery Program: A Case Study," unpub. MS., Woodrow Wilson School of Public and International Affairs, Princeton University, June 1952, p. 44.

squeezed out of the paper completely; in other words, he cannot "trust" the paper—it has no map-making function for him, it does not communicate significance to him, at least in the short run. With repeated exposures, however, the newspaper becomes familiar; at least it can be located in the reader's frame of reference. And to the extent that some rough congruity is established between the world as the reader thinks of it and the world as the paper represents it, the editors are once again the authorities for news.[18]

The raw stuff of a newspaper—whether one calls it news, stories, information, or whatever—comes into the newspaper offices from many different sources, in a more or less steady flow. Here, in fact, is the true "flow of the news": not its abstract unending march from events themselves, but the physical processing of specific dispatches and stories, coming in a steady file through the bottleneck of slow transmission systems across the desks of news editors. In all except a handful of American newspapers, the foreign affairs news comes almost exclusively over the news agency teletype machines, where the concept of the "flow" is particularly appropriate. The information or news comes unordered, in the sense that the items do not contain within themselves notions of their relative importance; it is rather like a do-it-yourself kit where the parts are unlabeled. How are these pieces put into the order that is implicit in the make-up of a newspaper? What are the circumstances and the criteria and the influences that help to shape decisions on the final product, which looks so predeter-

[18] Cf. *The Press and Its Readers*, A Report Prepared by Mass-Observation for the Advertising Service Guild, London Art and Technics, Ltd., 1949, p. 96: "The reader's preference for one particular paper is based on a complexity of different points almost impossible to unravel. He likes a paper that he is used to, that he knows well enough to be able to find his way around in." The report speaks also about "the personal feeling of attachment which grows and spreads itself over the whole paper once people have taken it for any length of time and once they have become accustomed not only to the individuality of its features but also to its peculiarity of presentation and general lay-out." (*Ibid.*, p. 109.)

mined when it hits the doorstep or the newsstand? What follows by way of an answer to this question is not meant to be a formal disquisition on how a newspaper should be put together; there is an ample literature of journalism concerned with that subject. We are interested rather in observing how, in practice, foreign affairs material is handled in the editorial processes, and we particularly want to trace through some of the themes that we have seen to be guides in the earlier choice of news by correspondents.

Some General Considerations. The daily task of constructing the segment of international reality takes place in a particular kind of setting, both institutional and social, aspects of which have some relevance here. For one thing, the editorial functions involved in the processing of news are dispersed, to an extent that varies, *inter alia*, with the size of a paper; but except for papers of very small size and circulation, anywhere from two to a half-dozen or more people are involved in the selection, layout, editing, and headline writing of foreign policy news. Effective decisions are made, therefore, at a number of different points, although the general news editor and the telegraph editor, who presides over the bank of news tickers, together with whatever assistants they might have, make the major decisions involving selection and layout. These men do not, of course, start the editorial process *de novo* each day; they approach the task with an experience and a perspective that have both long- and short-term components. Over the long term, particular classes of stories pre-empt the leading news spaces—economic reform, war, international political competition. As the Alsops have pointed out, in the 1930's it was the New Deal, and since 1945 it has been the political confrontation between East and West.[19] In the short run, the editors carry in their heads the knowledge of what the news

[19] Joseph and Stewart Alsop, *The Reporter's Trade*, p. 26. For a confirming picture of the things that captured the interests of Washington correspondents during the Roosevelt years, cf. Leo Rosten, *The Washington Correspondents.*

has been—and what they have made it—over recent days and weeks. Hence they come to their tasks every day with half-formed and unarticulated notions of what the news is apt to be *like*.

When they get to their desks on any given day, they confront two stern realities: there is a paper of a specified size that must be filled, and the job of filling it has to be handled at a rapid pace. The cycle begins at a late hour, to take advantage of late news items (and the latest variant of earlier items); as press-time nears, the pressure becomes intense, lifting slowly as the major decisions are made. Considering that "the news" is ever new, one might expect that the job presents the editorial workers with the prospect of infinite variety, challenges never faced before; in fact, however, it is highly routinized, like most jobs. Walter Lippmann put it very expressively: "Without standardization, without stereotypes, without routine judgments, without a fairly ruthless disregard of subtlety, the editor would soon die of excitement."[20] Watching this process, and tracing the fate of the foreign affairs news as it makes its way through the stages of selection, the observer is struck by two things. First, the practitioners do not have the time for serious reflection on the meaning of their choices while they are in the midst of making them. They may give careful thought to the problem in between times, but it takes a substantial effort to replace the reflexive choice with the conscious, deliberate selection of news items meant to illuminate a particular pattern or image of international affairs. Second, the judgments that are made at nearly every point in the editorial process are made on implicit grounds; the editors are generally unable to give meaningful, non-tautological explanations for their choices.[21] Yet they are very well

[20] Lippmann, *op.cit.*, p. 267; his forty-year-old description of this process is still fresh.

[21] Cf., e.g., the reasons for the rejection of foreign news stories reported by Casey and Copeland; 20 per cent of the rejected stories were turned down because of "lack of space," 18 per cent because of "lack

attuned to each other; the extended network of interactions that bear in on the news editor and then out to the copy editors functions for the most part in silence. The work of one person may be modified by another further along the chain, but the number of judgments that are explicitly questioned by any of the participants is small, and even then of minor import.

Some Bases of Choice. Despite the implicit, reflexive, routinized character of the editorial task, one can observe certain persistent influences and sources of judgment being brought to bear on the treatment of foreign affairs news.

(1) The commercial criteria that we have seen reflected in the judgments and choices of the foreign affairs correspondents originate in the management and editorial offices of newspapers. For the newspapers themselves are economic enterprises, no matter what else they may be, and the interests of circulation are registered on the news desks, by and large, as pressures for the kind of coverage that is presumed to sell papers—lively, contentious, sensational, dramatic, personalized, and so forth. We say "presumed to sell papers," because the judgments about what a reporter has called "the stuff that sells papers" are less than rigorously or scientifically derived; they are generally the intuitive reactions of publishers and editors to past performance, and very few independent tests are made to discover whether it is bad management, for example, or the taste of the readers, or changes in the character of the communities, or something else again, that accounts for the success or failure of particular newspapers at particular points in time. Papers with extensive foreign affairs coverage, and papers with very little, both justify their choices on the

---

of appeal or interest to the readers," 17 per cent because "the stories were considered to be lacking in news value and significance." The remaining rejections involved such things as timing, technical considerations, problems of style and make-up. (*Op.cit.*, p. 88.) For comparable data, see David Manning White, "The 'Gate Keeper': A Case Study in the Selection of News," *Journalism Quarterly*, XXVII, No. 4, Fall 1950, pp. 383-90.

grounds that "we print what we know the public will want to read," which indicates how little precision or discrimination there is in these estimates. Nonetheless, there is a general consensus in newspaper circles that foreign affairs is not a staple in the reading diet of mass audiences—a reasonably correct observation that may or may not be related to the success or failure of particular papers. Even on newspapers with good foreign affairs coverage, the "public's news values" are understood to lie along other scales; an editor of such a paper remarked, "We don't have to make concessions to the public's news values." So, in all but a handful of daily newspapers, the presumption on the news desks runs against foreign affairs stories, and against extended analyses of complicated foreign policy issues. That is to say, the commercial criteria affect chiefly the amount of coverage and its general character, which are long-term decisions, rather than influencing judgments on a daily basis against one particular news item and in favor of another. The area and variety of foreign affairs coverage are enlarged from time to time, of course, but to the extent that commercial notions hold sway, the enlargement comes as a consequence of judgments about the "appeal," the "intrinsic interest," the "salability" of new and exciting or unusual events, rather than as a consequence of judgments, say, about their policy significance.

(2) The policy preferences of editors and publishers, and the substantive theories they have that invest specific developments with policy significance, constitute further bases for the choice of foreign affairs news—in some newspapers, that is. Since no effort has been made to investigate this proposition in a representative sample of newspapers, it is offered here only as a possible factor to look for, rather than a constituent element in editorial choice of foreign affairs news everywhere. All we can say for sure is that news judgment in some newspapers is affected rather strongly—though never exclusively—by the theories and preferences of the editors and publishers,

while in other newspapers there appear to be few consciously or strongly held views on these matters, so that foreign affairs news judgment is substantially informed by other standards. It is difficult to resist the belief that there are more newspapers of the latter kind than the former, although the evidence to support this is circumstantial.

The American newspapers that are noted for their coverage of foreign affairs—indeed, the newspapers that are rated the highest according to general professional criteria both by newspaper editors[22] and by faculty members in American schools of journalism[23]—are virtually all staunch defenders of a liberal international foreign policy, in the same sense that we applied the phrase to the foreign affairs reporters earlier. The *Chicago Tribune* is the major exception to this generalization. And there is ample evidence that the coverage of foreign affairs in these papers reflects the example of the European Recovery Program, which in the view of close observers within the press was systematically supported by both reporters and editors, who gave space to the proponents of the program and largely ignored its opponents. In another case, extensive coverage of a tariff matter was explained by the editor who was responsible in these terms: "The briar pipe case is a classic example of an incident that seems trivial to some people on the surface of it, but which we are really convinced is extremely important." One finds similar editorial justification for special coverage of many different aspects of American foreign relations. The correspondents for these newspapers are aware of and responsive to the foreign affairs interests of their news editors, so that the latter are then supplied with material they can publish without paying conscious attention to the reasons why they are doing so; after all, it *is* "the news." "We are great

[22] The study, conducted by Edward Bernays, is reported in a full-page advertisement for the *St. Louis Post-Dispatch*, in the *New York Times*, April 18, 1960.

[23] John Tebbel, "Rating the American Newspaper—Part I," *Saturday Review*, May 13, 1961.

internationalists," said a reporter from a border state; "the editor has strong viewpoints on issues."

These editorial preferences and theories may come into play within the bounds established by the ruling commercial considerations, and also at their margin. For these are among the factors that will lead one news editor to run an interpretive background story, or a story from a foreign newspaper, while another editor will restrict himself to the daily news items. And they are among the factors that help editors pick and choose among the daily foreign affairs stories that cross their desks, since they do not have room to run them all.

(3) Not many newspapers, as we said above, appear to be run by men with consistent and well-developed conceptions of the international environment, who exercise their own judgment in producing a newspaper noted for its foreign affairs coverage. Most newspapers are run by men whose interest and experience are confined to regional or state or local affairs, who do not specialize in foreign affairs, and who lack the understanding, the theory, that tells them the foreign policy significance that might attach to particular stories.[24] Their world revolves around the community and its issues, whether they be political, economic, or criminal. Yet these newspapers *do* publish some stories on foreign affairs. How do they choose among the available offerings, and how do they determine how these stories should be played in relation to the rest of the daily fare?

[24] Robert Merton's distinction between "cosmopolitans" and "locals" seems appropriate here—even though in a community context he might classify editors as cosmopolitans. See his "Patterns of Influence: Local and Cosmopolitan Influentials," in Paul F. Lazarsfeld and Frank N. Stanton, eds., *Communications Research, 1948-1949*, New York, Harper and Bros., 1949. See also Alvin W. Gouldner, "Cosmopolitans and Locals: Toward an Analysis of Latent Social Roles," in two parts, *Administrative Science Quarterly*, II, No. 3, December 1957, pp. 281-306, and II, No. 4, March 1958, pp. 444-80. The IPI study, *The Flow of the News*, reports that "Two-thirds of the American managing editors replying to an inquiry of their views on the qualifications of deskmen handling foreign news, were highly critical . . ." (p. 81).

Where editors lack their own theoretical or substantive criteria for distinguishing the significance of the individual elements in the stream of events, they borrow the judgments made by others in whom they have some confidence. These judgments about foreign affairs news come from two major sources. First, and most important on a daily and continuing basis, is the wire service news budget—a résumé by each news agency of what *its* news editors think are likely to be the most important stories in the daily run, for both the morning and afternoon papers. These lists—one from each agency to which the newspaper subscribes—are in hand when the telegraph editor confronts the thousands of words spilling out of the machines, and when the news editor approaches the task of making up the day's newspaper. They provide, in a sense, the labels that are not intrinsic in the news items themselves. The news budget gives an editor the comforting knowledge that if he accepts the news judgments therein, he will be in the company of hundreds of other editors (who are all fulfilling the wire service news editors' prediction of what "the news" will be that day). Not only is it hard to go wrong that way, but to diverge from that judgment is to fly rather manfully in the face of what the editor himself knows by that time *will be* the news. This is especially true of those items that appear in more than one news agency's budget; on the other hand, items that are unique to a particular budget may force an editor to exercise his own judgment—or to seek outside help from still other sources in making choices. The budgets, furthermore, put international and foreign policy news into a context of domestic news from a variety of arenas, so that the editor can know not only the top foreign policy stories but also the relative importance assigned to these stories in the larger field of news.[25]

[25] Walter Gieber portrays in even sharper terms how the wire editor "is caught in a strait jacket of mechanical details. . . . He is concerned with the immediate details of his work rather than the social area in which news is made and given meaning." ("Across the Desk: A Study

In addition to the budget, and as a kind of independent check on it, editors sometimes borrow news judgments from other newspapers. The outstanding guide in this respect is widely acknowledged to be the *New York Times*. Louis B. Selzer, addressing the 1956 convention of the American Society of Newspaper Editors as editor of the *Cleveland Press*, observed that whereas newspaper readers were interested in local situations, newspapers gave most of page one to "news from remoter and less controversial areas.... They then check with the *New York Times* to see if their judgments are upheld."[26] Joseph Kraft said of the *Times* that its coverage alone "makes it indispensable as a basic news source to editors and writers, politicians, statesmen and professional men all over the country."[27] The news judgments of the *New York Times'* editors are transmitted by the wire services and by the *Times'* own syndicate, which sends its clients not only a selection of its news stories of the day, but a list of its page-one stories, and those of the *New York Herald Tribune*, too.[28] Although the *Times* may have a pre-eminent position here, it is not the only guide; to quote a reporter from a western publication, "The *Times* is the only really important paper nationally.... The influence of other papers is largely regional—but in a list of papers which influence other editors I would put the *Post-Dispatch*, the *Courier-Journal*, and the *Chicago Tribune*." Warren Breed also suggests that while the *New York Times*, *New York Herald Tribune*, and *Christian Science Monitor* have a special significance as "opinion leaders" among the press, the larger newspapers in every area serve as a guide to the editors of the smaller papers. "The influence goes 'down,'

---

of 16 Telegraph Editors," *Journalism Quarterly*, XXXIII, No. 4, Fall 1956, p. 432.) As a consequence, press association recommendations of news are accepted more or less mechanically and consistently.

[26] *Problems of Journalism*, 1956, p. 154.

[27] Joseph Kraft, in *Esquire*, November 1958, p. 126.

[28] Warren Breed, "Newspaper 'Opinion Leaders' and Processes of Standardization," *Journalism Quarterly*, XXXII, No. 3, Summer 1955, p. 283.

from larger papers to smaller ones, as if the editor is employing, *in absentia*, the editors of the larger paper to help 'make
up' his page."[29] Obviously this "arterial pattern," as Breed calls
it, is circumscribed, and not only by the limiting factors he
mentions, such as big local stories, competition among papers
in the same city, and particular situations where the larger
paper may be suspect.[30] Even if they would like to model themselves after big city papers, the smaller papers will often go to
press before or at the same time as the larger ones, and thus
the latter are not available as guides to that day's news display.
But even yesterday's paper provides a check on one's news
judgment, and a check against too exclusive a reliance upon
the wire services' judgments.

The importance of the news budget and of other newspapers in establishing the significance of stories, and the
interaction between these two sources, may be seen in the
following incident. When the Subcommittee on National Policy
Machinery of the Senate Committee on Government Operations, under the chairmanship of Senator Henry M. Jackson,
held its first public hearing on February 23, 1960, the public
witness was the Hon. Robert A. Lovett, who had once been
Secretary of Defense and Under Secretary of State. In his
testimony Mr. Lovett, a Republican who had served a Democratic President, was outspokenly critical of the national
security effort being made by the Eisenhower Administration.
Lovett's remarks were given front-page treatment in the *New
York Times*, but the AP handling of the story was described
as "routine" by someone who followed these developments
closely; that is, it was given no extra nudge, so it had "no
play in the Associated Press budget." (In the Associated Press
the budget items are selected by the general news editor and
his assistants, with the help of suggestions from the AP
bureaus themselves, which are closer to the stories being
covered.)[31] As a result the story was either "buried" by most

[29] *Ibid.*, p. 278.   [30] *Ibid.*, p. 281.   [31] *Ibid.*, p. 283.

editors, or it was overlooked completely; "it wasn't even in the *St. Louis Post-Dispatch*, for instance." But the AP is a servant of its members as well as their master, and when some of the editors of the member papers discovered that they had "missed"—i.e., not had their attention specifically directed to— a story that was given a big play in the *New York Times* and other bellwether newspapers, they vented their spleen on the AP. The result was a number of round-up and follow-up stories about the Subcommittee by the AP in an attempt to regain lost ground, plus the assignment of a special AP reporter to cover the Subcommittee for a while.

☻   Conclusion

The correspondents for the wire services and for the few newspapers that maintain an independent foreign affairs coverage follow a path of news that is narrowed at the start both because it proceeds within the framework of what they understand editors and publishers to want by way of variety and amount of foreign affairs news, and because it is subject to collegial definition of what the news is at any given moment. Beyond this initial influence on the shape of foreign affairs news as it ultimately appears in the newspaper, there is the extraordinary significance of the editorial choices, the judgments of importance, made by a comparatively few people, especially in the news agencies and in what are sometimes called the "quality" media.[32] Their decisions constitute a powerful thrust toward the standardization of news, national as well as international, in a country that has no truly national newspaper to do the job. Indeed, these processes may be said to do for the newspaper press what network news does for radio and television, although of course the several news systems are by no means independent of each other. Those who are disturbed by the potential influence and great responsibility

[32] Cf., e.g., James N. Rosenau, *Public Opinion and Foreign Policy*, New York, Random House, 1961, pp. 81-83.

that, in these circumstances, rest in just a few hands[33] may be a bit reassured by the fact that this is substantially an unconscious accretion and exercise of power. Those who make the effective decisions at each stage in this process feel themselves to be rather more in the grip of the news than in command of it. Later we shall have occasion to speculate on some of the consequences of the differential exposure to foreign affairs information that exists even within this framework of standardization.

[33] E.g., Breed, *op.cit.*

CHAPTER V

THE EYE OF THE BEHOLDER:
POLICY MAKERS' VIEWS OF
THE PRESS

———————•••———————

◐   A N   I N Q U I R Y into the role of the press in foreign
policy-making that examined only the behavior of
the press would be one-sided, for it would miss the range
of interactions that complete the circuit between press and
policy maker. The "mirror" that the press holds up "by
which its readers can see the world"[1] is not fashioned exclusively by the initiatives of the press, nor is it the product
solely of the criteria of judgment that mark the news-gathering
and editorial processes. Foreign affairs news comes out of an
interplay between the correspondents and the men of responsibility whose thoughts and actions are the objects of the
correspondents' interest. The figure of the mirror, indeed, is
rather inappropriate on a number of accounts; the glass that
the press holds up is refractive rather than reflective, and the
beams that come out of it strike the policy makers as well
as a larger public. The readers, in particular, include both
the members of the press itself and those who dwell in the
policy-making structure—that is to say, those who manage
the prism are also managed by it. And so in our search for an
understanding of the significance of the press in the foreign
policy process, we must look at the uses to which the press is
put by foreign policy officials, and the patterns of thought
that shape those uses. The policy maker both contributes to
and extracts from the fund, or the flow, of foreign policy news;
and both the putting in and the taking out help to define the

[1] V. O. Key, Jr., *Public Opinion and American Democracy*, p. 390.

nature of the press's participation in the process of foreign policy-making.

◉ A Guide to "The Press"

There were, by recent count, 1,761 daily and 546 Sunday newspapers in the United States;[2] obviously these are all part of the ill-defined, amorphous institution known as "the press." Equally apparent, however, is the fact that no one, not even a large extractive industry like the United States government, can assimilate or even be exposed to more than a small part of the institution. In previous chapters, when we referred to the press, we meant the sector of it that produced the bulk of the foreign policy news and analysis; and we were interested particularly in the correspondents who specialized in this subject. What does the foreign policy press look like to the officials in the Executive and Legislative branches of the American government who have foreign policy responsibilities? There are several layers in the foreign policy makers' image of the press.

The "Prestige Papers." It should occasion no great surprise to discover that foreign policy officials recognize that there is a small and specialized foreign affairs press in the United States; and that the single most important newspaper, by general admission, is the *New York Times* should also be a familiar datum. The *Times*, which regards itself as a newspaper of record, a daily contribution to history, is read by virtually everyone in the government who has an interest or a responsibility in foreign affairs. Some typical comments in the State Department: "The *New York Times* is read more generally than any other newspaper, owing to its more exten-

[2] Edward W. Barrett and Penn T. Kimball, "The Role of the Press and Communications," in American Assembly, *The United States and Latin America*, p. 96; since there are frequent changes and combinations in the newspaper business, and different definitions of what constitutes a newspaper, any such figures must be regarded as an "order of magnitude" of the present situation rather than a precise accounting.

sive coverage." "The first thing we do is read the newspaper—*the* newspaper—the *New York Times*. You can't work in the State Department without the *New York Times*." "The *New York Times*," a former Assistant Secretary of State reminisced, "was of particular importance." A Congressman called it "everyone's Bible of information," and a Senator's Legislative Assistant said that the *Times* was "every man's CIA around here." Outside the State Department one frequently runs across the familiar story: "It is often said that Foreign Service Officers get to their desks early in the morning to read the *New York Times*, so they can brief their bosses on what is going on." This canard is easily buried: the "bosses" are there early, too, reading the *New York Times* for themselves.

The importance attached to the *Times* may be seen in some examples of its use. A freshman Congressman wanted to reach the State Department, the White House, and his fellow members of Congress with his foreign policy ideas, but he felt that his junior status in itself gave him no platform in Washington from which to reach this audience. So he chose to communicate to the foreign policy-making community by writing letters to the editor of the *New York Times*, for publication, hoping to make a substantive contribution to foreign policy that way. In another circumstance Senator Monroney, Democrat of Oklahoma, worked closely with the *New York Times*, seeking coverage of his proposal for an International Development Association—favorable or unfavorable—as an essential ingredient in his efforts to organize public support.[3] His reasons for wanting *New York Times* coverage were these: "First, he believes *The Times*, especially the Sunday edition, is read by some of the most influential individuals throughout the nation and indeed the world. Second, he knows that often what appears

[3] James A. Robinson, *The Monroney Resolution: Congressional Initiative in Foreign Policy Making*; see esp. p. 5: "Indeed, adverse testimony by a high-ranking official would not necessarily have been unwelcomed inasmuch as it too would have attracted attention."

initially in *The Times* will be picked up by other newspapers. And third, he likes to circulate reprints of such articles and editorials which he thinks will, because of their source, carry great weight."[4] And the conjecture of a Senate staff person that Senators had read the *New York Times'* stories about the Senate Foreign Relations Committee's studies of American foreign policy in 1959-1960, but had not read the studies themselves, is also a commentary on the importance of this particular newspaper.

The *Times* has long been regarded as *the* American "prestige paper": "In each major power, one newspaper stands out as an organ of elite opinion. Usually semi-official, always intimate with the government, these prestige papers are read by public officials, journalists, scholars, and business leaders. They seldom have large circulations, yet they have enormous influence. . . . We find, then, that despite local and individual variations, the prestige paper has come to be an impertant and respected institution. Governments, politicians, and businessmen depend upon it. One might ask what would happen in Washington if the *New York Times* stopped publication and no other paper took its place. There would certainly be a deterioration in American political intelligence."[5] But if a prestige paper is defined by its importance to the political and governmental elite, then the notion of a single prestige paper has to yield, in the foreign policy field at least, to a plural concept.

There can be no question that the *New York Times* is of prime importance; but it has distinguished company on the desks of foreign policy-making officials, very few of whom limit their consumption to one or even two newspapers: the *Washington Post*, the *New York Herald Tribune*, the *Wall*

[4] *Ibid.*, p. 3.

[5] Ithiel de Sola Pool, *The "Prestige Papers,"* Hoover Institute Studies, Series C: Symbols, No. 2, Stanford, January 1952, pp. 1, 8. See also Wilbur Schramm's discussion of the prestige papers in *One Day in the World's Press*, p. 5.

Street Journal, the *Christian Science Monitor*, the *Baltimore Sun*, the *Washington Evening Star*. Collectively these papers, with extensive foreign affairs coverage and in many cases independent sources of news via their own staffs of foreign correspondents and foreign affairs reporters and analysts, form the prestige press in the foreign policy field. Their relative importance varies, obviously, from individual to individual; but one can hardly avoid recognizing the significance, in Washington, of the *Washington Post* and to a slightly lesser extent (perhaps because it is an evening paper) the *Star*. The following comments are typical. A Senator: "I read the *Post*, of course, and the *Star*, and the *New York Times*";[6] a State Department official: "I read the *New York Times*, of course, and the *Post*, and the *Star*"; a former State Department official: "Everyone in the State Department reads the *New York Times* and the *Washington Post*."[7] Running behind these papers in the number of daily official readers, yet carefully scrutinized within the policy-making institutions themselves, are the other newspapers on the above list. Every day, for instance, the News Office of the State Department prepares, for the higher-level officials in the Department, a two-page survey of major foreign affairs news stories in these leading eastern morning newspapers. Many of these officials are quick to state the virtues of these other newspapers; for example, "The *New York Times* has the best coverage, in extent, but for balanced, objective reporting, in depth, the *Christian Science Monitor* or the *Baltimore Sun* may be better."

If one hypothesizes that the order in which newspapers are

[6] Cf. Donald R. Matthews, *U.S. Senators and Their World*, p. 206: "Most . . . [Senators] read the Washington papers, the *New York Times* or *Herald Tribune* (sometimes both), plus several leading home-state papers every day."

[7] In May 1953, the *Washington Evening Star* reported that 95 Senators and 406 Representatives bought its weekday issues. Cited in Franklin L. Burdette, "Influence of Noncongressional Pressures on Foreign Policy," *Annals of the American Academy of Political and Social Science*, Vol. 289, September 1953, p. 95.

read has some impact on the relative attention paid to each—on the plausible assumption that the major items will be read most thoroughly in the first newspaper one takes up, and even that, under the pressure of work, only one newspaper will be read on a number of days—then there is additional reason to upgrade the *Washington Post.* For the *New York Times* is often the second newspaper to reach the foreign policy specialist in Washington, the *Post* usually being the first. In fact, for many of these people, the *Post* is the doorstep newspaper, and it is read over the breakfast table. They will then pick up the *Times* on the way to the office, or it will be on their desks when they arrive. The *Times* is uniformly regarded as the authoritative paper in the foreign policy field; in the words of a State Department official in the public affairs area, "You can't work in the State Department without the *New York Times.* You can get along without the overnight telegrams sooner." But our judgments must be based on the practices of these men as well as on their expressed attitudes, and their practices put the *New York Times* in the position of *primus inter pares.*[8]

The prestige press, then, does not consist simply of *one* newspaper whose publisher and editors have determined to make it quantitatively, if not qualitatively, distinctive in the foreign affairs field; rather, it is an amalgam of the eastern metropolitan newspapers of higher quality and better coverage that are available to the policy makers on the day of issue. There are others, too, not yet mentioned, which perhaps belong on this list; these are the better newspapers whose regional circulation does not include Washington in any substantial way, such as the *St. Louis Post-Dispatch*, the *Louisville Courier-Journal*, the *Milwaukee Journal*, the *Minneapolis Tribune*, to mention just a few. These papers *do* get to Wash-

[8] Cf. Key, *op.cit.*, p. 405: "The *New York Times*, the New York *Herald Tribune*, the Washington *Post*, the Baltimore *Sun*, and a few other newspapers command the attention of a highly politicized and very influential audience."

ington, and they *are* read, but because of their regional interest and their time of arrival they are not serious competitors for the early and daily attention of foreign policy makers; they are more likely to be scrutinized as the best examples of the flow of foreign policy intelligence to the "provinces."[9]

To sum up, then, the prestige press is not a unique newspaper that policy makers depend on for their political intelligence; rather, it is a larger network of communication that helps to define for the policy maker the current political universe. Washington survives when, from time to time, the *New York Times* is not published; it may be sorely missed, but there are a half-dozen other papers that collectively fill the gap. (There may even be secret relief when the pressure to read, and respond to, the *New York Times* is temporarily lifted.) The larger network of communication is marginally, not centrally, affected.

This general description of the foreign affairs communication environment among decision makers in Washington needs to be qualified slightly in one respect. As some of the above quotations indicate, the member of Congress from a non-eastern constituency has a more compelling reason to read newspapers published in his state or district than has any particular official in the Executive branch (although the job of some persons in the State Department is to keep track of what a range of newspapers from all over the country are saying). These Congressmen may also be more inclined than the typical foreign policy official in the Executive branch to read the higher-quality newspapers with regional circulations in the South, Midwest, and Far West, even when they arrive late, both because the newspapers are likely to be familiar and because of a political desire to keep in closer touch with currents of opinion in the rest of the country. Yet this does not

[9] This conclusion does not seem to be weakened by the well-publicized announcement on May 14, 1962, that the White House was dropping its twenty-three subscriptions to the *New York Herald Tribune*, replacing them with the *St. Louis Post-Dispatch*.

seem to alter the basic point made earlier, for Representatives and Senators cannot rely on district or home-state newspapers for national and international news if they cannot get those papers on the morning of publication (quite apart from the question of how much national and international news they may contain). The Congressman has too great a need to be kept up-to-date to indulge a possible preference for a constituency newspaper. The New York Congressman who said, "I know damn well that Representatives and Senators from the West Coast rarely even look at the *New York Times*" was over-stating his case. Members of Congress may, on the whole, prefer the *Washington Post* to the *New York Times* among the eastern papers; but those from the West Coast as well as from the East Coast who specialize in international policy are among the *Times*' readers. One western Senator, in fact, was so impressed by the paucity of foreign news in the home-town papers that he began sending the front page of the *New York Times* back home to keep his friends informed on foreign affairs. The pattern seems to be that, insofar as Congressmen get information from newspapers (rather than from personal contacts, for example), they get their national and inter-national political news and views chiefly from the New York and Washington papers, and their state and local political news plus a segment of local opinion from the constituency papers. Since they have other lines of communication to local political situations anyway, and are not generally acting in the immediate context of such situations, the delay in getting this news from district newspapers is supportable.

The News Agencies. For most newspapers in the country, as we noted in a prior chapter, the flow of national and inter-national news from the wire service tickers represents the well into which they must dip for their coverage of national and international affairs. Thus wire service coverage may be regarded as a vast, continuous, unedited newspaper—much more extensive in its coverage of foreign affairs than virtually all newspapers in the country, since no paper that relies on this source publishes all the information it produces. Moreover, not only do the wire service teletype machines define the outer limits of foreign affairs coverage for most newspapers and for many policy makers; they also may be regarded as "tomorrow's paper today," or "this afternoon's paper this morning." They give the news a number of hours before it can be obtained from ordinary newspaper sources.

For both of these reasons, the news tickers occupy a prominent place in the foreign policy makers' world. The State Department's News Office maintains Associated Press, United Press International, and Reuters news tickers; the *Agence France-Presse* ticker in the State Department is located, for language reasons, in the Bureau of European Affairs. And there are also several tickers in the suites of the Secretary and Under Secretary. The machines in the News Office are monitored constantly; eight copies come off each ticker, and additional copies are often duplicated in order to distribute the news items to all the relevant areas in the Department. The News Office rates the tickers as very important; "in fast-breaking situations, the tickers beat [State Department] cables by four or five hours—and in some cases by up to twenty-four hours." And the fact that the Secretariat has its own teletype machines may be taken as circumstantial evidence that the steady flow of news over the tickers is regarded as too important to be slowed down by the human processes of getting the clippings delivered from the News Office. The tickers are used and appreciated in the geographical bureaus of the Department, too. It was said, for example, that "the NEA people [Bureau of Near Eastern and South Asian Affairs] get their information from the tickers, not from newspapers or from correspondents per se." An official in the Bureau of European Affairs said that the tickers were "a faster medium" than reports from the posts abroad. In the Bureau of African Affairs: "We follow the Congo on the ticker and in the press, and you get a quicker report of what is going on than you do through official reports." This same theme is repeated in other Bureaus, in an acknowledgment of the importance of the private news agencies in the communications network that sustains the foreign policy makers.

The same general pattern prevails in the Department of Defense also, where the News Division has the AP and the UPI wires. These teletype machines are also monitored steadily, with eight copies being printed and clipped; and "the relevant clippings" are sent to "the interested people" in the Department. And as in the State Department, officials in the Department of Defense acknowledge that they "often see things first on the ticker."

In the Legislative branch the situation is not very different. There are AP and UPI tickers in the lobbies off the Senate and House floors, and they run just as long as anyone is around to read them. Page boys cut the sheets and hang them up, numbered consecutively, where they are read continuously whenever the Houses are in session. A member of one of the foreign affairs committees said, "The tickers are used steadily; this is the first source of information—many hours before we read it in the press."[10]

Considering the attention that men of top political and governmental rank pay to the wire services, one must include these services as part of the larger "prestige press." Each of them has its own staff of correspondents all over the world. Thus, each news agency represents an independent source of news about world affairs, more extensive in coverage and more rapid in impact than the best of the "prestige" newspapers, which maintain their own staffs of correspondents abroad and in Washington. The political importance of wire service news is additionally—though indirectly—heightened by the Wash-

---

[10] Cf. D. Matthews, who remarks that the tickers "are regularly consulted by all the Senators"—an overstatement, no doubt, but it makes the point. (*Op.cit.*, p. 206.)

ington newspapers, which rely very heavily on the news agencies for their international news.

The "Press" as People. Foreign policy-making officials also see "the press" as the output of particular reporters and columnists whom they respect or whom they believe to be influential in the political community even if they themselves do not think very highly of them. There is very widespread agreement on who these able and influential individuals are: Walter Lippmann, Joseph Alsop, Marquis Childs, James Reston, C. L. Sulzberger, Hanson Baldwin, Chalmers Roberts, and John Hightower are mentioned most frequently. And all of them, it might be noted, appear in the newspapers that make up the foreign policy "prestige press." These men are put in a somewhat special class; their columns or stories are a kind of personal communication rather than the output of an impersonal communication system. One person with experience in both the Executive and Legislative branches remarked, "I look for by-lines as well as subject matter." The following comments are illustrative of the predominant attitudes toward these men as representatives of the press. A Senate staff man: "A man like Reston must be considered as a statesman."[11] From the State Department: "There are too few Lippmanns in the world"; and "You count on your Lippmanns, your Childs, your Restons, etc., your better columnists, to carry the straight story, without attribution." There are, to be sure, less exalted expressions of respect toward these same men, and even some strong dissents from the very attitude expressed here; some people in the State Department, for example, pointed out that Lippmann does not make the correspondent's customary rounds in the Department and remarked that, if he did, he would not make so many "silly statements" in his columns. One went so far as to say, "Generally all columnists are pretty

[11] Cf. Joseph Kraft, in *Esquire*, November 1958, p. 123: "On some big matters the State Department informs him [Reston] almost automatically, as it would the representative of a major power."

terrible." But on the whole this "inner circle" of foreign affairs reporters and columnists is esteemed for the excellence of its contacts, and for its intelligent, insightful, and responsible use of information delicately and privately given. In a spiral of cause and effect, the doors of high-level policy officials open more easily for them; and when the policy makers evaluate a columnist as responsible and intelligent in their *own* dealings with him, they will more readily respect the rest of his writings as similarly authoritative, intelligent, and responsible.

Foreign policy makers see the press in a personal way in still another respect: the press also enters the world of foreign policy-making through the personal relationships among policy makers and correspondents who gather and comment on foreign affairs news in Washington. (Comparable relationships exist among American foreign correspondents and American embassy personnel abroad.) Personal friendships between government officials and newsmen are common, extending right up to the Presidential level,[12] and more-than-casual acquaintanceships are even more numerous, owing to the constant contact between officials and the reporters on a steady "beat," and to the fact that the foreign affairs reporters, who have high status among the Washington press corps, move in many of the same social circles as the government officials. A Senator even reported an instance where a close friend among the correspondents substantially influenced his judgment on a vote in the Senate: "I had damn near decided to vote against . . . [a particular proposal], just for the hell of it, to let the Administration know what I thought of their lousy way of doing things. I called this guy in, to talk it over with him. He pleaded with me not to do it—to vote for the proposal. . . . He was so intense about it, and so much better experienced [substantively] than I, that I gave him the benefit

[12] Cf. Worth Bingham and Ward S. Just, "The President and the Press," *The Reporter*, April 12, 1962.

of the doubt, and voted for the program against my better judgment."

Informal interplay, where it does occur, is valued by both sides—by the reporter who must establish good contacts to do his job well; and by the official who wants to see the press do a good job of presenting the issues (or at least his side of them), and who also knows that a good reporter has more ideas and information than he ordinarily uses in his columns in any one day. For the correspondent, like a traveling salesman, gets around a great deal, and hears a lot of things that may not rate as publishable news but that are nonetheless relevant and of interest to policy-making officials. The correspondent learns, too, that his relationships with officials develop best when he can trade bits of information—when he can give as well as get, and thus be useful to his sources instead of being, from their point of view, an endlessly prying nuisance. In this way the correspondents become direct personal communications links among the participants in the foreign policy-making process, over and above the intermediary function they may serve through the stories they write; they make their rounds carrying the germs of policy thought from one interested party to another. One State Department official, for example, who remarked that he was not in direct contact with reporters because he sat in a "protected position," nevertheless named about ten leading foreign affairs correspondents as personal friends: "I'm lunching today with a correspondent. . . . I do it often, with a number of them. I get ideas from ———, and he gets them from me. He knows all the top people here. We have a public duty to the press, to help them cover foreign affairs adequately." Another officer in the Department said that "about 80 per cent of my contacts with reporters are on a personal basis—reporters whom I know personally, some of them since we were in the 'field' together." A staff assistant to a Senator, both of them active in the foreign policy field, reported that "Sometimes reporters call you to give you information. Almost always this requires a friendly relationship and a sympathetic issue-orientation. A reporter will interview a Cabinet officer, and then he will call me and tell me what he said—and he may ask me what I think of it, too. Reporters are human, and they get swept up in issues."[13] Personal contact of this kind between reporters and officials is much more specialized, intermittent, and unevenly distributed than are their other points and varieties of contact; its qualitative importance would be very difficult to measure, to be sure, but it is too prominent a form in which the policy world experiences "the press" to be overlooked.

⊖   Patterns of Attitudes Toward the Press

Not all foreign policy-making officials, by far, have close personal relations with correspondents; indeed, the mutuality of trust that characterizes such a relationship is narrowly circumscribed, in the sense that many officials do not come into direct contact with foreign affairs reporters at all, and those who do are far from indiscriminate with their favors. Because the attitudes toward the press that circulate at any time among the policy makers are more or less related to the behavior of these individuals toward the press, it is relevant here to inquire into the nature of those attitudes and the particular patterns that may be found among them. It has been claimed, for example, that the attitudes of career officers in the State Department are more favorably disposed to the public affairs function within the Department, and to the press, than are the attitudes of men who come to the Department from the business world;[14] this is too simple a formulation to stand for very long, but it does at least suggest what a "pattern of attitudes" might look like.

At one level, it might be true to say that among those officials

[13] For another instance of reporters getting "swept up in issues," see Robinson, *op.cit.*

[14] Robert Pell, "The State Department Spokesman," *America*, July 2, 1962.

who have any contact with correspondents there is only one orientation toward the press that has any meaning—and that is ambivalence. The "love-hate relationship between us and the press," as a Deputy Assistant Secretary of State phrased it, pervades the remarks of many thoughtful persons in the Executive branch, and even of some of the foreign policy people in the Congress. Sometimes this comes out in the form of remarks that the press as a whole is both good and bad in its impact—as in the general comment from a former sub-Cabinet official that 20 per cent of what the press had to say on foreign policy was constructive and 80 per cent destructive. Sometimes the love and the hate are explicitly attached to different constituent parts of the press. It may be a case of some reporters being regarded as "responsible" and others not; for example, "You have to learn what reporters you can trust, and which you can't"; or, "You have to be careful with the press—you need to *know* the guy." Or it may be put as a reporter-editor problem, where the foreign affairs reporters do a good job but the editors do not use the good material. Sometimes it may come out in the form of a direct relation between the esteem in which a reporter is held and the nervousness he causes—the abler the correspondent, the harder it is to keep his nose out of what the officials feel are especially sensitive policy areas. As a general proposition, it might be said that the most favorable factors in the ambivalence tend to be the product of successful personal relations with particular newsmen over periods of time, whereas the unfavorable elements are a response more to the headaches that the press may have caused an official without his having been personally involved with the correspondent, than to direct instances of rough handling by the press. In any event, considering the large amount of negative feeling toward the press, a considerable number of respondents insisted that their own personal relations with the press had invariably been good.

Another way of looking at the ambivalent attitude toward the press—although officials themselves do not express it this way—is to see it as a reflection of the fact that the press performs a number of different roles in the foreign policy area, some of which are favorable or neutral to the policy maker's cause, while others are adverse. The press is thus a useful instrument to the policy maker in some of its manifestations, and an annoyance in others. The role of the press as critic, for example, may not unnaturally induce a considerable amount of hostility on the part of the official, even while he acknowledges the function of criticism in a democratic society, and even as he responds very favorably to the opportunities that the same or other correspondents present, via their neutral roles, to the advancement of his interests.[15] Since the press manifests its roles in different and particular guises, it is not surprising that ambivalent attitudes are found almost everywhere, even among those who profess to have uniformly favorable or unfavorable images. There are some officials, for instance, who emphatically repeat that the press and diplomacy are fundamentally antithetical—that the press must proceed on the principle of openness while diplomacy can only develop in a protected place; but significantly even these people have learned how to live on good terms with the press, and how to use it to further their own policy purposes. One often hears officials say that the press is helpful where it is responsible, and harmful where it is irresponsible. But the context just as often suggests that the true order is the reverse: where the press is thought to have been helpful, it is then regarded as responsible, and where it is judged to have been harmful, it is then viewed as irresponsible. But what is helpful and what is harmful in any circumstance depend on how particular individuals define their interests. Ambivalence, in other words, is compounded from a range of negative and positive attitudes

[15] President Kennedy's experiences with the press along this line are instructive; cf. Bingham and Just, *op.cit.*

that are partly ideological and partly instrumental in character, and that are a response to the various roles the press performs.

Let us, then, look separately at the constituents of love and hate in the policy makers' image of the press. Perhaps, in the process, we can shed a little more light on the things that cause both this hate and this love, and thereby contribute to the development of better "understanding" on both sides. Although the question of how to "improve" the relations between the foreign policy agencies and the press is not a central focus of our inquiry, one cannot be totally indifferent to this problem in the democratic management of foreign affairs.

Favorable Attitudes. Far and away the most frequently expressed comments in defense of the press concerned the characteristics and qualities of the correspondents themselves, and their helpfulness in the processes of foreign policy-making. The fact that favorable attitudes cluster around these two points is not accidental. The personal qualities of newsmen, and their helpfulness from the viewpoint of the policy maker, are different aspects of a larger instrumental attitude toward the press on the part of the foreign policy officials.

Foreign affairs reporters and columnists in Washington are commonly (though by no means universally) well-regarded, even by foreign policy officials who are highly critical of the press on other scores. These correspondents, specializing in foreign policy, are able to talk to policy makers in a language they understand, and they are sufficiently familiar with the issues of policy so that they can ask relevant questions that the policy officials find difficult to answer openly. In the course of the daily encounter between the two, which generally revolves around substantive policy matters, the official develops a respect, sometimes freely acknowledged, sometimes grudgingly given, for the correspondent: "They're a pretty savvy group of guys." "A fact of life in a free society is a corps of very intelligent, shrewd, indefatigable newspapermen. Some are tremendous . . . and can hold their own in any college political science department." "Reporters are clever, adept, well informed, responsible; I have great respect for them." "Good reporters are remarkably astute. . . . They are agreeable, interesting, knowledgeable people. They read a lot." "There are many qualified newsmen who are respected by government officials."

One of the characteristics most frequently cited by officials in favor of these correspondents is their trustworthiness, as attested by favorable experiences with them in the past. The reporter in an institution like the State Department, it should be noted, can function effectively only if his lines of communication through the institution are in good working order. He therefore feels obvious pressures to *be* trustworthy, for he knows that the reporters who violate confidences, or who undermine the policy positions of their sources by their revelations, or who cause their sources trouble as a by-product of their search for a front-page angle, will soon find themselves with no sources other than the handouts, or releases. Trustworthiness is thus a prerequisite to tenure in this "elite" group of reporters, and the long periods of service cited in Chapter II are presumptive evidence that certain standards of performance along these lines are regularly being met. A top-level career officer said, "I've never been *badly* let down by any of them; I've had good experiences. . . . You can take the senior and responsible correspondents into your confidence." A desk officer: "This is something that strikes the officers—press officers and desk officers alike—the freedom with which they can speak. The press is responsible and is able to distinguish between what it can publish and what it cannot." A former political official in the mutual security program: "Most policy people have their pet newsmen. . . . They are people with whom they can consult and whose judgment and discretion they respect." Not all correspondents are trusted equally by everyone, of course; certain correspondents and columnists do have nearly universal reputations for reliability, but they circulate chiefly at the upper levels in the foreign policy establishment. Below them the situation is more segmented; networks of trust are more limited in size and scope, and the over-all pattern is made up of these limited but overlapping areas of profitable experience.

The "helpfulness" of foreign affairs correspondents, which is perhaps the key to all the other favorable attitudes, is not wholly separable from the latter, since being helpful is a product of both personal qualifications and characteristics of performance as seen by the policy makers. This component of favorable images of the press reveals more clearly than any other how the foreign policy officials tend to judge people and performances by an instrumental criterion. If the reporters and analysts side with the Administration in its general foreign policy orientation, and if that basic predisposition is translated from time to time into articles or stories that help rather than hinder the officials in their pursuit of their vision of policy, and if, in the times in between, the reporters are governed generally as much by conceptions of desirable foreign relations as by conceptions of how to make the front page, then they are deemed to be helpful—that is to say, responsible—reporters. A White House aide during the Truman years remarked, "Most of the newsmen are liberal, and they gave the Administration a good break." A sub-Cabinet official in the same administration said, "I think the press did a good job. Explaining to the people is really their best role. . . . In such instances as the Greek-Turkish aid program, the Marshall Plan, and so on, they made a real contribution." It should be made clear that the requirement is general enough so that a reporter does not have to become a spokesman for a man or an institution in order to be regarded as helpful; but at a minimum he cannot contravene the larger assumptions governing both means and aspirations in the prevailing foreign policy.

This is, of course, a familiar subject to the careful reader, for it involves the neutral roles of the press and the potentialities that those roles contain for exploiting or "using" the reporter for policy purposes—only here we are looking at it from the standpoint of the official rather than the newspaperman. It would be too strong to say that the *really* helpful correspondent, in the official's eyes, is one who lets himself be used by the policy makers for goals that may or may not be shared by both of them, but this is surely an important element in the instrumental syndrome. For reporters to share the policy makers' image of desirable foreign policy is not necessarily difficult, nor does it necessarily or even often involve toadying; the typical foreign affairs reporter himself, remember, is strongly in favor of liberal international commitments. This personal orientation is part of his motivation in foreign affairs reporting, and so long as American administrations stay on this path in their foreign relations, the correspondents, as we said in an earlier chapter, may even welcome a chance to be "used" on particular occasions. A State Department official described the situation this way: "We have no press in this country that is an available tool for creating understanding, domestically or abroad, of foreign policy. We use it from the point of view of 'news' . . . where you give them the straight dope, to set them straight or to impress upon the reporters the seriousness of a matter. . . . You count on your Lippmanns, your Childs, your Restons, etc., your better columnists, to carry the straight story, without attribution. That is as near as you can come to using the press to convey policy, to directing the press as to what to say."

A reporter may sometimes be helpful, in the same sense of serving the policy maker's purposes, even when he is ostensibly critical of policies or relationships with which the foreign policy makers are identified; this is the case, for example, when the reporter expresses some criticism that the policy maker would like to express but is not free to do so in his official capacity. But since it is not clear to what extent these critical newspaper accounts are initiated by policy officials— "we can reap the benefits, but it is hard to organize such pieces to begin with"—we cannot be sure whether "helpfulness" of this kind is an accidental by-product of the reporter's critical function, or an example of the press's lending itself to the policy maker's purposes. In either case, however, the officials look benignly on the reporters so long as their points of view converge. Clearly, though, "helpful" can only be defined with reference to a particular set of personal or policy interests or preferences, and what is helpful to those who share these interests may be regarded rather differently by those who have other interests or purposes.

A corollary to the fact that instrumental considerations are foremost as a basis for policy makers' favorable attitudes toward the press is that ideologically based reasons for being favorably disposed toward the press are much less in evidence, and where they are expressed they are generally rather weak and unconvincing. One might have expected, on *a priori* grounds, that men who give some years of their lives to public service might have an ideological superstructure that justifies their own effort and relates it to a philosophy of democratic government and public participation. If ideologies or rationalizations of this kind do exist, however, they are not often articulated. Only a handful of foreign policy officials couched their approval of press activities in the foreign policy field in terms of the requirements of an informed public. For example, "The more news you can give out, the better. . . . The more people know, the better." "You have to have an informed public. You have to tell them what the problem is, what they are in for." "I am convinced that the people do not go wrong if properly informed. This is the real contribution made by the columnist to foreign policy—to create understanding, to educate." The ideological component may be even further diminished by the fact that a few of these officials had some public relations responsibilities; at least this makes it a little difficult to separate ideological from instrumental factors in their defense of the press.

There are, finally, some institutional and some personality factors that appear to be associated with favorable images of the press. There seem, for instance, to be certain personality types, certain kinds of people, who manifest a sense of self-confidence and of control over their environment that enables them to look on the press, on balance, more as a structure of opportunities than as a natural antagonist, an enemy. Instead of timidity or fear in the face of the press, they display a mastery, an instrumental competence (even though they may also have some negative feelings about the press). A high State Department official noted that government officials tended to favor caution and secrecy as ways of dealing with the press, adding, "But if you know what *not* to tell and *what* to tell, you can establish a confidential relationship and help to get across the favorable side of what you are doing, rather than the nit-picking side." A desk officer in the Department said that he preferred as many direct relations with the press as possible, with fewer and fewer intermediaries: "You get a better feel this way; you keep better control over what the State Department is saying publicly." And from the public affairs area of the State Department: "If we want a reporter to have our viewpoint, we've got to give it to him." It is not an exaggeration to say that there are those who "naturally" find it easy to deal with the press—to establish the "confidential relationships" with correspondents—while others find it so difficult that they consistently manage to avoid all contact with reporters; and the latter quite apparently outnumber the former. Considering the size of the State Department alone, for example, and the small number of regular foreign affairs reporters, and the fact that they trace overlapping paths through the Department (there are few exclusive contacts between reporters and officials; the reporters need multiple sources both for verification and to cover their traces, and most officials act on the understanding that "you can't play favorites with reporters"), it is obvious that relatively few people in the State Department have the confidence to discuss policy issues regularly with the press. In one Bureau it was reported that only four people besides the Public Affairs Adviser talked regularly to the press: the Assistant Secretary, a country-desk man, a regional organization man, and the economics specialist. "Individually, over a week, they will have from six to eight contacts with the press. Only the Assistant Secretary sees the press as a group—and then only once every two or three months, for a background briefing. So our regular contacts with the press are small."

It is sometimes argued that there are institutional factors at work here, in the sense that the top-level officials can talk to reporters with the confidence that comes from their positions of authority, while lower-level personnel are more reluctant to put their careers at risk in these encounters. This line of distinction is reported by a few State Department officials, and by some reporters, too, but the latter, despite their claim that the working-level "Indians" provide the best information, have a predilection for the more authoritative "chiefs," and thus their observations about the openness of officials may be colored by their preferred lines of access. Two sets of considerations can be introduced here, however, which suggest that confidence vis-à-vis correspondents is not a function solely or even substantially of rank, although this proposition cannot be regarded as explicitly testable by means of the data obtained in this study. In the first place, even on a random basis it is easy to find the confident-competent syndrome at all levels in the State Department, as well as fearful personalities at all levels, including the highest. There are instructive differences to be found, for example, in the press conference behavior of Secretaries of State Dulles and Herter; Dulles used all of his contacts with the press, including the formal conference, as an opportunity to lecture, instruct, propose, test out, and in general convey his own preferred conception of things, while Herter held his conferences less often and was notably more hesitant, cautious, unrevealing in his comments. Secondly, the State Department's public affairs institutions and procedures, which are designed to restrict the number of authoritative Departmental spokesmen, have the paradoxical effect of cloaking the junior officials in the Department in anonymity, since only the senior officials (and the News Officer) may be quoted directly or referred to as a State Department spokesman. This initial protection is sustained by the reporter's ethic never to reveal his sources, and together they are a major reason why "leaks" in the State Department are very rarely traced back to their source. This being the case, the hierarchical reasons for timidity or reserve in the face of the press, on the part of junior men, seem to lose some of their strength. As a senior official put it, "If it is not for attribution, it will not hurt anything." Nonetheless, it may still be true for some officials that self-confidence—the attribute of personality—develops slowly over time and with experience, and is thus indirectly related to rank in the Department. This possibility ought not to be excluded, even though the data at hand suggest that the relevant experience may be acquired in months rather than years, and thus be relatively independent of changes in rank.

There are other institutional differences in attitude toward the press that are frequently put forward and deserve some scrutiny. It is sometimes argued, for example, that the P-area people—the Public Affairs Advisers, the men in the News Office and in the other offices and divisions of the Bureau of Public Affairs—who are professionally concerned with the State Department's public relations, are more likely to be favorably disposed toward the press, while the desk officers—the substantive people, the Foreign Service professionals—have a fundamental antipathy toward the press and other "outside" institutions. There is quite a bit of secondary evidence that supports the main burden of this distinction; most Foreign Service Officers are not in direct contact with the press, whether or not their instinct is to avoid it, as one of them asserted. And in the P-area, officials talk freely of their "constant battle" with the desk officers on behalf of "maximum disclosure." "We wish to make full information available, and appear a little bolder; Foreign Service Officers are cautious. . . ." Here, too, we lack the data properly to evaluate this hypothesis, but we can at least indicate some qualifications that should be considered.

In the first place, the distinction itself is not wholly valid, since many persons in the P-area are Foreign Service Officers on normal assignment. The Public Affairs Adviser in each Bureau of the State Department is normally a Foreign Service Officer; and one can find among them men who, on balance, favor the press and know how to work with it, and other men who have an unconcealed hostility toward it. Furthermore, since the P-area is conventionally suspected by reporters as the source of an official line, and held in low repute as "the gateway to the obvious," desk officers are cultivated as alternative sources of information; and thus there is circumstantial evidence that more than just a few desk officers *are* in contact with the press. The line of distinction that seems most valid here, as elsewhere, is not between P-area people and desk people, or even between political appointees and career officials, or between civil service personnel and Foreign Service Officers, but between those people in *all* classifications and at *every* level in the Department who are confident in their dealings with the press, and those who are not. Regardless of whether it is chiefly a matter of personality, or whether training and experience are also involved, the press-oriented personnel are a relatively small proportion of the total. As a very rough approximation, the State Department's contact with the press is regularly maintained by perhaps no more than 10 per cent of its staff, and probably considerably less than that.

The imprecisions and uncertainties that mark this discussion of patterns of confidence toward the press suggest the need for more extensive investigation of the subject. The problem is large in dimension, since large numbers of people are involved, and difficult in scope, since one suspects that the details of many contacts with the press will not be quickly volunteered. The State Department formally talks with one voice, informally with somewhat more. No doubt the managers of the Department prefer these contacts to be reasonably few, yet there is no apparent reason why anyone should prefer that the talents that sustain these contacts should be randomly or accidentally distributed throughout the Department. On the contrary, if more were known about their location and character, the State Department could easily make an effort to see that people with the requisite skills and personality attributes were regularly put into areas where the Department's public information needs were the greatest, and thus where they could do the Department the most good.

Thus far we have been looking at the character and distribution of favorable attitudes toward the press chiefly within the Executive branch, and most particularly in the State Department; a word may be appropriate here on the differences between Executive officials and Congressmen in these respects.[16] Congressmen as a group are rarely able to dispose of the kind of information that bears profoundly on the state of political relations among nations. A handful of Congressmen are regularly kept informed on aspects of foreign policy by the State Department, but since it is understood at both ends of Pennsylvania Avenue that it is difficult to "maintain security" in the Congress, the flow of information is carefully circumscribed. Members of Congress thus are not generally

[16] For an extensive discussion of the Congressman's general orientation toward the press, see Douglass Cater, *The Fourth Branch of Government.*

in a position to be good sources of foreign policy information, nor are they generally cast in a role that requires them to put a "straight story" across. They have no continuing public relations functions in regard to foreign policy, except insofar as foreign affairs committee members (and in times of perceived crisis larger numbers of Congressmen) may deliberately associate themselves with a foreign policy proposal to move it through Congress, or to "close ranks" nationally. As a result, rather few members of Congress are sought out by correspondents on foreign affairs matters, and even fewer can summon them.[17] A member of the Senate Foreign Relations Committee with little seniority expressed his situation this way: "My contact with the press is very limited; I'm not a focal point for the press. I suppose I could call press conferences, but you don't do it unless you hold a position on the Committee that makes it seemly. . . . But from time to time . . . a reporter will come to get my view on a particular item. . . . Sometimes what I give them appears in a story, and sometimes it doesn't." Another Senator with a strong personal interest in foreign affairs and a committee assignment that impinges on foreign policy said, "My contacts with the press are restricted to the _____ [regional] newspapers, and they have no application to foreign policy."

This being the case, tapping the average legislator's attitudes toward the press in the foreign affairs area taps in an indiscriminate way his attitudes toward the press in general; and insofar as foreign affairs can be separated from other policy areas, it taps his attitudes as a *consumer* of foreign policy material rather than a producer of it. The favorable attitudes that are mentioned most often by Congressmen should be judged in the light of these considerations; they are very largely limited to the personal qualities of the news reporters themselves, but without any explicit instrumental over-

[17] Donald Matthews makes this point also, talking about all news of national scope. (*Op.cit.*, pp. 202-3, 216-17.)

tones such as were found in the case of Executive agency personnel. Congressmen are impressed with the over-all ability of the reporters, generalizing from the ones they see every day on Capitol Hill; they mention their trustworthiness, their responsibility, their fairness and objectivity. These judgments are made in the absence of explicit criteria, and particularly criteria of self-interest, such as "helpfulness."

Unfavorable Attitudes. On a frequency basis, about a third more respondents (78 in all) in the Executive and Legislative branches expressed negative attitudes toward the press than made favorable remarks (60). While intuitive impressions based on casual conversations as well as on the interviews themselves had suggested that negative attitudes were more likely to be expressed, this was not borne out by the frequency count; the number of negative comments made by these respondents was greater than the number of favorable comments only by the same ratio (one-third) as the respondents expressing them were more numerous. A more explicit and sensitive measure of intensity of feelings might easily turn up a different set of findings, however; for example, there were no admirers of the press who matched the depths of hostility expressed in remarks such as these: "The level of education [of the working members of the press] is very low; by and large they are a group of incompetent men. They really don't know anything about foreign policy. . . . With few exceptions the daily reporters have not enough brains to understand what is going on." Or, in the Defense Department: "You have many snoops coming around and looking for information. . . . ——— has dinner with correspondents now and then, but we make every effort to avoid them. They make a career out of snooping."

In fact, virtually all dimensions of this hostility directed at the press in the foreign policy field call for closer scrutiny; the negative feelings themselves are often expressed so generally that it is difficult to isolate or assign an underlying reason to them. And since hostility toward the press seems to be generalized from one policy area to another, it is difficult in cases where officials have more than one interest or responsibility to know whether evaluations of the foreign affairs performance of the press are the cause or the result of generalized press attitudes. Even the extent of governmental hostility toward the foreign policy press needs to be established in a more reliable way; the evidence at hand tells us that it is very widespread, slightly more than 50 per cent of our governmental respondents having taken the occasion to make negative evaluations of the press. (Only 40 per cent had expressed favorable attitudes, and about 20 per cent of the total were on both lists.) But were the rest being honest or merely cautious, which is surely an appropriate response in these circumstances? A very able and observant public affairs person in the State Department remarked, "A free press is absolutely essential to the democratic process, in this country or in any country. Most people in the State Department will say they believe this, but 90 per cent don't really mean it." This is obviously impressionistic, and perhaps hyperbolic, but it might turn out, under a more representative and more impersonal mode of data-gathering, to be a better approximation to reality than the 50 per cent figure.

What are some of the reasons behind the antagonism toward the press? A few lines of objection seem to be particularly salient; they may also be familiar, since they tend to be the converse of those supporting favorable images of the press. Among foreign policy officials in the Executive branch, the major complaints about the press are that it is unreliable, irresponsible, and "unhelpful." And like the constituents of the favorable attitudes, these three seem to be closely related, perhaps even being different manifestations of one large animus.

The theme heard most often was that press coverage in the foreign affairs field is unreliable, in the sense that the reporting is uninformed and inaccurate, and the reporters themselves unequal to the task; the news product as a result is distorted and untrustworthy. "If stories were based on fact all the time, they might not come out so well." "Most young reporters don't know what they are talking about in this field." "The press has distorted stories, has confused issues, and often jumped to wrong conclusions." "I give the guy [a magazine writer] the true facts, and he gets depressed: 'That's not the way I heard it.' His trouble is, he's been reading the papers." Officials often supported their charges of "meretricious journalism" with examples drawn from newspapers no more than a week old, and in several instances only several hours old. The most violent criticism was directed against the *New York Times*, which published an AP story about an alleged new proposal that the reporter had been told was not true, and which joined it to a photograph of officials conferring elsewhere on a different subject. The official explained the story as the consequence of a UPI report: "The guy can't let the United Press report go unmentioned by Associated, so he writes this story, which implies that the State Department is planning a new . . . program, that 'reports' of the plan are being made by Departmental personnel rather than the United Press, and that these guys in the picture are sitting around discussing it."

An obvious reason for this line of criticism lies in the greater access of policy officials to relevant information about issues; they know the "insides" of stories, or at least a *version* of the inside story, and they repeat with conviction the often heard complaint, "I've hardly ever seen a correct statement of a situation about which I knew the facts." Not only do they have more knowledge of the subject than the reporter, but they have some background of prior cases, and also some knowledge of the hit-and-run aspect of the reporter's relationship to any particular subject in the first place. So when they see newspaper accounts of stories they know something about, they are likely to be skeptical about the adequacy of the reporting. Some of the officials are prepared to "set the reporter straight," on a background basis or perhaps when the story is no longer in the news; while others let the errors stand, on the ground that to alert the reporter to them is to give away too much information, and to encourage reporters to go on "fishing expeditions" in order to be told the "inside story." The extent of the distrust that an official feels toward foreign affairs coverage, and its significance for his communications behavior, are less clear than one might expect, however. While a policy maker may repeat that no one can believe what he sees in the paper, and underscore his argument with a current example, he nonetheless is an avid and careful reader of foreign affairs news in his morning newspapers, and he extracts from them some very substantial and positive things (see Chapter VII). Perhaps the controlling hypothesis is that the less a policy maker knows about a subject or an issue, and the more remote it is from his area of professional interest, the more likely he is to accept a news account as reasonably accurate, at least pending positive evidence to the contrary. For if a foreign policy official automatically disbelieved *everything* he saw in the paper, he would be disoriented, cognitively unequipped to make the appropriate associations between his own areas of foreign policy work and all the others.

Closely related to the theme of unreliability is that of irresponsibility; and, as we noted earlier, the degree of a reporter's responsibility is also closely identified with the degree to which he is thought to have been helpful from the policy maker's point of view. But there is an independent sense in which the concept is used. Reporters are held to be irresponsible when they write their stories not in terms of manifest foreign policy content—the essential content as interpreted by the foreign affairs specialists—but rather in terms of news values like controversy, conflict, and sensationalism that are likely to capture headlines and front-page space; when, in other words, there is a "distortion" of emphasis and significance resulting from the application of different standards of evaluation. "If a reporter is fully briefed, and he then jazzes the story up and distorts it to get it on page one, for example, that is irresponsibility." "Many of the foreign correspondents are quite unscrupulous and actually distort the news for the sake of headlines. The ethics of the press, unfortunately, are not too high." But most of the time, irresponsibility cannot easily be separated from notions of damage to particular foreign policies or to our general foreign policy position— again, an instrumental attitude. Some officials regard this kind of irresponsibility as an inherent feature of the press in the American political system—one that flows from the independent existence of the institution and from its ruling criteria, rather than from the ethics of particular reporters, editors, or publishers. For example, one of the foreign affairs correspondents' best friends in the State Department said: "The requirements of news writing are essentially opposed to the objectives of foreign policy. The major criterion of news is conflict; news concerns all the bad things in our international relationships. Our basic objective in foreign policy, on the other hand, is to find accommodations between countries . . . . We minimize our differences with countries outside the Communist circle . . . but the press wants to maximize conflict. So they make legitimate differences much larger, to the point where they become 'conflict.' "

More often, however, officials are less philosophical and more particularistic in their criticisms. They complain that the press has not been helpful (i.e., has failed to publish material that would further particular foreign policy interests) or that it has been actively unhelpful (i.e., has published material that officials would prefer to have remained unpublished), in specific contexts. By "making life difficult" for those who are, in their own eyes, trying to do a constructive job in foreign policy, the press is regarded as behaving less than responsibly. A former Assistant Secretary of State recalled: "Some of the correspondents were helpful. . . . However, there is something quite wrong with newspaper people. Sometimes they don't have any morality whatsoever. If they can steal a secret, they will, and then use it for what they want. For example, when we were consulting with our NATO partners about the integration of Greece and Turkey into the system, the whole story broke in the newspapers before we had completed our consultations. This made things pretty awkward for us. And this type of thing happens constantly." In the public affairs area one official said, "The press is always lousing things up. . . ." And another: "The press throws a lot of sand in a lot of gears—in negotiations of policy within the State Department, as well as with other countries."[18]

Perhaps the clearest illustration of how attitudes toward the press are related to a measure of its helpfulness or unhelpfulness is contained in a pair of observations by a person who was closely involved in foreign policy formulation in the State Department during the Truman Administration. First this official expressed himself in strongly negative terms, and told the following incident: "On several occasions we got into deep trouble with the press. Once we had a big argument . . . [within the Department] regarding the future of British, French, and German relations. The question was, do you try to build up something on the Continent between the Germans and the French, at the risk of excluding the British from whatever develops there? . . . This debate was published in ——'s column, and it threw fat into the fire. It scared the French, who were trying to work out a way to live with the Germans but hadn't found it yet. . . . I think the publication of this debate set the cause of Franco-German *rapprochement* back two years." Subsequently this person characterized his prior remarks as "dramatic overstatement, to clarify the issues.

[18] There can be little doubt that Walter Lippmann's proposed exchange of Turkish for Cuban missile bases as the key to a solution of the Cuban crisis in October 1962 was regarded in the State Department as at least a ton of sand.

Of course, you do have a lot of friends in the press; they can be of tremendous help to you. I've been scared at times, fearing I've been indiscreet, but nothing happened." He then told of having had lunch with a columnist, during which he described how a particular State Department official had been instrumental in establishing the Marshall Plan. "Two days later, at breakfast, I turned to ———'s column," and found the whole story reproduced there. "I went to the State Department that morning with trepidation, fearing that at our morning meeting people would start asking questions, and the roof would fall in. But there was only the barest mention of the piece, and no adverse reaction in the State Department, because it was a helpful article."

The pattern of Congressional hostility to the foreign affairs press differs in one important respect from this picture of the Executive pattern. Congressmen share the Executive officials' negative attitude toward the unreliability of newspaper accounts of foreign affairs developments, and toward the irresponsibility of the press as a consequence of what one Senate staff member called its "vested interest in controversy." The criticism of Executive policy makers at the unhelpfulness of the press, however, is a minor theme in the Congressional outlook, reflecting a smaller institutional concern with the problems of secrecy and of public relations in the foreign policy field (and perhaps also the fact that the Congressman learns a great deal about what is going on in the foreign policy-making institutions as a result of the probings of the press). In place of the Executive official's hostility toward the press for "lousing things up," Congressmen and their staff assistants are perturbed by what they feel is a lack of objectivity in the press; the apparent biases of reporters and columnists, and their attempts to influence the shape of foreign policy—i.e., the manifestations of the press's "participant roles"—seem to the legislators to be inappropriate, whereas the Executive policy makers have long since become accustomed to them.

Significantly, there were very few negative expressions of an ideological nature, such as might reflect dissatisfaction with the press's performance of its "obligations" to the electorate. One can only conclude that here, too, the evidence supports the proposition that the grounds for disliking the press, as for liking it, are overwhelmingly instrumental rather than philosophical—one more dimension of the pragmatic character of American politics.

It seems clear that the basic ingredient in the foreign policy makers' reluctance to meet the press—the reverse of the sense of confidence and mastery that we noted among those who are the reporters' regular lines of access to foreign policy—is a pervading sense of fear. This fear grows out of the official's inability to control what the press will do with the information it gets. The opposite of the sense of confidence, then, is the sense of insecurity, an unwillingness to take any risks in the press's handling of information even at the loss of whatever policy advantages or initiatives might accrue as the consequence of good coverage. Even Congressmen are not immune to these feelings; for example, a Senator remarked that he did not feel free to make statements on foreign affairs to the press because "the press people would twist them." He preferred to "pose questions," instead. Even the confident people experience the fear that things will come out badly, but they are willing to run a few risks; and so they take their chances even as they try to lower the probabilities of disaster by choosing the reporters and the subject matter with some care. And they have a powerful ally in the general understanding among reporters that officials can shut off some sources of information if reprisals should be necessary. There is an egg-shell fragility to their sense of having good relations with the press at any particular time. Speaking of Acheson's unhappy experience with the press, a friend and colleague said, "The best of men can have the press turn on them quickly; they turn like tigers." Another former State Department official said, "From the standpoint of the State Department, the White House, the Pentagon, the press is looked on as a dangerous, unattractive beast, which you can lead along for a little bit of the way, but which is likely to turn and bite you at the slightest opportunity."

CHAPTER VI

CONTRIBUTIONS TO THE PRESS:
THE OUTWARD FLOW OF NEWS

———————•••———————

THE ATTITUDES that foreign policy officials entertain toward the press—the animosity and the fear, the confidence and the ambivalence—are ultimately reflected in the flow of information from these officials to the press. In prior chapters we have looked at reporters and editors as important shapers of foreign policy news; here we shall look at the policy makers themselves as sources of news by virtue of the things they choose to say about American foreign relations. (An official is also a source of news as a result of things he *does*, but the less he says about these acts, the more the flow of information about them is shaped by the interests and standards of the press.) In the light of very widespread instrumental attitudes toward the press, and the prevalence of negative feelings about it, what can we say about the flow of news out, about the foreign policy officials' contribution to press coverage of foreign affairs?

In discussing the policy makers' contribution to the fund of information and ideas out of which the daily newspaper is formed, we have to keep in mind a simple distinction between what we might call voluntary and involuntary contributions—between those freely offered and those yielded up in response to varying amounts of extractive pressure and skill. The former represent a range of initiatives on the part of policy makers, the latter a range of initiatives on the part of the correspondents. But in either case the officials who make the contributions are among that small number who have regular contacts with the press—those whom hostility or fear has not driven into a protective isolation. On any given day, the policy makers' contribution to press coverage of foreign affairs is a mixture of voluntary and involuntary elements, in varying compounds.

We can distinguish three different kinds of voluntary contributions to foreign affairs coverage, representing three different levels of exploitation of the press in the service of foreign policy. The first of these is the "handout," or the formal statement or release, offered to correspondents, who generally regard it either as a form of official propaganda or as unimportant and irrelevant information—and sometimes as both. The handout puts the greatest strain on the wire service reporter, who interprets his obligation to report "hard news" so that it includes much of what the officials give out as news. One of these reporters, as he went over his notes after a State Department briefing, muttered angrily about the State Department's obtuseness and propaganda, adding that the official who handled the briefing was "the only person who went around saying that the Western Allies were in no real disagreement [in late 1958] about how to approach the Soviets in negotiations over Berlin." But despite his feelings on the subject, he still phoned the story in to his office. The men who are responsible for the handouts are aware of the negative sentiments that surround their work. A few of them are so sensitive to the propaganda overtones of the handout that they lean over backwards to strip the releases of any major policy significance; for example, "The news we give them [the reporters] on our own initiative is news of visits of foreign dignitaries, economic aid programs, and agreements with other nations." But in general the handout is designed to give the correspondents "stuff that might not come to their attention"— that is, information that Department officials think is important but that the reporters are unlikely to turn up in their stylized pursuit of news, and especially material that presents the State Department's interpretation or preferred explanation of developments. These help to "set the story straight" as far as the Department is concerned, although they do little to alter the reporters' image of the handout as propaganda.

The second level of voluntary contribution to foreign affairs coverage includes the more serious efforts to keep correspondents informed on major or continuing aspects of American foreign relations. These are invariably *ad hoc* efforts through informal channels, and their general purposes may be summarized as letting the leading correspondents and analysts— particularly those who are read by other correspondents— know what is going on in crucial areas, and what the state of Departmental thinking is in these problem areas, so that newspaper comment will not get divorced from reality as the officials see it. One "danger" in such a divorce, as we shall see in Chapter VII, is that the policy makers may subsequently be forced to adapt themselves to the correspondents' view of reality. Stated this way, the instrumental component in these informational efforts is obvious; it is equally apparent in many of the voluntary contacts between correspondents and informed working-level officials, where the very act of informing the reporter in a particular context inescapably involves communicating a particular ordering and interpretation of a set of facts. But these instrumental elements should not obscure our understanding that this is the context in which the press is unobtrusively kept informed—not for attribution and sometimes not even for publication—of the developments that are currently sensitive and therefore not likely to be the subject of official releases or statements.[1]

The third type of voluntary contribution consists of the deliberate instrumental use of the press in order to achieve specific foreign policy objectives. The identification of these occasions, in which information on particular issues is fed

[1] See Chapter V, footnote 11: "On some big matters the State Department informs him [Reston] almost automatically, as it would the representative of a major power." (Joseph Kraft, in *Esquire*, November 1958, p. 123.) For this process at work in the developing stages of the Marshall Plan, see Joseph M. Jones, *The Fifteen Weeks*, p. 237.

to particular reporters or newspapers, is generally difficult, because so many of them are either not acknowledged, or never described in the detail that permits the observer to discriminate among their varied purposes. They usually represent unorthodox political maneuvers, designed to influence the decision-making of particular individuals by shaping their communications environment; hence they are treated with the degree of secrecy commonly associated with security classifications, lest the maneuver backfire or the channels through which information has been flowing be compromised. Because of the secrecy that surrounds them, it is impossible to know just how frequently they occur, and therefore what their comparative importance is among the various types of contributions to the press.[2] For the same reason it is also difficult, from a distance, to distinguish in particular cases between this type and the second type of voluntary contribution.

The staple in the diet of the foreign affairs correspondents, however, consists not of the dishes they are offered but rather of the bones they manage to dig up for themselves. This is the result of the fortuitous intersection of their own preferences and those of foreign policy officials. Unless the reporter's co-operation has been enlisted in the service of a foreign policy cause that he is informed about and sympathetic to, he is inclined to be suspicious when "significant" information is freely offered to him; he wonders what the motive is, and where "truth" lies, and he is not satisfied until he has gone digging around on his own, checking with other sources, and extracted the information that he thinks approximates the true story. A highly respected correspondent phrased it as follows: "I think one's attitude to the State Department . . . depends on whether they can come to you with a piece of information, or whether you go to them with a request for some

[2] It is interesting, in this connection, that Douglass Cater's Chapter 7, "Intelligence and Counterintelligence: Part II—*A Disquisition on Leaking*," is among the shortest in his book, *The Fourth Branch of Government*, pp. 128-41.

information. If they come to you, there are grounds for skepticism or caution." The foreign policy officials, on the other hand, are not disposed to give away information on current policies unless some instrumental purpose can be served by doing so. "If publicity is going to make it impossible to attain certain important objectives, the government is entitled, in the foreign affairs area, not to telegraph its punches." The policy officials would rather let the reporters come to them with specific questions; in that way they protect themselves against the possibility of giving out information for which there is no present "demand," as well as having the protection afforded by the recourse to "no comment." "The ordinary reaction of the desk officer, and the higher officials in the State Department," reported one of the desk officers, "is that the safest way is to have the least dealings with the press. This is their natural protective instinct. . . . Few desk people cultivate reporters . . . all the seeking-out is done by the press, not by the desk officer." Both the correspondents and the officials, then, prefer to work on the principle that foreign affairs reporting is extractive. Even in the public affairs area of the State Department, it is acknowledged that "our contacts with correspondents are usually a result of their initiative."[3]

An important consequence of this preference for "involuntary" contributions to foreign affairs coverage is that, as the initiative is passed to the correspondents, so is a large part of the responsibility for the definition of news; here is created the need to keep a few leading correspondents informed on a personal and informal basis, to keep them "on the track." Furthermore, with the initiative in the hands of the reporter, an important task of the State Department official is to "keep

[3] Cf. the remarks of Luther A. Huston, Director of Public Information, Department of Justice, on February 26, 1960: "I think that probably two-thirds of my own time . . . is devoted to answering queries and getting information asked by the members of the Washington Correspondents Corps." (From a letter quoted in William L. Rivers, "The Washington Correspondents and Government Information," p. 87.)

up with the news"—i.e., with what is already in the newspapers—so they will know what to expect by way of further requests for information. It would not be a great exaggeration to define the government's basic public information programs in the foreign policy area in these same terms. The important phases of those programs, especially the press conferences and news releases, are substantially guided by a process that might be called "playing reporter"—that is, the officials prepare for the reporters' initiatives by going through the same steps as the reporter does in *his* search for news. By thoroughly exposing themselves to the current market in news, they can predict with reasonable accuracy the questions that the correspondents will be asking on any particular day.[4] On the basis of these predictions they are able to make sensible advance preparations of their answers. A colorful description of this process comes out of the State Department, although the same kind of thing takes place in the White House and the Department of Defense, too: "We do a two-page summary of news stories of interest to the State Department. . . . We can look at the summary, and determine what the questions will be like that day at the noon briefing. We have regional men [i.e., regional specialists] here, and when we figure out what the questions will be like, these men go bird-dogging to the area desks, talk to the people there, and get the latest poop and the latest feelings about things—for example, like when the story in the paper doesn't square with our reports—which we use to prepare for the questions." In other words, the major influence on the daily pattern of public information out of Washington on foreign policy comes, circuitously, from the press rather than from the officials responsible for foreign affairs. There is a larger political significance in this, involving questions of public participation and political control in a demo-

---

[4] Even amateurs can do a good job of second-guessing the reporters; cf. Fauneil J. Rinn, "The Presidential Press Conference," unpub. Ph.D. diss., Department of Political Science, University of Chicago, 1960, pp. 20-22.

cratic society. Those who are concerned about "managed news," about the control that the government exercises over the citizen's view of the world, may find comfort in the fact that in ordinary circumstances the press still bears the largest responsibility for the shape of foreign policy information. But those who are concerned about the substance of those images of the world will note that the way the press goes about shaping that pattern of public information is not characterized by any orderly or systematic approach to the substance of foreign affairs, nor by any explicit understanding of what public information might usefully consist in.

The Congressional approach to press coverage of foreign affairs is a similar mixture of voluntary and involuntary contributions, but here the extractive principle is the more usual, the number of Congressmen involved is small, and the total contribution is much less—three observations that follow from our prior discussion of the pattern of Congressional attitudes toward the foreign policy press. Even the foreign policy leaders in the Congress, those who can summon reporters, feel inhibited in the foreign policy area,[5] and prefer to "answer questions" rather than to "call in reporters," although they will of course give them advance copies of occasional foreign policy speeches in order to maximize publicity. On their part, the reporters themselves are more interested in the foreign policy votes than the foreign policy views of the large majority of Congressmen; they reserve their efforts for those few people, on the foreign affairs committees or in leadership positions, who are likely to have reliable information about foreign policy

[5] For other evidence of Congressional restraint in the foreign policy field, cf. *The Congressional Quarterly*'s study of open and closed committee hearings during the 1961 session; the House Foreign Affairs Committee had the highest percentage of closed meetings (64 per cent) among the group of 28 committees that met at least 35 times during the session, and the Senate Foreign Relations Committee was tied (with the House Ways and Means Committee) for second place in this group, with 61 per cent of the hearings closed. (xix, No. 51, week ending December 22, 1961, pp. 1961-62.)

itself or about legislative possibilities concerning foreign policy issues.

● The Channels of News

An elaborate network of formal and informal channels is at hand for use by officials in their efforts to feed information to the press, and by correspondents in their attempts to elicit information and comment from officials. Most of the institutions that sustain or comprise these channels have been abundantly described elsewhere;[6] the only point in discussing them further is to delineate their usefulness to the men involved in them.

The most important of the formal organizations within the Department of State is the Office of News, formerly the News Division, the Director of which is the person most frequently identified in reporters' accounts as "a State Department spokesman." The Office of News has a staff of about twenty men, who have geographically and functionally organized responsibilities for news distribution, who monitor the teletypes, and who run the latest news through the Department. The Office is the reporters' formal point of access to the Department; the Director holds a "briefing," a small-scale news conference, every day at noon, which provides the Department with a regular outlet for routine statements, announcements, charges, replies, and so forth, and which offers the reporters an opportunity to ask some of the more obvious questions that the morning newspapers will have generated. The noon briefing, an outgrowth of Secretary of State Hull's daily meetings with the press back in the 1930's and 1940's, is attended by approximately 30 reporters, mostly from the leading domestic and foreign wire services, syndicates, and newspapers, and most of them will depreciate its importance, given the slightest opportunity. One of them remarked, "Some

[6] See, for example, Cater, *op.cit.*, and Lester Markel, ed., *Public Opinion and Foreign Policy*.

days . . . we sit out there all day and get propaganda. Other days we get nothing from them." After the morning flurry of preparation for the noon meeting with the correspondents, the staff has the time to "field" the less obvious questions that individual reporters may put to them in more private audience. And when the News Office cannot handle a question satisfactorily, either alone or after consultation with the policy people, it will put the reporter in touch with officials in the Department who are closer to the substantive problem.

Another formal channel of news is the Public Affairs Adviser attached to each geographical and functional bureau in the State Department. The Public Affairs Adviser's (PAA's) primary responsibility is, in the words of one of them, "to flag the substantive people, and force them to focus on the public relations problems of our foreign policy." In practice, however, the PAA himself handles many of the public relations problems, and "we have to field a lot of hot ones the press hands us." The PAA's are also an important point of access for the reporter, and, like the Office of News, if they cannot effectively work out an answer to an inquiry in consultation with the country desk, they will put a correspondent in direct touch with the appropriate political officers. "The desk officer knows what is going on in the country—much more so than we do, who cover the whole *area*." This self-appraisal is shared by most of the reporters, who also see the PAA's as lesser parts of the "handout" system, as cogs in the Department's propaganda machine. We can recall here a reporter's characterization, quoted earlier, of the PAA's as "a gateway to the obvious." But since the obvious is often of value, the PAA's lead a busy life. "We are available to the press twenty-four hours a day. . . . We talk on a background basis only [i.e., attributable only to 'State Department officers' or 'official sources,' and not to be quoted]. . . . Or we can give background material without any attribution at all."

The formal press conference is another important institutional channel of news, but a comparatively infrequent one. Few Secretaries of State in recent years have met the press as regularly and often as John Foster Dulles. His press conferences were generally scheduled the day before the President's, and were approximately as frequent; they were also well covered by reporters. Part of the interest in those conferences developed from the fact that Dulles was likely to answer questions by enunciating new lines of policy, often taking his staff by surprise. For most Secretaries, however, the press conference has been an occasional device, and their obvious lack of enthusiasm for it has been reciprocated by the correspondents, whose reportorial habits and notions of journalistic skill do not easily accommodate to the increasingly public nature and public functions of the press conference. Some of the leading correspondents, in fact, make a point of not attending press conferences. Within the confines of the questions raised by the reporters, the press conference offers the Department a chance to state its positions; and the Secretary is free to make whatever additional statements he wishes. Most observers in the Department are prone to call the conference a "vital and important" institution; but the view from the top is a little different. The man on the spot is likely to be more impressed by the potential difficulties and dangers than by the opportunities and advantages, which is why Secretaries of State have had such little recourse to it, on the whole. A former Secretary of State criticized the institution on the grounds that news was made "by the reporters asking questions, not by the President or the Secretary of State who wants or has something to say." A high official in the State Department called the press conference a "dubious sport": "The problem arises because of the disparity of your audiences. It is like having just one vaudeville act for both a men's smoker and a church social." There are, of course, other functions and purposes that are served by formal press conferences— the often-drawn parallel with the British Question Hour is suggestive of these—and there are other lines of criticism that would need to be brought into an over-all assessment of press conferences, but we are not attempting such an assessment here. Our present purpose is rather to point out those gross features of the press conference that bear upon its usefulness as a channel for the dissemination of foreign policy information.

Speeches constitute another formal device through which officials can contribute to press coverage of foreign affairs. Talks by policy officials may constitute official declarations of policy, or merely explanations and restatements of it; the chief difficulty with these as a way of getting wide distribution of the views enunciated is the official's lack of control over the uses made of them at the receiving end. The task of getting good newspaper coverage of speeches may be facilitated by preparing good press releases that tell the reporters what the speaker's important points are meant to be, and by some judicious phone calls reminding reporters of the talk and conveying some sense of its significance. But even then most officials habitually describe press coverage of their speeches as capricious. One official reported the following experience: "I gave a major speech in Kentucky once . . . which got no publicity. Six weeks later, I gave much of the substance of it in an off-the-cuff address here in Washington, and it got big press coverage with no effort on my part. In the first instance, there was even a good press release, and yet it was not picked up nationally—only locally in Kentucky. And then you appear here casually, and you get wide coverage. I wouldn't say there is no rhyme or reason to it—just that it is hard to know what the rhyme or reason is." The reporters, however, take refuge in the concept of "news," and if their passing judgment is that they are being treated not to important declarations of policy but rather to restatements of position, their disposition either to accept it as "news" or to ignore it as "propaganda" is strongly influenced by the number and nature of the other things that are "in the news" that day.[7]

It should be clear from these remarks that the formal lines of news distribution in the State Department and in other agencies having foreign policy responsibilities are adequate and satisfactory only for the more formal or routine types of messages about foreign affairs, and for the declaratory aspects of foreign policy—that is, when the announcement of an official position is itself an important or even an essential part of the policy. Since there are many of these items in contemporary foreign policy, these lines are busy most of the time. They are much less efficacious for the not-for-attribution material relating to on-going foreign relations or the non-declaratory phases of policy; and so they are not the channels that are used by officials in offering, or by correspondents in eliciting, these kinds of information. And while the correspondents have to cover the former class of material in the performance of their neutral role as objective recorders of daily history, they are usually more interested in the latter class and so they work hard at the cultivation of the necessary informal channels.

These informal connections range from the structured background briefings that Department officials will manage on particular occasions, to the casual private conversations on a personal level between a correspondent and an official. The former are sometimes hard to distinguish from press confer-

[7] This holds not only for reporters' reactions to speeches but in general for all information volunteered by officials through these formal channels. For example, in the confusion of developments in the Congo in the summer of 1960, the public affairs people in the State Department thought it was important to balance the Soviets' picture of their contribution to the United Nations' troop lift to the Congo by telling the American people about the United States' contribution to the troop lift. The Department issued a handout, and accompanied it with a press release, giving the statistics on the American effort; there was even an official on hand to answer any questions about what the Soviets had done. The officials were disappointed, but not greatly surprised, that very little of this was carried in the press as an independent story. One of them said, "To the press this was an old story. . . . [The correspondents] blame it on the city room: 'Don't blame me, it's not news.' "

ences, the latter from ordinary discourse between individuals. The distinctive feature of a "backgrounder" is that the material given the reporter cannot be quoted or attributed to particular officials, or identified as the official viewpoint of the Department, nor is it considered binding. The purpose, most generally, is to enlighten and instruct the reporters, to let them share the thinking and perspectives of the policy officials, "so that they know what they should know about important policy matters"; "so they will act responsibly"; "so they will not go off halfcocked." Another important purpose is to get politically useful information into circulation without revealing the source. Some officials insist that only the Office of News gives out news, and that in their own background discussions with reporters they provide only a context or perspective; but apart from the non-attributability of the latter the distinction may be meaningless to a reporter. Context or perspective lends meaning to events, and may be "newsworthy" in itself. In fact, the distribution of the foreign affairs correspondent's time as between the News Office and his own contacts throughout the Department shows that the distinction between news and perspective is a distinction without a difference.

Informal sessions with reporters can be varied to meet almost any kind of circumstance. Assistant Secretaries of State have regularly held background briefings of a relatively well-structured sort. Secretary Dulles would often have a dinner discussion with a small group of correspondents, senior in status, who stood by, as it were, ever ready for a hint from on high that the Secretary would welcome a dinner invitation. Some of Dulles' critics suggest that the hints came whenever the Secretary was getting especially rough treatment in the press. The practice itself, however, is a common one, and many friends of Secretary Acheson attribute his difficulties with the press to his refusal to "play favorites" among the foreign affairs correspondents in this fashion. The luncheon conversation with a reporter is another very common practice among policy officials, but it is only one variety of what an official called "backgrounding *à deux*"; other forms are curricular, in the sense that they are a sanctioned use of the working time of those officials who have the inclination and competence to deal directly with the reporters. And, of course, there are extensive personal friendships between correspondents and officials, of a kind that facilitates the interchange of information not otherwise shared between the two institutions. There are thus multiple opportunities for officials to "plant a story" in private, and as a result there is a steady flow of information pertaining to current developments in foreign relations—called "leaks" by people who have not given it out themselves—from all sides of the Department.

Criteria Governing the Distribution of News

The foreign policy official who has some reason for talking to reporters has no trouble finding a way. There are, to be sure, some fine points that he may want to consider in making his choice of the most appropriate channels—whether to make a public speech, for example, or to make a statement at the start of a press conference; whether to pass the word along to a small number of leading columnists, or to talk to a particular one; or whether to prepare a handout, etc.—but these are not separable from the specific issues of substance that he wants to discuss and the reasons that lie behind them, since his choice will be shaped in some measure by his estimate of the effects of handling particular policy ideas in particular ways. Questions of purpose, therefore, are relevant in any consideration of approaches to the press. What kinds of regularities can we discover in the reasons for the distribution of foreign policy information? What are some of the criteria governing the channeling of foreign affairs news to the press?

Ideological Considerations. The point was made in the preceding chapter that ideological or philosophical reasons for being favorably disposed toward the press are weak, and subordinate to instrumental reasons. The same rank ordering exists among the two sets of considerations with respect to the actual distribution of particular items of information, although a new factor is involved. Decisions to release or reveal specific bits of "news" are more likely to be made—or at least justified—on general ideological grounds, the more their content is routine and declaratory or peripheral to policy matters. The public affairs personnel, partly because they are responsible for the bulk of the routine material, and partly because their jobs are defined in this fashion, are much more likely than the policy people to advance the general criterion of "informing the public" as the basis for decisions on what information is to be given to reporters. But even in the public affairs area the rationale is perfunctory and suspect; since anything that is given to the press serves to "inform the public," the criterion itself is non-discriminating. It may even be worse than that: because the criterion embodies democratic virtues that are politically equivalent to "home" and "mother," it permits the user to embrace any kind of public information policy or practice he wants, releasing or withholding information on other bases but justifying the output as a desire "to make more and more information available to the public." This is not to argue that manipulators of public understanding are deliberately hiding behind the mask of a democratic philosophy, but rather that the philosophy itself induces an unknowing self-deception among people who have extremely difficult decisions to make, and have no other way of explaining or justifying their choices; they sincerely believe that their selections are motivated by an effort to inform the public—"we try to keep the public honestly informed"—but that would be the case no matter what selections they made.

There are other versions of ideological criteria that are less comprehensive in a philosophical sense but more effective and honest discriminators of information that should or should not be given out. These are articulated more frequently by officials with policy responsibility and they reflect a greater concern with practical questions and with purposeful or instrumental reasons for "informing the public." One of these is a concern that the American public be alerted to developing problems, "to clouds on the foreign horizon which may, indeed, threaten our very existence,"[8] in the hope that responses to crises can be carefully fashioned in advance rather than convulsively adopted in the midst of the event. The choice of news to this end, to "directing the attention of the public to certain items," seems to be made after estimating the extent of Congressional and public participation in particular acts of policy-making, and the likely direction that these involvements will take if left alone. It is also motivated by longer-run concerns about the stability and continuity of American foreign policy, by desires to put American participation in international politics on a predictable and sustaining basis. Another yardstick of this kind—i.e., a practical concern with the state of public information—is provided by rough estimates of the level of public anxiety. If the public, whether sampled through the press or by other means, seems to be worried about particular aspects or manifestations of American foreign policy, then these suggest obvious guides to the choice of subjects and of materials to be discussed with correspondents.

Promotional Considerations. The capacity of the foreign policy maker actually to get material into the newspaper is a product of several factors that we have already discussed, and it seems a worthwhile digression at this point to recapitulate a few of the more salient ones. Working *for* the official who approaches the correspondent with some information are all those features of the reporter's orientation that we summarized in Chapter II as the neutral roles of the press. We pointed

[8] Edwin M. J. Kretzmann, "New Perspectives in Foreign Relations," a lecture delivered under the auspices of the Walter J. Shepard Foundation at the Ohio State University, April 4, 1958, p. 14. Mr. Kretzmann was then the Public Affairs Adviser in the Bureau of Near Eastern, South Asian, and African affairs in the Department of State.

out there that one consequence of the reporter's felt obligation to transmit information "objectively" was to make him peculiarly susceptible to being "used" by policy makers who come bearing information shaped to suit their own purposes. Working *against* the official, however, are the reporter's awareness and distrust of the official's interest in a particular version of reality, and a disposition to disbelieve official versions and even to disbelieve the story as it emerges from any single quarter of the foreign policy establishment. Also working against the official is a definition of news values that discriminates against the policy maker's patient search for accommodations, in favor of the controversial and contentious elements of political competition. What the balance of these forces, and any other relevant ones, may be in any particular situation or setting seems to depend on the interests and frames of reference of the participants, and especially on the degree to which the reporter and the policy maker can make common cause, either explicitly or implicitly, on the purposes that might be served by any particular body of information or version of reality. Let us look now at some of the interests that are promoted by officials through the release of foreign policy information, so we may have a better sense of where the policy maker's interests and preferences intersect those of the reporter. We shall look at three different kinds of promotional considerations: policy promotion, institutional promotion, and personal promotion; and we shall consider each of these in a general political context and in a narrower context of bureaucratic politics or of Washington politics. It is not always possible to make sharp distinctions among these different kinds of promotion; in a political milieu, particularly, institutional interests tend to become identified with a given set of policy interests, and the positions of particular individuals are hard to disentangle from the record of their institutions and the fate of its, and their, policies. And in these circumstances, it is possible for individuals to push one set of interests as the best means of achieving a different set. As a Senator observed, "The best politics is to inform the people about policies and problems." Where we can account for these situations, we shall; but where latent criteria are not apparent, as is most often the case, there is little we can do but keep the possible interconnections in mind, focus on the manifest content of the considerations that are put forth, and treat the varieties of promotion as if they were distinct types.

Policy Promotion. The advancement of policy interests is by far the most frequently articulated motivation behind the distribution of foreign policy news; it is expressed about as often as institutional and personal advancement combined. Even so, it is hard to know exactly how much oil one has struck here; the main pool of policy promotion is probably hidden from view under layers and layers of private inhibitions against disclosure, inhibitions that are reinforced by Congress's well-known dislike for anything that might resemble domestic "propaganda."[9] So the closer one gets to the possible use of the press on behalf of policies not yet stamped with the official imprimatur of Congressional or Executive authorization, the more one feels that the well of reliable information has begun to run dry. There are no inhibitions, however, against supplying information to the press in order to organize general public support—usually defined no closer than that— for policies that are agreed and adopted, and may thus be regarded as official. On the contrary, this is thought to be part of the continuing problem of citizen education in the foreign policy field, and an obligation rather than a competitive challenge for the State Department. "The P-area has encouraged Departmental officers to go out and accept invitations to speak around the country, to explain our policies. . . ." "The utility

[9] William L. Rivers summarizes the record of Congressional opposition to government publicity. (*Op.cit.*, pp. 78-83.)

of official releases has been proved; it is a democratic manner of obtaining public support for our foreign policy."

Despite all the reasons for reticence, there is still ample evidence that the press is used extensively to gain broad public and political support for policies and programs that are not yet official or authoritative, in the sense that they have not yet been approved by Congress, as well as to strengthen ever-fragile declaratory policies by clarifying and restating the positions and intentions of authoritative (if unidentified) officials. It is no great surprise to hear a State Department official say, "For a long time, august officers in the State Department have been using the *New York Times* to advance official views on policy. . . . By using the *Times* at least we know these views get picked up by other papers." Executive officials seem in these respects to share the reporters' conception of the foreign policy-making process as a network that runs from the Executive to the press, and thence either directly to the Congress or first to the public and then on to the Congress, which can translate the "public will" into votes or other expressions of judgment on Executive proposals or policy declarations. A former Assistant Secretary, for example, said that "Competent journalists helped to persuade the American people and Congress of the validity of many policy decisions that attracted national attention. The Marshall Plan and Point Four are examples." Many other observers both in the press and in the State Department have described State Department-press cooperation in "selling" these pillars of postwar foreign policy to the public and the Congress.[10] A more recent example of the use of the press to shape the thinking of Congressmen in advance of Congressional consideration of an issue involved Secretary Dulles and the Eisenhower Doctrine. Dulles reportedly fed a steady stream of information to newsmen, particularly to James Reston of the *New York Times*, for three days before he put the proposal to Congressional lead-

[10] Cf. Joseph M. Jones, *op.cit.*

ers. By then it was presumably too late for the Congressmen to do other than acquiesce in the widely publicized policy.[11]

What part the press accounts actually played in the political history of these policies is, of course, a matter more of conjecture than of demonstrated fact. We have no fully satisfactory evidence one way or the other on these questions, even though the myth is further supported by the major Congressional critics of the Marshall Plan, particularly, who argued repeatedly that the press put the policy "across" by a daily parade of favorable stories, while it systematically ignored the viewpoints of the opposition and denied them access to the news columns.

Congressmen, too, have gone to the press from time to time, in the hope of generating a measure of interest and support for foreign policy proposals that they themselves had tossed in the Congressional hopper. These proposals, however, are usually at the fringes of political policy and do not represent a major initiative in foreign policy (though there have been notable exceptions to this over the years). One Representative piloted a bill through Congress in support of which he himself had written articles, "and I have cooperated with or inspired newspapermen to write articles on the program." Senator Monroney also courted newspaper coverage of his resolution urging the Executive to consider establishing an International Development Association as an affiliate of the World Bank.[12]

On still another level, the press is used to build up support, or at least some political resonance, for proposals that are still contesting for acceptance as policies within the Administration.[13] The annual consideration of the defense budget has

[11] See the account in Kraft, *op.cit.*, and the reference in Cater, *op.cit.*, p. 136; see also the *New York Times*' accounts for December 30 and 31, 1956, and January 1, 1957.

[12] James Robinson, *The Monroney Resolution.*

[13] Cater reports the instance, during World War II, when Admiral Ernest J. King "used the background conference to publicize and help nullify what he considered an ill-conceived plan to take General George C. Marshall away from his post as Army Chief of Staff." (*Op.cit.*, p. 131.)

often been preceded and accompanied by newspaper stories patently fed to reporters by the supporters of one or another of the military services. In the long controversy over a nuclear weapons-testing policy, also, the protagonists have quite obviously gone very often to the reporters in the hopes of building up their case. Several of the reporters, in fact, had strong feelings of their own on that subject, and were easy to find and to "exploit"; they became rather active participants themselves in the struggle for position and support. The importance that the press assumed in this struggle over policy may be gauged from the report that some of the Atomic Energy Commissioners were "surprised and disturbed that their testimony about the need to resume testing of atomic weapons received no attention from columnists or in newspapers."[14] Less spectacular, perhaps, but not greatly different in kind, have been the uses of the press in the developing contest over a new American foreign trade policy to fit a changed international economic environment, of which the European Economic Community is a part. Concerning an earlier stage in the fashioning of new economic institutions, specifically the effort to transform the OEEC into the OECD, a public affairs area official in the State Department said, "This is very important, but it has no sex appeal. The problem is how to lay it out in an interesting fashion, and get a cynical reporter to see the long-term importance of it."

Another policy use of the press involves a forward-looking strategy on the part of an official who wants to establish himself as a logical source of policy ideas or statements on questions that are not currently active but might be in the near future. For example, "When you see something coming up, you can steer a conversation with a reporter around to a description of possibilities. . . . The reporter may not remember what you say, but he will come back if the issue does materialize, knowing that there is thinking on it here." This cultivation

[14] *U.S. News and World Report*, July 11, 1960, p. 24.

of channels for use in future policy situations is no doubt a motivation behind many of the overtures that officials make toward correspondents, even though they do not often express it so openly. More frequently it will be said, for example, that "The best thing is to have close personal relations with the press, so they know what they should know about important policy matters, and hence are on your side." All of the intimate social and professional contacts that officials maintain with reporters, and that have been discussed in different contexts before this, are relevant in this context, too.

In the framework of government and politics in Washington, as in the larger political system, the press is a useful handmaiden in the competition over policies. For this is the place where direct political support is needed if one view of policy rather than another is to prevail; and all the reasons that send men to the press in the search for general public support would seem to be even more compelling in this political arena.[15] There are, of course, a lot of ways to exert influence in a political community, and the newspapers are only one of them. Furthermore, we are simply not able to say with certainty how the newspaper compares with all the others in the flow of information relevant to decisions in the foreign policy area. But we can see, in the prominence of the newspaper in the life of politicians and political decision makers, in their over-all attitudes toward the press, and in the proliferation of public relations devices, the marks of a widely held conviction that having the newspapers "on your side" in terms of favorable coverage and treatment helps to create an impression of how the political winds are blowing, and is thus a significant instrument for shaping the attitudes and expecta-

[15] Henry M. Wriston cites a State Department report identifying administrative inadequacies, which deny officials the machinery to participate in policy deliberations, as a prime factor in leading officials to take their case to reporters and Congressmen. ("The Secretary and the Management of the Department," in American Assembly, *The Secretary of State*, Englewood Cliffs, N.J., Prentice-Hall, 1960, p. 80.)

tions and predispositions of others. And so the stream of information is directed to reporters as the developing policy situation seems to dictate; one is told again and again that "this is going on all the time" in the foreign policy field, although the circumstances are apparently thought to be too sensitive to discuss in any detail. Several sketchy references may suggest the range of possibilities, however. A State Department person, contemplating the need "to go up to Congress in a week or so" and ask for more funds for a particular purpose, remarked: "It would certainly help if they could be reading in the press all about the problem, and if they knew what they are in for. I spent yesterday working on ———— [a journalist] on this." Another official talked about getting material into the New York and Washington papers to try to influence Congress directly or indirectly. In another instance, a staff assistant for a Senator had been trying to get the Senator to "say something" about the need for a particular foreign policy move, "but with elections in the offing he throws up his hands in horror." The assistant was then called by a prominent correspondent on a story related to the subject in question, and took the occasion to give the correspondent the same policy argument that he had been giving the Senator. "This appeared almost in my words this morning on the front page of the ———— [newspaper]. Now I'd like to lay this on the Senator's desk and say, 'If you won't take my words for it, see what the ———— [newspaper] has to say.' I won't do this; but it is done rather often."

Institutional Promotion. The promotion of foreign policy institutions within the general political system is like most institutional advertising with which the reader is familiar; it involves the use of the press not to push a particular policy directly, but rather to "sell" the organization that produces it, thus creating a favorable environment for existing policies and for future ones. The building blocks for institutional advertising in foreign affairs include the quality of the personnel as well as the achievements of the past, which are projected into the future in the form of over-all trends of policy. And like other organizations trying to build up their corporate image, the foreign policy institutions are concerned about the presentation and handling of the materials on these subjects—the packaging of its various policies.

The processes involved are perhaps most visible in the case of those foreign policy institutions that are created to handle a particular aspect of American foreign policy, and whose continued existence depends not only on the life of the problems it is meant to do battle with, but also on broad general impressions of what the organization does, how important it is that these things be done, and how well the organization does them. The United States Information Agency is hobbled in its efforts to promote itself, because Congressmen have been on guard against the possible diversion of resources from foreign to domestic public relations; again, there is no direct evidence on this point, but circumstantial evidence—most outstandingly its vulnerability during the McCarthy era in the early 1950's—suggests that the USIA has thereby been disadvantaged relative to other foreign policy agencies in the search for a climate of political acceptance. The foreign aid agencies, on the other hand, have had quite a different experience. It would be nonsense to attribute the difference to this one point—among other points of difference have been the massive Presidential support for the foreign aid program over the years and the relatively greater ease in citing the effects of foreign aid than of foreign information —but it would be equally foolish to ignore the greater opportunities that the aid agencies have had to sell their program via the correspondents. A Foreign Operations Administration representative with some public responsibilities expressed the faith that led the institution to the press (although it does not tell us much about the kinds of "facts" that are presumed to be useful): "Public opinion could restrict our operations, but if the people are given the facts and are exposed to them correctly, they will come to the logical conclusion that the program is worthwhile." The FOA also demonstrates that the broad impressions of the work of foreign policy institutions, on which they may depend for public support, may rest on superficial information rather than on highly germane data that are central to operations; another officer in that organization said, "We have to find where the public interest most naturally lies [meant not in a political sense but in the sense of 'What attracts people's interest?'] and then use feature stories as examples of the whole program. For example, we used the visit of the Greek monarchs as a vehicle to explain what the United States has done in Greece."

Confronted with one popular stereotype of the diplomat as a social dilettante, and another public image of him, sired by Senator McCarthy and nurtured by successor groups on the extreme right, as a Machiavellian in the service of Communist powers, the State Department has a constant interest in developing a more favorable public conception of the Foreign Service Officer. At one level this is handled in a conventional way, as the Department supplies material to the hometown papers on the travels and activities and promotions of Foreign Service Officers who do not otherwise break into print—all this in an effort to raise the prestige of the Officers and of the Foreign Service. At a higher level, the image of the diplomat is inseparable from the work he is engaged in; the stream of information about the current framework of diplomatic activity, consequently, has a component of concern—perhaps not always made explicit—with the reputation of the men conducting it. There is thus a third image of the diplomat, which, while perhaps not deliberately shaped by the State Department, seems to be encouraged by it: the diplomat as the competent troubleshooter who can move in and pacify turbulent political situations, as the first-team negotiator who takes charge when diplomatic bargaining becomes hard and serious, as the unflinching confronter of Communist bosses on the periphery of the free world, and so on. Departmental spokesmen constantly complain about the reporters' penchant for the spectacular and the personal in their reporting about foreign affairs, yet in their news releases and statements one can detect a willingness on the part of officials to cooperate, at least, with these criteria in the interests of a more favorable image of the diplomat.

On the higher levels in the State Department, there is a major and continuing concern with the public relations problems of the institution. Indeed, this is the *raison d'être* of the Public Affairs Advisers: to keep a watchful eye, at the operational level, over the public relations aspects of the Department's work. But even further, the modern Secretary of State is as much a public relations man for his Department as he is a policy formulator or an administrator, and those Secretaries who have not performed aggressively in the first role have seen the Department's prestige and political capacities reduced. One of the major anomalies of recent years was the extraordinary political resilience of Secretary Dulles in the face of severe and persistent policy criticism, which seemed on occasion to match the worst that Secretary Acheson had met. It is being suggested here that a major factor in Dulles' political strength was his restless concern over his, and the State Department's, domestic public relations, even at the occasional expense of relations abroad—a concern expressed through his readiness to meet reporters and his apparent frankness in discussing current policies, both of which were carefully engineered to get maximum policy and public relations miles per gallon.[16]

[16] In these respects Dulles seems to have been cut from the same cloth as Secretary of State Charles Evans Hughes; see John Chalmers Vinson's chapter on Hughes in Norman A. Graebner, ed., *The Uncertain Tradition: American Secretaries of State in the Twentieth Century*, New York, McGraw-Hill, 1961. For an analysis of Dulles' public information strategy before he became Secretary, see Bernard C. Cohen, *The Political Process and Foreign Policy*, chap. 7.

Most foreign affairs correspondents had enormous respect for Dulles as a consequence of his attention to their business, even though they did not always have equal enthusiasm for his policies. Other Secretaries and their chief assistants have sought promotional advice from correspondents (where they have not received it gratuitously), and on one occasion in recent years a prominent reporter's criticisms of the State Department's press relations was so trenchant that he was offered a job on the Policy Planning Staff, "a real job, working with us in the other direction." The reporter turned this opportunity down, however, as did another well-known correspondent to whom it was subsequently offered.[17]

The press is also used to try to build up the position of foreign policy institutions within the governmental circle. The careful programming and staging of Congressional hearings to maximize favorable coverage are an obvious example, but substantially greater opportunities to create an institutional image exist in the Executive branch. The need is also greater there, because of the competition from other Executive agencies and because of the dependence on the Congress for agency funds. A Washington correspondent has described the period from January to June each year as "the period when Congress is considering appropriations and each agency is passing out carefully selected information to make itself look good."[18] How much is actually accomplished this way, however, is a matter for further study; in an environment where all institutions are understood to have a deep interest in the outcome of all competitions in which they are involved, the information they release may be received with skepticism,

[17] Two foreign policy reporters, William Jordan and Ernest K. Lindley, subsequently joined the Policy Planning Council in the Kennedy Administration, although not ostensibly in a press-relations advisory capacity. A third, Arthur Sylvester, accepted the position of Assistant Secretary of Defense for Public Affairs.

[18] Quoted in "News Under Kennedy: Reporting in the First Year," *Columbia Journalism Review*, I, No. 1, Spring 1962, p. 13.

if not suspicion. As a Congressman put it, "One knows that Hagerty, Lincoln White, and Murray Snyder are doing a selling job, so one discounts it." It is a common feature of Congressional criticism that the State Department "uses the press as the organ for its propaganda program." But even if the intended audience is not entirely convinced, it may still be the case that a residue remains, and also that the less perceptive citizen who reads from a political as well as a geographical distance is getting a picture of reality that is drawn by an interplay of divergent institutional interests that are not at all apparent to him.

Personal Promotion. It is sometimes difficult to distinguish incidents and possibilities of personal advancement from the other varieties of promotion discussed above, especially since personal interests are almost always associated with institutional or policy interests and are not likely to be made explicit by the person involved. Personal promotion may be regarded as one manifestation of politics, both electoral and administrative, in which a variety of interests may be served at one time. Despite the hazards of attributing any particular resort to the media in the foreign policy field primarily to considerations of personal advancement, such interpretations of political motivation on the part of others are being made all the time by participants in the foreign policy process.

Congressional use of the press for these purposes is relatively easy to observe, even though there is not a great deal of it in the foreign policy field. Efforts of Congressmen to get favorable publicity for their speeches are well known, as is their introduction of foreign policy resolutions that are meant only as a sop to their constituencies. The members of the Foreign Relations Committee are often described as feeling more responsible for American foreign policy than most of their colleagues, yet even there, "Members who want to cultivate the press leave hints around, and the reporters can develop a story." And one frequently runs across suggestions that the few Senators who have achieved national prominence as foreign affairs specialists in the post-World War II period, like Vandenberg and George, have done so partly through their mutually accommodating relations with reporters.

On the upper levels in the Executive branch, where the stakes in political ambitions and political reputations are high, there have been some spectacular illustrations of personal promotion as an apparent criterion governing the distribution of foreign policy news. The long-drawn-out dispute in 1957 between Secretary Dulles and Harold Stassen, Special Assistant to the President, on US approaches to disarmament and arms control was often joined in the news columns, as first one and then the other would give his version of the issues and his thoughts on his opponent's position to reporters in background conferences.[19] Eight years earlier, according to contemporary observers, Secretary of Defense Louis Johnson carried on a feud with the State Department and Secretary Acheson by the daily release of material to the press; the subsequent replacement of Johnson after the Korean War began marked the failure of his efforts. A critic of President Eisenhower expressed the belief, which he said was held by "many people in the State Department," that the White House's handling of the U-2 incident in 1960 was dictated by his staff's concern for building up the image of the President at home; this is no doubt an oversimplification, yet it is of interest because it indicates the readiness of foreign policy officials to read personal promotion in the behavior of other officials toward the press. Some policy officials also suggested that their colleagues are governed in their conversations with reporters by a desire to impress the latter with how much they know, and to seek praise from them.

It would be a distortion to conclude that foreign policy news is heavily shaped by these personal considerations. Yet if

[19] See the *New York Times* and the *Washington Post*, e.g., between March and August, 1957; see also Cater, *op.cit.*, p. 135.

foreign policy keeps increasing in importance among the live issues in American politics, we may expect to see more people trying to establish their political reputations by dealing in foreign policy information. And the problem of determining the relevant "reality" through the public prints will be that much greater.

External Policy Considerations. Paralleling the uses of the press to promote foreign policies at home are its uses to promote policies abroad; here we shall bring together and extend the remarks made at earlier points in this chapter on the external, or foreign policy, purposes behind the distribution of foreign affairs information.

There are two sides to the coin of external policy considerations, two manifestations that seem to be of equal importance. There is the giving of specific material to reporters as an instrument of policy to influence the behavior of others in foreign countries, and there is the withholding of specific material from reporters in order to prevent undesired influences on behavior abroad. Since the international impact of foreign affairs information is cited as the chief reason for restraint in the release of information at home, it is appropriate to consider these negative criteria along with the positive ones.

Foreign policy officials are reluctant to discuss in detail the active uses of the press to promote particular foreign policy interests, and so one ordinarily hears more about the restrictions that external policy requirements impose upon a domestic public information policy than about the opportunities they offer. Assistant Secretary of Defense Arthur Sylvester, however, was unusually frank in asserting several times during the 1962 Cuban crisis that news was a "weapon" in the hands of the government, and that "information is power." Soon after the crisis had passed, Sylvester spoke about "the inherent right of the government to lie to save itself when faced with nuclear disaster. . . ."[20]

[20] See his speech to the Deadline Club in New York, December 6, 1962, as reported by UPI.

The reasons for the general reluctance to talk this way are twofold at least. For government officials to acknowledge that some news items—those that are not so obvious that they need no acknowledgment—have foreign policy objectives is to involve the American government explicitly in enterprises that look like "interference" in the internal affairs of other countries, running the risk that the efforts will backfire and also that future attempts to communicate with foreign governments through the press might be excessively discounted. And for officials to acknowledge these things is also to complicate and compromise their relations with the correspondents upon whom they depend to give prominence to the items. These correspondents may or may not understand the latent significance of a particular story, and that they themselves are being used for policy purposes; but even if they do understand and accept these things, the moral requirements of objectivity and independence for the press mean that they cannot passively accept their being made explicit. Indeed, James Reston has claimed that the "whole controversy" between the press and the government during the Cuban blockade arose only when Assistant Secretary Sylvester made the government's intention explicit: "As long as the officials merely didn't tell the whole truth, very few of us complained; but as soon as Sylvester told the truth, the editors fell on him like a fumble."[21]

As negative criteria—as reasons governing the non-distribution of information to correspondents—external policy considerations affect a sizable range of topics. The most obvious, perhaps, involve diplomatic actions and negotiations, where political advantages or bargaining positions might be undermined or lost if they were given out too early, or where the opportunities for slow and delicate compromise in sensitive areas might disappear if they became the subject of daily newspaper discussion. "We don't expect General Motors to

[21] See his column, "Washington," in the *New York Times*, November 2, 1962.

issue descriptions or pictures of its new automobiles to its competitors months in advance of their release; why should the United States government be put in that kind of a position with respect to *its* competitors?" "You cannot carry on negotiations for a missile tracking station on a small island . . . if there are going to be constant newspaper announcements about it." The constraints on the distribution of information to reporters during the blockade of Cuba in the fall of 1962 are an especially vivid illustration of this criterion.

Secondly, there are subjects that fall under the ban for reasons best summarized as the sensitivity of other peoples or governments, which is to say that large aspects of our foreign relations are dependent on "good will," and hence that the propriety of revelation may be a more significant criterion than the truth as far as foreign governments, policies, and officials are concerned. Governments, like private persons, do not publicly call attention to the frailties or infidelities of people they have to live and work with; nor do they publicly reveal their true thoughts about someone else's manners, intentions, and aspirations when to do so would be disruptive of ordinary good relations; nor can they claim full public credit for good works if the persons thus benefited are embarrassed by the revelations.

As a third class of subjects calling for restraint we might include the range of foreign policies still to be bargained for and negotiated at home; just as there are points where publicity may help one out in the process of policy-making, there are times when to tip one's hand is to guarantee victory to one's competitors. These are not always external policy considerations, to be sure, but one suspects that foreign policy officials sometimes handle them as such because secrecy in the name of the national interest has social sanction, while secrecy for the sake of narrow political advantage is always under attack from the press.

As positive criteria—as reasons governing the distribution

of information to reporters—external policy considerations are no doubt more potent than an outside observer can judge (or than a participant can record). We can easily discover the important use of the press, however, in declaratory policy or declaratory aspects of policy, where the statement or announcement of intentions, of programs, of past performances—indeed, of any aspect of foreign relations—is itself a vital element in the policy. The wide dissemination of information about Christmas food packages abroad, about the Congo troop airlift, about aid programs where the economic effects will not be felt for months or years; the more focused communication through the press to foreign governments, dropping hints about a willingness to talk or restating firm obligations of support or deliberately obscuring our likely responses by ambiguous forecasts (e.g., a "keep-them-guessing" policy such as we have relied on for the defense of Quemoy and Matsu)—these are a few examples of the communicative or declaratory aspects of foreign policy. They illustrate how the press as a system of communication has become an integral part of the battery of instruments by means of which American foreign policy makers try to influence the expectations and the behaviors of other peoples and governments—friends and allies as well as potential enemies and countries with wandering affections.

It is not always possible to distinguish between the substantive political component of policies and their declaratory overtones, because some courses of action must be verbally communicated before they can begin to be effective and thus the declaratory aspects are essential parts of the policy. On the other hand, there is little possibility for confusion about the use of the press for the direct exchange of remarks and viewpoints with foreign governments, where the discourse itself constitutes the entire political relationship; this scoring of minor points in an endless exchange of charges, denials, and countercharges has been a characteristic policy weapon in the Soviet-American cold war since 1945. The press may also be employed in countless other ways to support particular policies or lines of policy, ways that are neither declaratory nor propagandistic. Cater points out how it has been used to focus public attention (and thus political attention) quickly on potentially dangerous situations, and to put pressure on an ally in order to induce concessions in subsequent negotiations.[22] The practical effect of these uses of the press is to alter the political pressures on our competitors or opponents, or at least their perceptions of future degrees of opposition or support; Secretary Dulles' news conference warning to the French of an "agonizing reappraisal" of American policy if the French defeated EDC is a good example.

The Testing of Reactions. The "trial balloon," the calculated indiscretion that is designed to test reactions to new policy ideas, constitutes one of the best—or at least the most widely—understood reasons for the distribution of foreign policy information, even though it is far from the most common use made of the press by foreign policy makers. By definition the technique is reserved for new, potentially unpopular decisions; these may be ones for which there are reasonable alternatives, so that if the reaction turns out to be adverse, particularly from the Congress, then a different decision can be made. But policies can be tested that will be put into effect in any case, the results of the testing providing data on which to base public information programs to make the policy choice more palatable. Implicitly, also, the flotation of trial balloons is the province chiefly of the higher levels in the foreign policy establishment, where authoritative decisions can be made on the basis of the data that the testing has provided.

Foreign policy officials defend as a practical necessity the use of the press to measure reactions both abroad and at home, but they give it far less attention than they pay to other

[22] Cater, *op.cit.*, pp. 134-35.

reasons for releasing information to reporters. Among its very considerable advantages for foreign policy officials are the speed of the data collection and the possibility of tailoring it to a very precise set of potential policy specifications. Alternative systems exist for estimating public reactions, particularly of wide and distant publics; for example, polls, the mail, local party officials, organizational representations and literature, and day-by-day scrutiny of ordinary press coverage. They are, however, much slower, and unless they are specifically undertaken by officials with particular questions in mind, they have the further weakness that they can be applied to new policy possibilities only as a result of inference and extrapolation from other and perhaps crucially different issues. But even among the near-by political community, the trial balloon can elicit within hours a sample of political responses to specific proposals that would require a greater degree of commitment as well as much more time and effort to evoke by such means as private exploratory discussions, for example. To be sure, there are problems in the interpretation of reactions that are stirred up by trial balloons in the press, too, but after some experience with the technique, the very pattern of reactions—the sources, the intensity, and so forth—itself furnishes clues to the way that the proposals will be received. The staff assistant of a Senator active in foreign policy said that the Senator tested reactions to new ideas this way: "The reaction of the *Washington News*, and to a lesser extent the *Post* and the *Star*, and even lesser the *Sun* and the *New York Times*, is an indication of the mass acceptability of the idea."

While the interview data at hand do not refer to it, one can imagine a situation where Executive testing of foreign reactions through the press might conveniently take place through the agency of a friendly Congressman. Testing out foreign reactions to new policy developments may be less disruptive of existing relations if the overtures seem to come from the Congress; if the response from abroad is too severe, the suggestion can be more easily disavowed and the official foreign policy agencies of the government are less likely to feel the chill wind from abroad.

Diversionary tactics. Some of the higher-level foreign policy officials who regularly deal in the material for many different news stories have developed a rationale for the distribution of information that a former official called "a diversionary procedure," the purpose of which was "to keep secret the things we really wanted to keep secret." He described it as follows: "The device was patterned after the legendary Russian family escaping across the snow in the sleigh, throwing out babies to the snapping wolves in order to propitiate them. Whenever we would meet reporters, _____ and I would ask each other, 'What baby shall we throw out today?' Then we would toss them a relatively unimportant bone, and they would . . . scramble so quickly . . . that they would not press us on the matters we wanted kept secret." Another former official in the State Department called a colleague of his "the wisest man in the State Department when it comes to the press. . . . His secret is that he selects what *he* wants to talk about, and he will never discuss things that are under negotiation." A public affairs official observed that "The best treatment is to take reporters into your confidence—or at least make them feel that you have." One can practice this form of control over the pattern of news only if one knows enough about a number of different foreign policy developments so that one has a good supply of babies to toss out. But there is a further requirement: before an official can draw reporters away from certain areas of inquiry by leading them down other paths of news, he has to have an understanding of what a correspondent will regard as a *divertissement*—that is, what kinds of babies are delectable to the wolves.

Knowledge of Reporters' Criteria. Foreign policy officials are such diligent and professional readers of the press that they develop over the years the same sensitivity to "news," the same understanding of what will sell in the market place, as the reporters acquire through their daily exposure to the work of their colleagues.[23] This is revealed, as we pointed out earlier in this chapter, in the capacity of officials to predict the questions that correspondents will be asking on any particular day. It is also apparent in the fact that officials characterize the "news values" of foreign policy in almost the same terms as the reporters themselves use.[24] Conflict and controversy, sensationalism, the "big name," that which is timely and "interesting"—these are the foreign policy reporters' criteria as understood by the policy makers, and as used by them both to get something in the newspapers and to try to keep it out. Since most officials deplore the conflict-controversy-sensationalism orientation toward foreign policy that ignores the "peaceful constructive work," they tend to be guided in their *active* promotion of news more by the other criteria: the personalization of issues, the fresh angle, the playing-up of features that can compete for reader-interest with the rest of the day's news output. Perhaps the real key governing the use of these criteria is found in the insight gained by some of the officials who are very successful in their relations with correspondents, to the effect that a reporter does not have a single fixed con-

[23] Donald Matthews observes the same phenomenon among the Senators: "Over the years, most Senators develop a 'sense of news'; that is, they are able accurately to anticipate what events will be considered 'news' by which reporters." (*U.S. Senators and Their World*, p. 203.) It should be remembered, though, that many officials and Congressmen were newspapermen earlier in their careers. In 1946, for example, George Galloway noted that "Ten Senators and 24 Representatives are now, or formerly were, newspaper editors and publishers or journalists. . . ." (*Congress at the Crossroads*, New York, Thomas Y. Crowell, 1946, p. 297.)

[24] A correspondent reported the following incident: "In 1954 . . . at the Foreign Ministers' meeting on Germany, the Russians demanded that Communist China be brought in. Dulles agreed [as a tactical device] that a committee should consider the matter and then report back to the Ministers. One of his assistants [a former newspaperman] then leaned over to Dulles and whispered to him that the press would report this as 'Dulles Willing to Admit Red China.' So when his turn came on the next round, Dulles changed his mind."

ception of a desirable story in mind; that he may be independent one day and follow the mob of reporters the next; that
his real attachment is not to a particular subject but rather
to turning in a good story no matter what it is about—"something that is interesting enough to print." When the reporter
is hard-pressed by the prevailing market for news, there is
little that the official can do to alter his focus short of dramatic
new revelations; but where the pattern of the day's news is
not clear cut, the discerning official capitalizes on his understanding of the correspondent's implicit criteria and shapes
his news offering accordingly.

Conclusion. These varied considerations that shape the
foreign policy official's approach to the distribution of news are
presented here largely in a classificatory way, with little attempt at ordering or locating them in an on-going political
structure. Hence they do not pretend to explain the press behavior of particular officials at particular times, but only to
point out the range and character of the influences that come
to bear on the release of foreign policy information. These
criteria are interwoven in a fabric of discourse between officials and correspondents, in which the initiative most often
rests with the reporter and the official has to make the best
of his opportunities to achieve the "mix" of interests that seems
reasonable to him. A more elaborate study is clearly indicated,
to ascertain the magnitude, location, and relative significance
of the different motivations behind this active use of the press.

Perhaps the most compelling argument for more systematic
knowledge of these motivations is that they are helping to
shape our daily image of what is relevant and important in
American foreign policy; and in the absence of satisfactory
knowledge about the reasons why these particular segments
of reality are the ones that "make history" today, we cannot
properly evaluate the information contained in the news
stories.[25] Are we reading about a potential crisis, for example,

[25] Cater makes this point with reference to "leaks." (*Op.cit.*, pp.
139-40.)

because there is a high probability that it will actually materialize, or because there is a high probability that it will facilitate a Congressional appropriation, or strengthen someone's hand in a forthcoming negotiation? A better understanding of how the press serves a multitude of political and policy-making purposes might well diminish its efficacy with respect to some of those purposes; but we are not even in a position to begin to judge the net balance of advantage and disadvantage on the basis of our present inadequate knowledge of the motivations and of the degree to which they serve their purposes in practice. We may get a better comprehension of the latter problem, however, if we turn now to what is taken *out* of the press by foreign policy officials.

CHAPTER VII

EXTRACTIONS FROM THE PRESS: THE UTILIZATION OF NEWS

⬤   CONTRADICTORY and ambivalent themes mark the approach of foreign policy officials to the press, and these contradictions and inconsistencies have been reflected in prior pages. The negative attitudes toward the press and the strong depreciation of its standards and accuracy, the view that one cannot trust the newspapers or believe them or take them at face value, are all aspects of a cynical, wary outlook suggesting that the official is relatively impervious to the contents of the press, that he regards it as something vulgar that he cannot rub out of his life but that he will not permit to upset the rhythm of his work and the order of his day. But as intense and as widespread as these feelings are, readership of the press and reliance upon its foreign affairs content are just as widespread and intense. Indeed, the evidence in this chapter suggests that the foreign policy maker typically takes more out of the press than any one of them readily admits to, or may even be aware of. The familiar saw, "All I know about foreign affairs is what I read in the *New York Times*," is meant as a confession of limited competence, and when it was uttered by a Presidential hopeful in early 1960 it earned the scorn of reporters; yet if the reference to the *New York Times* is meant generically, there is more truth in the statement than most practitioners feel comfortable with. The press is not wholly responsible for their education, to be sure, but it does serve them in some very important ways, supplying material that is not supplied elsewhere. What are some of the things that policy makers get out of the press that have a bearing on the foreign policy environment? And how well are the purposes that lead policy makers to communicate through the press actually served by these patterns of extraction from it?

⊜ Information

For the Executive. Although he is surrounded by official and unofficial private networks of communication designed to keep him informed, the policy maker in the State Department still turns to the press for basic factual information about the international political world he lives in—information from abroad as well as from his own immediate environment.[1] Why should this be so? What can he learn from this general public source that he does not get from his established internal sources of information? To a great extent the answer depends on how the internal network of communication serves different needs or requirements of foreign policy officials at different levels and with varying functions and responsibilities. These officials have certain common requirements for information, and other needs that are functionally specific.

Except for the top foreign policy-making officials, there is a specialization of geographic area and/or function among the people in the State Department. The official network of communication from representatives abroad is designed to keep these specialists informed with respect to their own specialization. As a Departmental official pointed out, "The embassies do not attempt to cover the news; they assume that people in the State Department read newspapers." A former high-level official said the same thing: "Most of the information you get, you get from the newspapers. . . . In the State Department the internal flow of communication is specialized; the

---

[1] E.g., ". . . reporters who called to find out what the crisis men [the State Department's short-lived twenty-four hour Operations Center, the "crisis desk"] knew about last week-end's surprises—the Friday midnight revolt in Argentina and the Berlin border closing Saturday night—found that the center was getting its word from the press." (*New York Times*, August 21, 1961.)

broad scope of developments is found in the newspaper." The same point was made by a foreign aid official: "Of course, government employees get their information from the news-papers. . . ." And from a former foreign aid official, "The *New York Times* is the primary information source for most of our foreign policy people." For the relatively few men at the top of the foreign policy establishment, the press also provides an independent report, outside the diplomatic channel, on what is happening around the world. The State Department long ago considered and gave up the notion that it might compete with the major news agencies by running its own network of news reporters around the world. Having taken that course, the Department became dependent on the wire services, and on the major newspapers with their own staffs of foreign correspondents, for its basic coverage of world events, and for an independent check on the more limited and private flow of intelligence within the Department. "The *New York Times* and other newspapers with their own corre-spondents abroad have angles that you may not be aware of as a consequence of reading only the official reports."[2]

Furthermore, the officials usually get their information sooner through the press than through official routes; owing to the coding and decoding procedures, official reports gen-erally run behind press reports. Ultimately, of course, officials have to work with the information and analysis supplied by their own "reporters" in the missions abroad; but their contact with the rapidly changing contours of the international polit-ical world at any moment in time comes more through the press than through their own facilities. And the more rapidly the changes take place, the greater dependence there is upon the press. A close observer said that "In fast-breaking situations, the tickers beat cables by four or five hours—and in some cases

[2] A *New York Times* reporter once asked Under Secretary of State Sumner Welles, "Do you know anything we don't know today?" To which Welles replied, "Of course not, where do you think we get our information?"

by up to twenty-four hours." Another State Department official, who has the news tickers clipped and sent up to him steadily all day, concluded that "the State Department sources run about twenty-four hours behind the press." Radio news also has a competitive time advantage, in a limited situation: the early morning news roundups often have later information than appears in the morning newspaper, and officials listen to them at home, some hours before they get a chance to see any of the same material on the tickers in the Department. It is not unusual, consequently, for an official to make a reference to a late radio news item in the Secretary of State's morning staff conference, or in other morning conferences within the State Department. Under these circumstances, the press cannot help but have some impact on the way the men at the top initially define international situations. "Your vision of the world," one of them said, "comes at you from the paper, it hits you at breakfast." The press's definition of the structure of international affairs, or parts of that structure, may even become the prevailing definition among these top officials—indirectly, because it is the one so many other people accept; and by default, because these officials are physically unable to read everything that comes into the State Department through official channels.[3]

It may be misleading here, in any event, to discuss the press accounts and the diplomatic reports as if they were two wholly independent streams of intelligence. The men who write the reports in the embassies are like regular newspaper reporters in the sense that they too are responsive to developments "in the news," and what they send in to the Department some hours later may be their own reaction to things they have seen on the tickers, or it may be in reply to requests

[3] The Executive Secretariat screens, summarizes, and selects cables for the top three officers in the Department, in much the same way as the editorial staff of a newspaper makes its selections of material for the paper—ostensibly with "different priorities in mind," according to a close observer, but the process bears investigation.

from Washington that were first stimulated by news reports. In this sense the press's definition of issues and the content of its news stories have a direct bearing upon the internal system of reporting. Furthermore, the local press in the foreign country has an impact on reporting from the field. In developing his own reports, the diplomatic official gathers his information from a variety of sources, prominent among them being the press of the country concerned. A Foreign Service Officer reminisced: "The embassies find out what the government to which they are accredited is doing, via the press. . . . In _____ I used to mine the local newspapers all the time, for my reports to Washington." In other words, the significance of the press is not merely that it gets to the foreign policy people sooner and perhaps over a wider range of issues, helping to define situations, but that in getting there first it also helps to shape the subsequent diplomatic reporting on the same issues. It does seem clear, in any case, that the reporting function of the diplomat—one of the classic triad of functions: reporting, representation, and negotiation—stands in need of reexamination in the larger context of the total flow of foreign policy information from abroad to foreign policy officials. There are some other points of similarity in the generally held conceptions of the diplomat and the foreign correspondent—for example, in the notions of desirable training, competence, language facility, and the like; but the smaller the difference, in practice, between regular journalism and diplomatic reporting, and the closer and more intimate the connection between them, the greater the significance that we must attach to the press in the stream of foreign policy intelligence, and the more relevant to the processes of policy-making become the standards by which press coverage is made and measured.

For the foreign policy specialists, the desk men and others who work on a narrow front, the press also provides an independent and more rapid view of what is happening in their areas of interest. But since the internal flow of specialized material is great, the informational contribution that the press makes directly to their work is proportionately less. A desk officer described it this way: "There will be a story in the *New York Times* from time to time which is *news* to us, and about which there is nothing on the cables from _____. But it is usually the structural problem, not a particular event, that gives rise to this story." The press provides these people with other information, however: it tells them what is happening around the world in areas other than the one with which they are primarily concerned. Since they neither have access to, nor time to read, the official reports from all over the world, these specialists—up to, and sometimes including, the Assistant Secretaries of State—rely substantially upon the press for their broader knowledge of international developments. It would seem to be the case, however, that the narrower a man's area of specialization, and the greater the distance between him and the staff level in the State Department, the greater is his dependence on the press for his larger view of the world.

The press also provides the specialist with domestic political information. The specialist lives in a bureaucratic world, and he is familiar with the political struggles that accompany policy ideas and proposals along the route to decision. Of necessity, he acquires internal sources of information about relevant developments and possibilities in proximate bureaucratic units, but here, too, his intelligence becomes more tenuous with increasing distance. And so he turns to the press for information about things that are happening and proposals that are being considered elsewhere in the foreign policy-making structure of the government. Robinson, for example, reports how a *New York Times* story announcing an agreement between Senator Monroney and the State and Treasury Departments on his resolution calling for an International Development Association stimulated renewed expressions of opposition from "a prominent financial official within the Administration."[4] Similarly, every announcement in the newspapers that Japanese peace treaty discussions might be in the offing evoked a wave of interested and critical participation from West Coast Congressmen who were concerned about a treaty solution to the fisheries problem.[5] Even the President keeps in touch with the administration of foreign affairs this way; a recent account described President Kennedy's phone conversation with a "top official" in which he discussed "a *New York Times* story dealing with expenditures of one of Chester Bowles' foreign journeys. Item by item, the President demanded explanations; the official, his brow wet with perspiration, dealt with them as best he could."[6] A Foreign Service Officer tactfully explained how the situation looked from high up in the State Department: "You cannot divorce foreign policy from domestic political situations and political events. By and large the traditional departmental methods of informing departmental officers do not suffice, so the press plays an important role in factually informing officers."

For the Congress. The Congressman's "need" for foreign affairs information is of a different order from that of the official in the State Department; his interests are rarely as specialized as the official's, and he rarely has to respond immediately to developments abroad. Despite this, the press is at least as important to members of Congress as a source of foreign policy information as it is to State Department officials,

[4] James A. Robinson, *The Monroney Resolution*, p. 13.
[5] Bernard C. Cohen, *The Political Process and Foreign Policy*, chap. 12.
[6] Worth Bingham and Ward S. Just, in *The Reporter*, April 12, 1962, p. 21. Cf. also V. O. Key's discussion of the role of the *New York Times* and the *Washington Post* "as a means for supplementing the internal lines of communication of the sprawling federal establishment." (*Public Opinion and American Democracy*, p. 405.) In another example, Douglass Cater claims that during the U-2 crisis, officials were "communicating with each other via the news tickers" rather than through the NSC. ("A Chronicle of Confusion," *The Reporter*, June 9, 1960, p. 17.)

because the Congressman's alternative sources of information are not so extensive, and because for most Congressmen this is apparently the most congenial way of keeping broadly and generally informed.[7]

The legislative policy maker who is at all interested in foreign affairs is not much different from an attentive citizen in his dependence upon the press; he reads the newspapers to find out what is going on in the world. A Senator remarked, "I can't overemphasize the informational function of the newspaper. We have to get our information just as the citizen gets his." The absorption of legislators in the press is legendary; Congressmen are always to be seen in the lounges reading newspapers or the news tickers, and the Senators and Representatives who have a specialization or a reputation in the foreign policy field commonly begin their day by reading from two to six newspapers, spending as much as two hours on them. Staff specialists for these legislators are somewhat more introspective and articulate about the relative place of the press in the scheme of things than are the legislators themselves; this may be due in part to their better capacities for observation and generalization than the Congressmen possess, and in part it may be a projection of their own experiences. Among these staff people, remarks like the following are commonplace: "The newspapers are part of your life, your existence. Things just soak in from the newspapers. Then you may pick up bits in articles here and there. . . ." "The newspaper is *the* source of foreign policy information—especially the *New York Times*, which is better than the State Department." "On a day-to-day basis, of course, it is still the press that supplies the information." "The press remains the only way in which one can get the whole impact of the world around oneself." A State Department official with long legislative

[7] Cf. Cabell Phillips, "The Mirror Called Congress," in Lester Markel, ed., *Public Opinion and Foreign Policy*; and Robert A. Dahl, *Congress and Foreign Policy*, New York, Harcourt, Brace and Co., 1950, esp. chaps. 1 and 2.

experience accounts for the endless reading of newspapers by Senators this way: "They are asked to comment on events, so they have to be up on them. . . . They are well posted on current problems."

The Congressman's dependence on his daily newspaper for his foreign affairs information is apparent in the inadequacy of his possible alternative sources of information. The links that Congress maintains with the State Department via the foreign affairs committees of the two Houses provide additional, not alternative, sources of information. The Department's internal sources of information are not sufficient even for the foreign policy officials there; by the time the flow of classified information reaches the Committee members, it is more like a trickle—intermittent, specialized, partial (for security reasons), except perhaps in the case of a very few and highly trusted Senators. A member of the House Foreign Affairs Committee suggested that Executive sources of information are like frosting on the press cake: "The Committee, and the leadership on both sides, get briefed by the Executive branch, so they get other information than what they get from the press." A leading Senator's staff assistant reported that "Consultation with Executive branch people only confirms what is seen in the press. . . . [The Senator] has said this many times." Further, some Committee members are distrustful of consultation with the Executive branch, seeing it as a form of dependence on the Executive and preferring the independence of press information. And among Representatives who are interested in foreign affairs but who are not on the Foreign Affairs Committee, there is disenchantment with the Committee, which further attenuates the flow of information from Executive sources through this channel.

Congressmen even look to the press as a source of information on what is going on in and around the Congress. Matthews' observation to this effect[8] holds up in the foreign

[8] Donald Matthews, *U.S. Senators and Their World*, p. 206.

policy area, where the newspaper seems to be a convenient and economical substitute for the heavy investment required to read Congressional studies, reports, and hearings. One Senate staff assistant ascribed this pattern to Congressmen's being "primarily 'mouth and ear' men—i.e., they pay more attention to what they hear than what they read. Most of what they read is likely to be in the mass media." Congressmen even treat foreign affairs information in newspapers with the deference, and accord it the authority, that those on the "outside" (including reporters) commonly accord to the information that comes *out* of Congressional studies or deliberations. The newspapers often provide the material that enables legislators, according to their own testimony, to ask intelligent questions of witnesses during hearings. And according to a member of the House Foreign Affairs Committee, Committee members regularly bring newspaper clippings into their sessions to authenticate points and to clarify problems or raise them for questioning.

In all of these cases, the "press" referred to is the prestige press that we defined in Chapter V, modified scarcely at all by the addition of constituency newspapers. For most Congressmen, unless they are from eastern metropolitan areas, constituency newspapers are not a source of foreign affairs news, either because their coverage is relatively skimpy—"only the bigger papers have the facts"—or because they arrive in Washington too late. A midwestern Representative said, "No citizen or legislator could rely on any _____ [home state] newspapers as sources for policy or for broadly based knowledge as a citizen." When constituency newspapers do arrive, they are used for different purposes, which are amply summed up in this remark of a Democratic Senator's Legislative Counsel: "Local newspapers are read for their state political news, for their news about employment conditions, general or new business developments, and for what they say about the Senator."

It may seem obvious at this point, if it has not earlier, that the press serves foreign policy makers in both the Executive and Legislative branches as a basic, standard source of factual information about foreign affairs and also about political developments within the American government that are relevant to foreign policy. Yet it is of more than passing significance that even though the press gives the policy maker his "big picture" and a large number of his smaller ones, this particular service does not constitute one of the standards by which press roles or performances are defined or judged. The informational role of the press—its central function—is aimed at the citizen; even the reporters on the prestige papers, while they presume that the reading public is intelligent and well informed and may even include policy officials, generally have a relatively unspecialized public audience in mind as the group they are trying to serve.[9] (The participant roles of the press, on the other hand, which *are* aimed at the policy makers, are defined in political rather than educational terms; foreign policy interpretations and preferences of newspapermen, rather than substantive information, are introduced into the policy-making process.) Although many reporters see the foreign policy official as an important part of their audience, nowhere do newspapermen seriously argue that an important role of foreign affairs reporting is, or should be, the provision of information to officials. Thus the informational standards of the press, even the "prestige press," are set by the assumption that the chief market for every-day reporting is the citizen rather than the responsible specialist; the latter is, accordingly, fed a popular diet for breakfast, and with that initial intellectual nourishment he is supposed to go forth to his office and do battle with giants.

[9] A *New York Times* editor remarked, "We know we cater to a certain class of persons—defined as those people in the New York metropolitan area who for some purpose or other need to be informed."

Ideas, Evaluation, Analysis, Interpretation

For the Executive. We can recall that most foreign affairs reporters and columnists are eager to be heard by policy makers; in their activist or reformist moments, they value participation as an important role for the press and as a useful outlet for their own interests and capacities. How much encouragement in this role do they get in practice from foreign policy officials (among whom we found very mixed attitudes toward newsmen and toward the press as an institution)? How well do these officials acknowledge the propriety of the correspondents' aspirations, as measured by the value they attach to their product? How open are the policy makers to the press as a source of intellectual stimulation and inspiration?

Policy makers quite obviously turn to the press not only for information but also for analysis and evaluation of developments and proposals, and sometimes even for new ideas on how to deal with the range of problems that confront them. Their attitudes toward the intellectual contribution of the columnists and reporters fall handily into three patterns, outlined below. The correlates of these attitudes are not readily apparent; in the data available neither political party nor rank in the policy-making hierarchy, the two most obvious variables, seems to make any difference in the receptivity of officials to ideas from the press. The implication seems to be that the differences are highly individual, much as we found competence in the handling of the press to be.

(1) While men who are professionally involved in foreign policy decision-making are quick to acknowledge their constant readership of foreign affairs analysts in the press, some of them are extremely reluctant to attach any great importance to the evaluations of these columnists or to admit that they contribute anything to the development of their own thinking. For instance, a former sub-Cabinet official described the effect of these writers as "mostly negative. They contributed very

few constructive ideas." Another official of the same rank said that "none of them, Lippmann and the Alsops included," were important. "Their ideas had very little substance and merit. They were of trivial influence." There may be professional pride involved here—as in a Foreign Service Officer's view that "it is damned infrequent that the Foreign Service would miss something"—as well as jealousy, an unwillingness to accord to any outside source the distinction of equality with, or superiority to, the thinking that goes on inside the foreign policy institutions. There may also be, in this attitude, a trace of suspicion that the columnists are grinding the axes of other, unidentified, participants in the policy-making process.

(2) A step above this negative position is occupied by officials who grudgingly acknowledge that sometimes the newspapermen do have something to say that is worthwhile. For example, "Occasionally some columnist will drop a new idea that will get picked up in Washington, but this doesn't happen too often." A former Assistant Secretary of State described his encounters with reporters in these terms: "Some of them would come to see you—even pester you. There would be an exchange of ideas. They often tried out a variety of ideas on you, most of which you wouldn't pay much attention to."

(3) And then there are the officials who willingly give correspondents and columnists due credit for an important, if limited, creative role in the making of foreign policy. A number of high-ranking policy makers have said, in effect, that reading the columnists is part of their job, and that their columns have often been discussed at staff conferences.[10] An Assistant Secretary of State remarked, "Our policy is made by intelligent men who will read the views of . . . thoughtful and informed columnists." A Presidential adviser said that

[10] See also Joseph M. Jones' discussion of Lippmann's column of April 5, 1947, "one of the most consequential columns he has ever written." (*The Fifteen Weeks*, pp. 228-29.)

"the judgment of men like Lippmann, Reston, and Baldwin is valued because they offer interesting ideas from time to time." A foreign aid official reported that State Department personnel will "often times" draft arguments that take their line of reasoning from a recent article by one of the columnists; and a public affairs official in the State Department displayed a fresh newspaper clipping with some ideas on an educational exchange program, which the official was using as the basis of a memorandum proposing action along the same lines. The relevant attitude seems to be that good foreign policy ideas are scarce enough so that one should seek them out and exploit them wherever they may be found; if the columnists have the edge over academic or other outside specialists in this process—and it is not absolutely clear that they do have, although it seems so—it may be because they are easier to exploit, being right at hand and writing as if they were a part of the foreign policy establishment.

On balance, then, it appears that the press is a steady and somewhat fertile source of policy analysis and ideas, affecting even people who claim to be unaffected by it. One might entertain the proposition that the impact of the columnists' views is in inverse proportion to the number and diversity of competent specialists who take part in the competition over policy alternatives. Where the specialist market is thin, as it has been on many occasions in both foreign and military policy, the remarks of the columnists seem to weigh more heavily in the balance than they do where the competition is active and intense. (In the latter case, it is also more likely that the columnists will revert to a reportorial role, and concern themselves not so much with the substantive ideas at issue but rather with the fact of political competition and controversy involving those ideas.)

The press also provides the foreign policy official with another kind of evaluation, which is no less important for being less obvious. It is commonly understood that, in the political realm, what is *thought* to be true is often a more relevant source of political inspiration than what *is* true. A former State Department official who has always been a very close observer of foreign policy-making put it this way: "The freedom of action of the diplomat is greatly limited; he has to work with the realities of the way people interpret events. The newspaperman is of the utmost importance in that field." A Foreign Service Officer involved in high-level decision-making in the State Department argued more explicitly that the policy appraisals made by persons outside the Department, representing a wider range of policy understandings, are themselves a vital part of the over-all problem that is being considered within the Department: "In assessing a given situation, you can't rely exclusively on Foreign Service reporting, or on staff papers prepared below in the Department. You have to rely to a great extent on analyses from outside—from newspapers, editorial reaction, Congressional statements, etc.—all of which reach us via the daily press. These are not primary considerations in our decisions, but you can't leave them out." Succeeding sections of this chapter will amplify this point by explaining how foreign policy makers extract from the press a sense of the way reality is perceived elsewhere in the political system—and, hence, a sense of political reality itself.

For the Congress. Members of Congress and their staff assistants are almost unanimous in acknowledging the usefulness of the press, and especially the major columnists, as sources of ideas, insights, and interpretations in the field of foreign affairs. Unlike the State Department officials, the legislative personnel by and large lack a personal competence and *expertise*, lack their own resources for the analysis of foreign policy problems. They do have staff research facilities at their disposal, including the Legislative Reference Service of the Library of Congress, but these are not designed to provide the interpretations, the speculations, the new thoughts about current developments that are the daily food of politicians and the stock-in-trade of political columnists. The Congressman is interested in knowing what others are thinking about these unfolding events and their possibilities, as a convenient basis for locating and formulating his own thoughts. There are boundless examples of Congressmen absorbing the foreign policy ideas and reflecting the stimulation of columnists, ranging from the well-known relationship between Senator Vandenberg and James Reston to the daily and unremarked culling of ideas for policy speeches.[11] Interestingly, the strongest and most explicit argument from anyone on the legislative side *against* the usefulness of the analytical content of the foreign affairs commentators came from a Senate staff person whose formative governmental experience in foreign affairs had been in the State Department.

Both Congressional and Executive people agree that Congressmen are more susceptible to the foreign policy suggestions of columnists than are Executive officials. In the eyes of officials, this susceptibility makes the press a desirable vehicle for exporting ideas to the Congress, in the hope of improving the chances for Congressional approval of Executive policy proposals. It also heightens the Executive officials' interest in the content of the columns, as we shall note in a subsequent section, because they learn what the Congressmen are reading and thus are likely to be thinking in the immediate future.

Foreign policy interpretation in the press has different implications for the policy-making system than are suggested by foreign affairs information in the press. We noted earlier that policy makers draw foreign policy information from a press that aims to supply it to non-specialized readers. In the case of analysis and interpretation, however, the audience assumptions of the journalists are more in line with the uses made of their product, for the work of columnists in comment, evaluation, and analysis is explicitly aimed at the policy makers

[11] For one such example, see Robinson, *op.cit.*, p. 3.

as well as at the ordinary citizen. The reader may recall, from our earlier discussion of the roles of the press, that the interpretive function is generally regarded as an extension of the information role vis-à-vis the general reader, on the grounds that "the facts" are meaningless without some interpretation. But the functions of criticism, of advocacy, of asking unanswered questions, and of participating in the policy deliberations and in the exchange of policy ideas are all aspects of the larger participant roles, which assume a dialogue between the correspondents and columnists on one side and the government officials and legislators on the other. This is not to argue, though, that what is done deliberately and knowingly by reporters is therefore done well; indeed, the attention that commentators turn to policy ideas is generally as wandering, haphazard, and capricious as the attention that their brother reporters turn to accounts of foreign affairs events or developments. The same uncertainty of standards as to what is newsworthy lies behind them both.

☻ Importance

For the Executive. Policy makers also draw from the press some measure of the comparative importance of events in the eyes of others—that is, the significance that is being attached to particular developments or issues as a result of evaluations made elsewhere in the political system. In their official capacities, policy makers are constantly processing large amounts of information from internal sources and from other specialized sources; these items have generally been evaluated, explicitly or implicitly, at their points of origin, but the officials at the receiving end still attach their own criteria of significance to them. They then may wish to check their own judgments of significance with still other people, or they may have the judgments of others brought forcefully to their attention whether they want them or not. The same kind of evaluative problem exists, though to a lesser degree, with respect to the information they draw all day long from the wire service tickers. Despite the processes of selection and editing to which wire service news is subjected (which itself constitutes one external measure of its importance), the material still comes out of the machines as a steady flow of relatively raw copy, and much of it has to be put into further order—to have final importance attached to it according to criteria that will hold up in the marketplace of ideas.

The newspaper, and the wire service news budget, supply a large part of this independent ordering of the importance of events. The editorial choices of a given newspaper represent the ultimate evaluative process in the cycle of news. The editors, on the basis of their own best judgments of what constitutes news—helped, of course, by the judgments of the wire service editors—attach orders of priority to news items, which they make manifest by the place in the paper to which they assign the items, by the amount of space they allocate to them, and by the size and character of the headlines they write to call attention to them. In turning to the newspaper press, policy makers are seeking (or receiving) a comparative evaluation of the importance of events; and in turning to particular newspapers or directly to the wire service budgets, they are seeking the evaluation of editors whose bellwether powers they respect, and/or of editors in whose theories of what is news they have some tested faith.

One can distinguish several different aspects of this search for comparative evaluation. The first is the simple one of ascertaining whether or not a subject has been brought into the newspaper (or onto the ticker) in the first place. An issue may have received no coverage because officials have succeeded in keeping it under wraps, or despite the officials' best efforts to bring it to public attention, or only because reporters or editors have not thought it newsworthy. In any case, policy makers are entitled to draw reasonable inferences about the political environment of decision-making when the issues have not been put on public display. Whether they have contrived to keep an issue "unimportant," or whether they have been unable to communicate to reporters their own sense of its importance, the absence of coverage tells them something about the salience of the issue in the world outside their halls.

Once a subject has "hit the papers," a more obvious aspect of the search for external judgments of its significance consists in discovering how the press rates it in comparison with all the other events and situations that are occurring at the same time. A State Department official who was once a newspaperman stressed the meaning that this use of the press held for him: "The press is more important here than the cables. There is a big difference in seeing a story on the front page, in comparison with all the other stories there, from St. Louis and everywhere else, and in the specialization of the cables. . . . The impact of the cables is not felt until it is seen in juxtaposition with other stories, on the front page of the *New York Times*." The *Times* is not the only benchmark, of course; all newspapers that foreign policy officials see serve the same end. Officials who read the *Times* and the *Washington Post* in the morning, and other papers in the course of the day, will read the *Washington Star* in the evening in order, as one official put it, "to see how the news of the day is played in the evening papers." And the two-page morning roundup or summary of foreign policy stories in the "prestige papers" that is prepared for the top officials in the State Department contains, for each story, its location in each newspaper that runs it.

Another manifestation of this particular use of the press is not properly the *search* for outside judgments of importance through the press, but their *imposition*, with the press attaching such importance to an item of news that government officials are obliged to take special cognizance of it. In other words, under certain circumstances the order of priority that the press attaches to policy items may be superimposed upon the significance originally or ordinarily attached to them in the State Department and elsewhere, and eventually even come to supersede those original estimations.[12] This is readily apparent, of course, when the issue takes on scandalous attributes, or when the press coverage stirs up unsuspected opportunities for partisan political advantage. But less dramatically, and less obviously, it takes place all the time. This constant process whereby policy officials adapt their own concerns to the priorities of the press may be seen in two ordinary contexts.

First, whenever foreign policy officials meet the press in more or less formal and open conference, they customarily prepare themselves ahead of time by a thorough exposure to the current questions of interest to the reporters, as revealed by contemporary newspapers. "We pull together the questions we know will be asked of him, so that he doesn't go in there unprepared." This is a wholly reasonable and obvious mode of preparation, but its consequence is that the official is indoctrinated, so to speak, in the momentary foreign policy perspectives of the press and he has to organize, or if necessary reorganize, his thinking to match that perspective. "You know that a story that is scattered in newspapers across the country will stir up a certain reaction."

Second, and more important, the constant access that reporters have to foreign policy officials means that the newsmen are an integral part of the policy-making structure, and on an hour-by-hour basis their passing concerns, their conceptions of reader interest and news values, their notions of a story, are translated into questions that are fed steadily into the "policy machine"[13] and cause it to shape its interests and activities in order to produce the answers. The daily and

[12] A *New York Times* reporter quoted a State Department official as saying, when the *Times* arrived after a delivery strike in December 1958, "Damn, here we go again, trouble, trouble, trouble; phone calls, people calling up, asking about your column, and Reston's."

[13] Robert Elder's description of the foreign policy-making structure: *The Policy Machine*, Syracuse, Syracuse University Press, 1959.

substantial process of preparation for the noon briefing of reporters in the State Department should be understood as part of the Department's continuous effort to understand and stay in step with the problems that seem to be bothering the press and presumably the public. This process reaches all the way up in the Department; the public affairs people, working with the two-page summary of the foreign policy news in the morning papers, raise some of the items for discussion in the Executive Staff meeting every morning. According to one of these officials, "Sometimes other people in the meetings will raise one of the items. These are items we may have to do something about. . . . There may be a story or an analysis that raises a question of policy. We may raise it at the meeting because we know we will be asked about it today, and we have to think about how to reply to it when we are asked." But this is more than just a morning preoccupation culminating in the noon briefing. At any time of the day a wire service item may bring the reporters into the News Office with questions, and when they come, "the people upstairs [i.e., the policy people] have to put their heads together to figure out how to field it." A public affairs man in one of the regional Bureaus offered a fresh example of how the policy officials have to adapt to the world of foreign policy in the press: "We are always calling news stories to the attention of the policy people. Today, for example, there is a United Press report of a US submarine observed off the _____ coast, which is reported to be armed with a nuclear capability. Well, we know what kinds of questions we are going to get asked tomorrow by the press. Have we cleared this with the _____ Government? This is part of . . . [our treaty arrangements] which has never really come up yet, and it will have to be interpreted." As we noticed at the end of the preceding chapter, their very success in foreseeing the questions that will come up is the best evidence that State Department officials, in thinking like correspondents, have assimilated many of their implicit criteria of importance.

Thus the press, in giving prominence to an issue, helps to nudge it somewhat higher on the list of items claiming the attention of foreign policy officials. This may then get translated into still further pressure on the State Department, into still another outside measure of importance, when members of Congress call up the Department to ask, "What about this problem I see in the paper?" There is great incentive, consequently, for the policy makers to turn to the newspaper to make sure that they know what is about to become important to them because people elsewhere think it is important—after their newspaper implicitly told them it was.

For the Congress. Congressmen understand the capacity of the press to lend significance to whatever issues are being discussed in its pages, just as they understand how they personally can use the press to create supportive publicity for themselves. In part, this understanding reflects the resignation of legislators in the face of a foreign policy environment over which they have no strong influence. Thus a Senator defined the principal role of the press as "picking up ideas that officials have dropped and then building up great publicity about those ideas." And a Representative attributed the lack of sophistication about foreign affairs in the House, and its attendant lack of impact on foreign policy, to the "great thrusts of attitudes they [the Representatives] cannot control." But we have made it clear in earlier contexts that legislators realize full well that the press can be an ally in gaining prominence for policy ideas in the Congress as well as in the Executive branch. A Senate staff member used the Bricker Amendment as a good example of a legislative issue in which few people were interested until the newspapers gave it coverage, thereby establishing an importance for it. "The important thing is . . . the fact that coverage is there to keep . . . an issue alive among the people."

But while members of Congress are conscious of the power of the press in raising up issues, they seem on the whole to be less aware than the Executive officials of the extent to which their daily notions of what they have to think about in the foreign policy field are influenced by the press. Where Executive foreign policy officials often turn to the press precisely to see how issues are being played, the Congressmen seem to be more willing to accept the order of priorities in the press as the "natural" order. It would seem that their own dependence on the press is so complete that they absorb most of the ordering of importance that takes place in the newspaper as an original formulation of reality, rather than as an outside source of evaluation that might compel them to alter other and preferred priorities, as is often the case with the Executive. In other words, the order that is in the press becomes *their* order, and as such its capacity to impress itself upon foreign policy officials in the Executive branch is augmented. This is manifested in the daily response of Congressmen, on and off the Floor, to the contents of the day's paper, as well as in the calls they make and the memos they send to the State Department. It is also reflected in their conviction, as outlined in Chapter V, that reporters should stick to the objective facts about an objective set of events, and allow these news events to speak for themselves. In other words, they believe that a responsible newspaper depicts an incandescent reality that the responsible legislator has to soak up and to which he must respond.

● Standards

For the Executive. The eastern metropolitan newspapers, alone and in conjunction with other newspapers from more remote constituencies, provide foreign policy makers in various parts of the government with standards by which to measure or judge what others involved in the political process are reading about foreign affairs. This is an important source of their insight into the way foreign policy issues are being perceived and assimilated into political structures, foreign as well as domestic.

In the State Department, the New York and Washington newspapers especially provide a guide to what groups elsewhere in the foreign policy universe are reading; this is one way in which the State Department keeps track of changes in the foreign policy perceptions of some of its most relevant audiences. In the higher reaches of the Department, it is claimed that the *Washington Post* editorials are read "because we know they are read on Capitol Hill." And at all levels in the Department—including the desk level, where there is the most direct contact with specific country problems—the *New York Times* is studied carefully (not merely read) because Department officials know that foreign embassy personnel in Washington accord it very great attention as the leading American newspaper and the one that is reputed to have the closest connections with the State Department. A desk officer put it this way: "A *New York Times* editorial has more weight with us *because* it has more weight with our clients, the embassies. This is why we have to read the *Times*. The embassy people read it too, and it becomes a common point of departure for their reactions and for ours." The columnists, too, are read with more care than the manifest content of their work might warrant, just because the officials know that they are read widely in Washington and also by attentive people all across the nation. "Reston almost makes foreign policy, to many people. . . ."

For the Congress. The press is even more useful to legislators than to State Department officials as a standard because of the very great differences that exist among the newspapers they see regularly. We have noted earlier that the eastern metropolitan newspapers serve the Congressmen as their foreign policy news source, and that, when the Congressmen do not come from these eastern metropolitan areas, their district newspapers serve as their source of state and local political and economic information and opinion. In time the differences that create these separate functions appear to be magnified, and the Congressmen begin to use the New York and Washington newspapers as a yardstick to measure what their constituents are—or are not—reading. This is not simply a way of comparing what they themselves are reading about the world around them with what their constituents are reading; in addition, they seem to accept the foreign affairs coverage in the leading eastern papers as the benchmark of top quality, and use it to measure the inadequacies of local press coverage. Thus a Senator commented, "I get an entirely different picture of priorities from my local newspapers than from the Washington papers. I want to know what the newspapers are telling *my* constituents about what is important in the world. I have to judge whether the emphases are accurate. . . ." And a Representative complained that "There is no rhyme or reason to foreign policy coverage in the_____ [constituency] papers. A story may get a big headline there, and just one inch of coverage in the *New York Times*. Some idiot of a night editor plays a story up out of all proportions."[14] Another Senator said that he attempts to discover what the home district press is thinking, and then compares this with the views of "the more reputable papers." This suggests, then, that whereas Executive officials are relativistic and instrumental in their extraction of standards from the press, scrutinizing material with special care because others are known or presumed to pay special heed to it, Congressmen derive from the major newspapers a more absolute standard of quality or adequacy of foreign affairs coverage. In other words, the Executive's use of the press in this sphere does

[14] The *New York Times* serves as a standard for reporters, too: a midwestern newsman said, with respect to coverage in his own paper, "I notice omissions and overplays, but only by contrast with the *New York Times*, since I don't see the tickers. . . . The *New York Times* is an automatic yardstick."

not necessarily require the officials to accept as valid the degree of importance that the papers in question assign to various subjects; all that matters is that other people are reading the same things at more or less the same time. But the Congressional uses do suggest, once again, that the Congressmen have accepted the measures of importance that the New York and Washington papers have assigned to various topics as being normal, correct, accurate representations of reality.

Congressmen also turn to the syndicated columnists as another way of discovering what their constituents are reading in the foreign policy field. Franklin Burdette has stated that the stories of syndicated columnists have an impact upon the mail that Congressmen receive from their districts, and hence they are "of marked effect in the political atmosphere of the capital."[15] By reading the columnists the same day they appear in the constituency papers, the Congressmen gain some slight time advantage, some advance notice of what these particular political stimuli look like.

○   Opinions and Reactions

For the Executive. Lastly, the press provides policy makers with the ingredient that has long been assumed to be its chief contribution: a measure of public opinion. Opinions in the press—editorial opinions; the viewpoints of columnists and commentators; the positions or reactions, spontaneous or elicited, of other policy officials and "newsworthy" individuals and groups that are reported in the news columns; even the views of the editors concerning the relative importance of items in the news—constitute one of the leading channels by which foreign policy officials can regularly and continuously tap an informed and articulate segment of public opinion. To be sure, this is not the only way in which policy makers gain an understanding of public responses to foreign policy, nor is it always the most relevant way. But lacking any other

[15] Franklin L. Burdette, in *Annals*, Vol. 289, September 1953, p. 95.

daily link to the outside, any other *daily* measure of how people are reacting to the ebb and flow of foreign policy developments, the policy maker reaches for the newspaper as an important source of public opinion, as the instrument of "feedback." In fact, many officials treat the press and public opinion as synonymous, either explicitly equating them or using them interchangeably. The over-all political impact of the press in this respect was described by one official as follows: "The newspaper is a source of a daily 'feel' as to what is going on, and the public reaction to it." Perhaps a better way to put this is to say that the press, which has elaborated the task of independently recording and criticizing the actions of government officials, is thereby the most important of the public audiences before whom the foreign policy makers act.[16] This is the policy makers' major segment of public opinion, a daily referendum of articulate opinion, a surrogate for the body of plastic notions held by the general public that tell the foreign policy makers very little about public feelings and public preferences. In other words, the policy makers reciprocate and support the reporters' contention that they represent and speak for the public in the democratic dialogue between the government and the governed.

That the press is used as a major source of opinion about foreign policy is both widely acknowledged and well understood. *How* it is used, however, is less clearly understood; there are important variations both in the way press opinion is perceived and in its political impact and utilization, and these merit our attention.

In the State Department, individual reactions to press opinion range from the extreme of apparently total rejection (after careful reading!) to the view that at times Department policy is fashioned in direct response to press opinion. The former is exemplified by the individual who, after identifying

[16] The Congress is not regarded here as part of the public audience, even though some foreign policy officials think of it that way.

press opinion as public opinion, protested a little too much, it seemed, that "Public opinion doesn't matter. . . . The official has set his goals, he believes in liberal trade, and all he wants is to get support for liberal trade, and he will not be influenced to believe the opposite. Protectionist newspapers do not influence us in the slightest degree." This man added, "I might be able to think of one case over the years where the State Department changed its policy as a result of newspaper coverage, but I doubt it." Another official combined the same personal attitude with a different historical interpretation: "The Executive tends to be very concerned with editorial opinion, although I don't know why they are."

The opposite position has been well expressed recently by the observation that "State Department policy [toward Cuba in 1958-1959] was dictated by the hue and cry in the press on the side of Castro." A high career diplomat also justified the Department's position on the same grounds: "I think every one of us who knew anything knew that Castro was playing the Communist game completely. Yet how many of the press of the country were willing to take that position? If the State Department, at the beginning, had said, in effect, 'We won't have anything to do with this Castro,' we would have been castigated and the State Department could never have stood up under the fire."[17] The view that the State Department is extremely responsive to press opinion is perhaps better expressed as the limiting effect of large numbers: press opinion is taken into account whenever the accumulating evidence indicates a very clear trend one way or the other. If there is large-scale opposition to a proposal, one official said, "it is likely to be carefully reconsidered. On the other hand, if it receives wholehearted support, it is likely to be energetically pushed forward." Another saw significance in a 75 per

[17] Quoted in *U.S. News and World Report*, July 4, 1960, p. 47. These quotations are used here to illustrate an attitude toward press opinion, not to pass judgment on our Cuban policy.

cent majority of general editorial opinion. By and large, however, it seems to be the negative majorities that impress the
officials with the constraints they impose on policy, rather
than the liberating opportunities that are contained in positive majorities.

The large middle ground between these (no doubt over-
stated) points of view is occupied by two basic orientations
to press opinion that are more in tune with the uncertainties
of political decision-making, with the absence of any large
and clear majorities of opinion, and with the recurring need
to build effective majorities or at least to read persuasive public
support in the signs and signals of opinion reaching policy
makers. For convenience we might call these orientations,
which are not at all exclusive, the evaluative and the
manipulative.

The evaluative orientation looks to press opinion for clues
to the structure of actual or potential political support for
alternative policies. Where policy is relatively firm, "the daily
trend of editorial opinion," according to a desk officer, "is less
significant." But where there is flux, he went on, "we are
interested in seeing editorials, to see what is behind them,
who wrote them, what weight they represent." Another official, whose work entailed a wider area of political interest
and participation, sought the same end by the opposite route:
"The editorials are anonymous so that one can't tell who
actually writes them. The articles of the syndicated columnists
are in a way more important than the editorials." The policy
officials at the higher levels are also on the look-out for signs
of potential opposition or support in the Congress; these signs
are more eagerly sought where the official has used the press
explicitly for the purpose of testing reactions to new departures
in policy. But in the ordinary way, too, the press is a source
of comment on the things that come out of the Congress as
well as out of the Executive; and by eavesdropping, so to
speak, on the Congressional fragment of the dialogue between

the public and the government, the foreign policy officials in the Executive branch get insight into the potential strength of Congressional sentiments. A former Assistant Secretary of State recalled, for instance, that "the response of newspapers to the points of view of particular Congressmen . . . would indicate whether the Senator [sic] was just frolicking or was reflecting a widespread opinion."

In the State Department the manipulative or instrumental orientation seems to be at least as pervasive as the evaluative orientation; it is certainly not limited to those officials whose primary responsibility is the Department's public relations, although these people do have a special investment in it. The manipulative orientation looks to the press for clues to the way policy is being received by newspapermen, in order to determine whether such policy needs to be better justified or explained. In the public affairs area, the reading of editorial opinion has often led Departmental officials to make strenuous efforts, formal and informal, to give editors all across the country what one official called "the feel of what we try to do." Another person said that editorial and press opinions were "the true measure of the relative success or failure of our own public relations function." The higher-level policy people are equally concerned with these questions, as we have pointed out before. The following observation, from a vantage point close to the top of the State Department's policy-making structure, is an excellent statement of this instrumental use of press opinion and reactions: "The main use of the press in making foreign policy decisions is alerting you to public reactions and to public interest—to the necessity for considering how policy decisions need to be interpreted when they are made public. You can only set forth the reasons [behind a policy] in an intelligent fashion if you know what the public is worried about. The press that we read here is the major source of our knowledge of public opinion." One might question whether this is in fact the "main use" of the press, even at levels in the Department where internal information flows abundantly, but the relevance of this employment of the press to political purpose is plain in any case.

For the Congress. It can be expected of elected representatives that they will steep themselves in the public opinion that they find in the newspapers. As a Senator described it, "Newspapers give us editorial reactions, personal reactions, of people who are informed, people whose reactions are an important gauge of the significance of developments abroad." Congressmen, as we have said before, use their constituency newspapers for state and local news and also for opinion information, since they are interested in the outlook of a particular public as well as an especially well-informed one. Surprisingly, however, this use of the constituency press for opinion information does not extend equally to foreign policy opinions, at least among Congressmen who are especially interested in foreign policy. These Congressmen, even when they come from remote constituencies, seem to pay more attention to editorials and other expressions of foreign policy opinion in the *New York Times* and the *Washington Post*— as much attention, perhaps, as they pay to the foreign policy information in these same newspapers. Since this is an unusual finding, we shall explore its possible sources.

One apparent reason for the relative downgrading of local press opinion is that in many district newspapers there is no editorial coverage of foreign affairs or other expression of the foreign policy opinions that circulate within the constituency, while in many other papers there is only occasional and scant opinion information. A member of the Senate Foreign Relations Committee said, for example, "The county seat papers in _____, which print principally local news, do not attempt to influence public opinion [on foreign policy]." If the representative is interested in keeping in touch with general editorial opinion on foreign affairs, he turns as a matter of convenience to those papers close at hand that print a lot of opinion information. Another reason for non-reliance upon the constituency press is that some Congressmen feel that press editorials on foreign policy matters have no resonance in the local communities. These Congressmen are looking for the "informed opinion" of more than just one editorial writer. Where they suspect, rightly or wrongly, that the editor himself has no audience, that his views are not going to create a wider body of opinion and hence do not anticipate or reflect such a body of opinion, the Congressmen are likely to rely more heavily on the eastern newspapers that are presumed to have a wide and significant audience for their foreign policy editorial opinion. A midwestern Representative expressed this well when he said that "Reading the local paper doesn't give me any opinion information, because no matter how good the editorial columns—and they are *the* foreign policy columns in the paper—I know that nobody reads them." In the same vein, a number of staff assistants remarked on the sensitivity of members of Congress to opinions that they think *do* have a market, even if they are not themselves part of it; one Senator's assistant observed, for example, that "Columnists are read for their opinions because they are so widely distributed." Still another reason lies in the content of the editorials that do appear in the district papers; the smaller the paper, the less likely is it to have editorial writers who can comment on abstruse or specialized foreign policy subjects, or who can say new and different things on more familiar subjects. Thus a Representative found most editorials worthless because they were "on the *obvious*, not the subtle, aspects of policy, and along the general thrust of attitudes. . . . Several of the great newspapers will discuss editorially the more important but less notorious aspects of foreign policy, but generally it is not done."

And still another possible reason for the opinion significance of the eastern press may be discerned in the circumstances of the political life of Congressmen. The longer a Congressman remains in Washington, the more his ties with his home district or state are subject to attenuation. He lives in a new community, an intensely political one, and if he is interested in foreign affairs he soon discovers that there is a lot of international politics in Washington, too. But his new foreign policy horizons are likely to have no counterpart in the editorial world of his constituency press; that may tell him some things, but it does not tell him how to respond to the stimuli that confront him in Washington. And so the Congressman turns to the editorial views that carry some weight in that community—part of a pattern that a Representative called "going Eastern"—thereby adding to the political importance of those expressions of opinion. A prominent Senator observed this process among Committee chairmen: "When a member of Congress becomes a committee chairman, his home electoral district becomes a necessary nuisance; consequently, to this Congressman, the influence of the home district paper is decreasing."

In the light of all this, it is not surprising to find, as Miller and Stokes have, that Congressmen have no clear perception of attitudes within their constituencies on matters of foreign policy; their data indicate a .19 correlation between constituency attitudes toward American involvement abroad and the representatives' perception of those constituency attitudes.[18] The near-absence of opinion information on foreign affairs in the district papers compels the representative to look elsewhere if he wishes to ascertain constituency opinion on foreign policy. But the absence of foreign policy news and opinion information in the local press also tends to cut down on the stimuli that will be reflected in whatever other conduits of opinion within his district the representative might employ. And beyond this, of course, if the representative avoids editorial opinion on foreign policy in his constituency papers because

[18] Warren E. Miller and Donald E. Stokes, *Representation in Congress* (forthcoming).

he thinks of it as politically meaningless even when it is substantively competent, then he is cut off still further from articulate opinion back home.

● Conclusion

It remains here to link this discussion of the classes of things that people in the government take from the press with our prior discussions of some of the characteristics of press coverage of foreign affairs. In taking information, ideas, standards, opinions, and a measure of importance from the daily parade of words in the newspaper, how are foreign policy officials and legislators affected by the things that reporters write about foreign affairs, by the way they write about them, and by the things that other officials and legislators try to get them to write?

We noted earlier that foreign affairs reporters tend to cluster around the story or stories that are getting the biggest "play" in the newspapers; that the biggest play is likely to be given to the dramatic, the controversial, the contentious, the personal element; and that this pattern of story choice has the effect of muffling other stories, on a day-to-day basis and also over extended periods of time. We pointed out, further, that in hopping from issue to issue, from crisis to crisis, the correspondent deals in political discontinuities. In drawing information from the press, then, the policy official confronts a grossly uneven, often misleading picture of the world and its political relationships and problems. And in extracting a sense of the public importance of foreign policy issues from the newspapers, policy makers are responding to criteria that, no matter what their merits, are not systematically relevant to the problems of American foreign policy that otherwise seem most urgent to them at any particular time.[19] This is not to

[19] A reporter who worked in the office of a high military official during World War II observed, "Even the best-informed Washington

argue that these issues may not be important in the sense that public apprehensions, interests, and energies have been focused on them; it is rather to indicate that the priorities of the official, which do bear at least some relationship to a coherent pattern of foreign relations, are modified by the priorities of the reporter, which are responsive to no such coherent pattern, and which reflect rather the problems involved in assimilating foreign affairs to the standards of a mass market. We may still believe that foreign policy ought to be responsive somehow to some order of political values that arises in the public marketplace, even when those political values have no intellectual rigor or coherence. But this leaves open the question whether the reporter's priorities should be accepted as the most relevant ones within the marketplace, or whether a more consciously responsible and responsive political leadership might have a larger share in the task of defining these political values.

Another relevant feature of press coverage of foreign affairs is its anchorage in the immediate present, in the wake of those things that can be observed to have happened. The foreign affairs correspondents, in terms of their own *modus operandi*, have only a limited freedom to move in various directions, asking more anticipatory or developmental questions about political issues or possibilities, much as a boat at anchor can maneuver in a very circumscribed arc. (And, to be sure, the policy official is not often willing to talk in these "hypothetical" terms either.) Consequently, information and ideas relevant to policy generally enter the stream of intelligence after a situation has developed rather than in anticipation of it. There are exceptions to this, of course; an obvious exception is where policy officials sense a developing problem and for

journalist is ill-informed on policy—and especially on foreign policy. . . . What impresses most press people when they are taken on the inside is that before they were so far out on the fringe. The press is a limited channel of communication."

their own (generally unarticulated) purposes make a major effort to get correspondents to treat it as news. But under more common circumstances, where officials are cautious in the release of information, the opinions and reactions relevant to foreign policy that are stirred up by press discussion, and that officials then take from the press, concern policy developments that are comparatively mature and are therefore resistant to a large variety of external pressures. The opinions and reactions that officials learn about, consequently, are less capable of being integrated into the stream of policy thinking and policy choice than would be the case if newspaper stories were built upon foresight and facilitated foreknowledge of the possible patterns and procedures of political choice. (This may, of course, be the reason for the caution of officials in the first place.)

There is perhaps a closer fit between the things that some officials try to contribute to the press in the foreign policy field and the things that other officials take from it, than there is between the ordinary needs of the officials for substantive and political information and the routine contribution of the reporter. The efforts that individuals make by way of institutional, personal, and policy promotion reach home, so to speak, in the information, the ideas, the measures of importance that other policy officials take from the press. We noted earlier, for example, in a different context, how an official might use the press to claim the attention of higher policy levels in the State Department for an idea or a problem that he could not bring to the top through regular internal channels.[20] This process is constrained only slightly by the anonymity of sources of stories or ideas or viewpoints. In some cases the

---

[20] Cf., in this connection, George F. Kennan's remarks on the injustice in these "countless occasions" when "the Secretary or the President has been more decisively influenced by some chance outside contact or experience than by the information and advice offered to him through the regular channels." ("America's Administrative Response to Its World Problems," *Daedalus*, Spring 1958, pp. 18-19.)

source, or at least the political location, of stories may be known to other policy makers, or surmised by them, and in other cases it may not even matter whether these things are known at first, so far as their import for others is concerned. The use of the press by officials to test reactions to specific possibilities is, of course, a more-or-less complete process in itself; for every input there is an output, even if it tells the official that no one is paying attention to him. But in a larger sense the policy makers' continuous combing of newspapers to discover reactions to policy developments tends to generalize and extend the significance of the "trial balloon" far beyond whatever narrow purposes might originally have been entertained.

Contributions to the press that are meant to divert reporters from more troublesome problems that policy makers wish to keep under wraps may have serious consequences to the extent that they succeed in diverting other officials as well as reporters. These kinds of diversions, which reach officials in the form of daily estimates of what others in high positions are thinking about or preoccupied with, must be added to the distractions that the reporters themselves provide in their eternal pursuit of the "big story" and of popular "news values." Together they suggest a daily surge of stimuli that impinge on the foreign policy official but have no necessary connection with the longer-range problems of political relations that define the floor, the walls, and the roof of the house he lives in.

There are, finally, some observations to be made here on the subject of policy coordination growing out of common exposures to political stimuli, no matter how discontinuous, or distractive, or irrelevant those stimuli may seem to be. When one ponders the utilization of the press in foreign policymaking, one cannot help but be struck by how much real coordination of policy in an otherwise decentralized political system is provided by the institution of the press. Common exposure, on a continuous basis, to large amounts of information on foreign affairs, and common understandings of the apparent importance of various issues, help to provide a common context for the specialized efforts of large numbers of participants in the enterprise of foreign policy-making.[21]

Without depreciating in the least the impact of the press upon even the specialists in the Executive branch, one might say that there is greater significance in the fact that Congressmen draw their understanding of the world of foreign affairs from a common pool than in the fact that Executive officials do the same. For one thing, the Executive official does not have the Congressman's constituency problem. The Congressman, as a political specialist, is constituency-oriented; and in the course of his ordinary local routine his exposure to foreign affairs information and salience would come to him in large part through constituency or regional media. Living in Washington, however, usually deprives a Congressman of ready access to the local media, and particularly to his local newspaper on the day of issue; but it does provide him, as a part of the new community he lives in, with a new set of newspapers that reflect the dominant public and political interests of that community. The result is clear: despite the wide range of individual backgrounds, despite the low coverage of foreign affairs and the diversity of emphasis that would be found among constituency papers, Congressmen in Washington are exposed in common to a larger amount of information about the world of foreign affairs, and they are also exposed to uniform measures of salience or importance. To be sure, these men bring diverse attitudes and policy orientations with them

[21] "When . . . [Walter Lippmann] returned not so long ago from Russia and later from Germany, his reports were part of the common conversation of the Capital. Every embassy . . . discussed them and reported them to their governments. Members of the Senate Foreign Relations Committee read them and questioned the Secretary of State on his points." (James Reston, "Conclusion: The Mockingbird and the Taxicab," in Marquis Childs and James Reston, eds., *Walter Lippmann and His Times*, pp. 237-38.)

that help to condition the way they seek and utilize information about foreign affairs; yet one might speculate that Congressional consideration of foreign policy might be considerably more acrimonious and unfocused and less consistent and relevant than it now is if its participants were differentially, rather than commonly, informed.

By giving policy makers in both branches an insight into the political perceptions of men with important roles in the political process, the press helps to create common understandings or interpretations of political reality. There is thus some significance for the governmental—and hence public—debate on foreign policy in the fact that both Executive officials and Congressmen draw on approximately the same sources for their wider knowledge of "what is going on in the world," and how important it seems to be. Certain kinds of behavior can thus be reasonably predicted, and mutual expectation can become the basis for policy planning. Despite the specialized and confidential character of the State Department's diplomatic channels of information, continuous and meaningful discourse among foreign policy-making officials in all parts of the government, at all times and at all levels, is possible within the bounds set by this independent source of information and intellectual structuring of policy.

No matter what latitude a Congressman may have in general to vote according to his conscience or to go along with his party on various policy issues, he may still find it necessary to try to "touch base" now and again with opinion in his constituency. But the parochialism that lurks in this necessity, and that is enforced on American politics by the electoral system, seems to be somewhat counterbalanced in the case of foreign policy,[22] perhaps by the continuous tapping of a different stratum of opinion in the leading metropolitan newspapers that circulate in Washington. In this respect, the press

[22] Cf. Miller and Stokes, *op.cit.*

may be helping to create for all Congressmen a common constituency that is a little closer to the national constituency of the Executive branch and that is commensurate with the national responsibility inherent in the shaping of American foreign policy.

CHAPTER VIII

THE PRESS, THE PUBLIC, AND FOREIGN POLICY

● AT A NUMBER of points in the preceding chapters we have referred to aspects of the problem of foreign policy judgment and decision-making by public audiences in the light of low-volume, discontinuous, *post hoc* coverage of foreign affairs in the American press. Here we shall confront more directly the significance of foreign policy coverage for the non-governmental side of the foreign policy-making process, beginning with the notions of the relationship of press to public and to foreign policy that prevail among practicing journalists.

The belief among newspapermen that the citizen's requirement for more and more information about public affairs must be met by wider and wider distribution of news and opinion[1] has its source as much in the historical development of the American newspaper as in the independent elaboration of a democratic political ideology. In the first half of the nineteenth century, the conditions of newspaper publishing favored journals of limited circulation, which were aimed at small and specialized communities of interest. It was only in the latter half of the century that a developing technology and an increasing urbanization made possible the larger journal that "synthesized the newspaper-reading audience by appealing in

[1] Expressed in different ways by reporters and editors, this view gets authoritative restatement in Theodore Peterson, "The Social Responsibility Theory of the Press," in Siebert, Peterson, and Schramm, *Four Theories of the Press*. See esp. p. 91, where Peterson associates "the press" with the viewpoint of the Commission on the Freedom of the Press, as expressed in *A Free and Responsible Press*, Chicago, University of Chicago Press, 1947.

a single paper to a wide range of interests."[2] Once the process was under way, competitive pressures sustained it; the increasing investment that newspapers represented in plant and in news-gathering facilities necessitated increased advertising revenues, which in turn meant that newspapers had to appeal to larger and larger publics by including in one inexpensive paper all the subjects and features that separate audiences had hitherto found in specialized publications. The big city newspaper had acquired much of its present form by the last quarter of the nineteenth century, and set the model for the papers in the rest of the country.[3]

One result of this homogenization of the newspaper was the homogenization of the concept of the newspaper reader; the special interests of special readers were substantially lost in the adaptation of the newspaper to the interests, standards, and pastimes of a mass public that was lightly educated and in the market for diversion and amusement. Foreign affairs, a special subject that would have been easy to handle in the era of special-audience newspapers, came to public attention just at the time when the newspaper had successfully absorbed all areas and all subjects. The means of giving it wide public distribution were thus at hand when the movement for more democratic control of foreign policy spread in the early twentieth century. The juncture of these two phenomena further strengthened the image held by journalists (and others) of an undifferentiated mass audience for foreign affairs who should be and could be reached by foreign affairs coverage in the newspapers and, once reached, would be an unparalleled force, by virtue of its informed opinions, for wisdom and peace in the conduct of foreign policy.

In its capacity to withstand the direct and indirect assaults that have been made on this image in the years since it took clear shape, the American press has demonstrated not only

[2] Bernard A. Weisberger, *The American Newspaperman*, p. 89.
[3] *Ibid.*, esp. chaps. 3 and 4.

its resilience but also its insensitivity to insight and knowledge. One of the earliest and most enduring attacks came from a young journalist; Walter Lippmann brilliantly dissected the theoretical premises underlying the role of the press in the public life of the American democracy, arguing that "It is not possible to assume that a world carried on by division of labor and distribution of authority, can be governed by universal opinions in the whole population. . . . Acting upon everybody for thirty minutes in twenty-four hours, the press is asked to create a mystical force called Public Opinion that will take up the slack in public institutions."[4] The burden of Lippmann's criticism has been supported in recent years by the main lines of social science research in the field of mass communications, and also in the specific area of public opinion and foreign policy. This research has pointed to the differentiation in exposure and receptivity of individuals to communications on various subjects, and has stressed the connections between this communications behavior and political, social, and psychological variables.[5] This line of inquiry in the communications field, focusing also on the different political and social roles of various audiences, has invaded modern schools of journalism and their affiliated research institutions as well

[4] Walter Lippmann, *Public Opinion*, p. 274.

[5] Communications research has been so extensive in the last generation that its output fills two standard bibliographies: Bruce Lannes Smith, Harold D. Lasswell, and Ralph D. Casey, *Propaganda, Communication and Public Opinion*, Princeton, Princeton University Press, 1946; and Bruce Lannes Smith and Chitra M. Smith, *International Communication and Political Opinion: A Guide to the Literature*, Princeton, Princeton University Press, 1956. Representative collections of material on the mass media include Wilbur Schramm, ed., *The Process and Effects of Mass Communication*, Urbana, University of Illinois Press, 1955; and Wilbur Schramm, ed., *Mass Communications*, 2nd edn., Urbana, University of Illinois Press, 1960. The relation between communications behavior and foreign policy has been explored in Gabriel A. Almond, *The American People and Foreign Policy*; James N. Rosenau, *Public Opinion and Foreign Policy*; Lester Markel, ed., *Public Opinion and Foreign Policy*; Bernard C. Cohen, *Citizen Education in World Affairs*; and Alfred O. Hero, *Mass Media and World Affairs*, Boston, World Peace Foundation, 1959.

as their professional journals;[6] yet it has not made much of a dent in the public philosophy of practicing journalists in the foreign affairs field, who seem to possess only the vaguest and most fragmentary notions of whom they are writing for, and the uses that this audience makes of their work.[7] But what are the essential facts of the situation, and what do they suggest by way of alternative possibilities on the part of the press? How much is read, and by whom?

We noted in an earlier chapter that the volume of international news was a small proportion of total news space in most newspapers, and that it was small in absolute terms as well. And we indicated then that if little foreign affairs news was published, even less was read, on the average (a most important qualification). The extent of such readership is suggested in the American Institute of Public Opinion's readership survey of 51 newspapers, conducted for the International Press Institute; of the daily average of 106 column inches of international news from home and abroad that was published, the average number of column inches actually read by adult readers came to 12, or about a half a column. It was further estimated that only two and one-third minutes were devoted to reading this material.[8] Other studies suggest the same general pattern of over-all readership of foreign affairs news.[9]

[6] Cf., e.g., the work of such organizations as the Institute for Communication Research, Stanford University; the Institute of Communications Research, University of Illinois; the Mass Communications Research Center, University of Wisconsin; the Communications Research Center, Michigan State University. See also *Journalism Quarterly*, published by the Association for Education in Journalism, with editorial offices at the School of Journalism, University of Minnesota.

[7] The practitioners are not alone in this respect, as is evident, e.g., in this argument by Theodore Kruglak: ". . . the owners of the American information media have the duty and obligation toward their fellow Americans to reexamine their European news coverage on the basis of their answers to the following questions: . . . 3. Do you think that your present reports are giving the people in your community enough material upon which to base an informed opinion?" (*The Foreign Correspondents*, pp. 122-23.)

[8] *The Flow of the News*, pp. 62-63.

[9] Cf. Hero's canvass of the literature, *op.cit.*, pp. 80-81.

These figures are likely to dismay anyone who is intensely interested in international affairs and who shares a philosophic concern for extensive public participation in foreign policy-making. They are also confusing to newspaper people, who often overlook the fact that these data represent an *average* of very different levels of interest in and exposure to foreign affairs news. The reactions of the press, in the face of this kind of evidence, are manifested in a continuing "debate" over who is to blame for the situation: the public, the newspapers, or both. One point of view claims that the reader sets the pace, that popular demand will not support greater coverage or more analytical content, and that the comparatively low volume of foreign affairs news in American newspapers represents the editors' normal response to lack of reader interest. A United Nations reporter, for example, said, ". . . I don't absolve reporters, editors and publishers and networks entirely of blame in this matter, but they cannot go beyond what the public demands."[10] And a columnist explained why foreign correspondents write material that does not get into the papers: "It goes back to exactly the same thing we've been talking about—the American people are too distracted, too busy, too indifferent. They don't want it."[11] This side of the debate has been able to introduce, as evidence to support its claim, the results of public opinion polls showing that the public is substantially satisfied with the existing amount of

[10] Pauline Frederick, NBC reporter, in UMBS series: "The United Nations Reporter."

[11] Marquis Childs, in *ibid.*: "The Foreign Correspondent." Cf. also Alfred Zimmern, *Learning and Leadership*, p. 46, as quoted in Robert W. Desmond, *The Press and World Affairs*, New York, D. Appleton-Century Co., 1937, p. 169: ". . . the evils complained of [especially sensational coverage, in this case] are not of the newspapers' own creation. They are a response to a public demand." And Edward W. Barrett and Penn T. Kimball, "The Role of the Press and Communications," in American Assembly, *The United States and Latin America*, p. 88: "The pessimistic view of what North Americans will read about Latin Americans prevails, however, even in circles fervently hopeful of an opposite result."

foreign affairs coverage in its newspapers, and is unwilling to see local or national news reduced in order to give more space to foreign news.[12]

In view of the strength of their conviction that the reader determines the character and amount of foreign affairs news that is published, it is interesting that so few newspaper people acknowledge the inconsistencies that it gives rise to: in particular, the common situation wherein the newspaper gives the reader only a minimal dose of foreign affairs news, on the ground that he is not interested in the subject and will not take any more of it, and then puts that small dose on the front page and in lead positions (in line with the recommendations of the wire service budgets), where it presumably responds to what editors refer to as "the public's news values."[13] This circumstance points to the role of the press in forcing foreign policy material to the forefront of policy attention even though the large majority of the population would be as happy to see it sink into oblivion—and indeed immediately consigns it there. It is in this sense that the press should be seen as a significant part of the public audience for foreign policy, a creator of a structure of policy attention that has a very limited additional public audience and may never even be recorded in the mind of the *average* newspaper reader.

The contrary position in this argument is that the state of foreign affairs coverage, and therefore of readership, re-

[12] See, e.g., results of AIPO polls conducted for the International Press Institute between February 16 and May 18, 1953, as reported in *The Flow of the News*, p. 58: "Would you like to have your newspaper reduce the amount of local or national news in order to give you more foreign news?" Would—8 per cent; would not—78 per cent; no opinion—14 per cent. Thomas A. Bailey, in *The Man in the Street*, New York, Macmillan Co., 1948, p. 306, reports comparable results (but no figures) in a 1946 poll.

[13] The only newspaperman I have discovered who seemed to be aware of this anomaly is Louis B. Selzer of the *Cleveland Press*; see his address, quoted earlier, to the newspaper editors in *Problems of Journalism*, 1956, p. 154. Selzer attributed the phenomenon to the influence of the *New York Times* on other editors around the country.

flects editorial choices, and hence that editors and publishers rather than readers are responsible for the current conditions of coverage. News from Latin America provides a current case study of a situation in which the blame for the lack of material in the press is assigned, explicitly or implicitly, to the editors. Barrett and Kimball quote a UPI general news manager, Earl J. Johnson, who said: "After more than 20 years of pushing Latin American news on the wires, I've concluded that very few editors are really interested. Much is said at inter-American press meetings about the importance of printing more news from Latin American countries. But not much is done about it when the North American delegates return to their desks."[14] An Associated Press house organ recently raised the question, "Is there a gap between what managing editors tell us they want and what their papers actually print? . . . Recently Max Harrelson spent two weeks in Canada, then wrote a five-part series on Canada-U.S. relations. William L. Ryan put in two months on a Latin American tour. . . . Harrelson's series was used in 11 of 40 AMs [morning papers] checked. Two articles by Ryan from Brazil showed in 14 of 50 AMs. . . ."[15] Leo Rosten candidly put the responsibility on the editors, with the argument that "giving the public what it wants" is another way of saying "what we [i.e., the editors] *say* the public wants."[16] Another important and familiar claim on this side of the debate is that the average reader is actually a lot more interested in foreign affairs than he is given credit for, and that his disinclination to read foreign affairs material in the press is due to the complexity of the material that is presented to him. The burden of altering this situation is thus transferred to reporters and editors, who are challenged, in Lester Markel's words, to present foreign news

[14] Barrett and Kimball, *op.cit.*, p. 96; Johnson's AP counterpart said much the same thing.

[15] Associated Press, "AP Log," March 2-8, 1961.

[16] Leo Rosten, *The Washington Correspondents*, p. 268.

"in terms that are correct, concise and, above all, clear."[17]

Finally, there are others who are frankly puzzled over the location of responsibility, or who regard it as a "vicious circle," with both parties equally at fault. Thus, "Newspapers do not emphasize foreign affairs because the people are not interested, and the people are not interested because they do not find much foreign news in their papers."[18] This position is no doubt closest to the truth in the sense that the pattern of coverage is a response to perceived interests and priorities at both ends of the line. When the editor fails to draw attention to a subject because the prevailing news judgments give priority to other topics, then the majority of readers who are only marginally interested are not persuaded that it is important enough to read; and the editor in turn looks at the readership figures and draws justifiable conclusions about what people are reading. But the vulnerable part of this chain of reasoning, and of the whole argument, is the failure of the vast majority of reporters and editors to differentiate among their readers[19]— to understand that some of the public *will* read more foreign affairs news if it is offered to them, even though there may be no new recruits to the over-all readership ranks of foreign affairs news. What patterns of readership are involved here?

Readership of foreign affairs news is a poorly understood subject despite the attention that has been paid to the problem of audience analysis in communications research. One reason for this is that efforts to delineate the audience structure of

[17] Lester Markel, "The Flow of the News to Marilyn Monroe," *Problems of Journalism*, 1960, p. 77.

[18] Martin Kriesberg, "Dark Areas of Ignorance," in Lester Markel, ed., *Public Opinion and Foreign Policy*, p. 62. Barrett and Kimball cite Herbert Matthews of the *New York Times* on "the vicious circle of Latin American coverage. . . . The failure to provide the news perpetuates the ignorance of the reader, and this ignorance leads to the lack of interest." (*Op.cit.*, p. 87.)

[19] In Chapter IV we noted that some correspondents expressed an awareness that they were writing for a less-than-mass market, but that on the whole, apart from a handful of newspapers and correspondents, this had little impact on foreign affairs reporting.

the media of mass communication have rarely focused explicitly on foreign affairs news as a classification of newspaper content. Another reason for the uncertainties is that the available data are apparently misleading, in the sense that they appear to overstate both the extent and the depth of newspaper reading in the foreign affairs field. To ask a sample of respondents where they get their information about foreign news events,[20] and to learn that between 44 and 50 per cent of the respondents get most of their foreign affairs information from newspapers and a similar proportion from the electronic media, implies a level of exposure and information-seeking that exaggerates the true state of affairs.[21] Similarly, to learn that "For their news on foreign affairs, more than 90 per cent of the population depends principally on . . . the radio and the daily newspaper,"[22] or even that about 90 per cent of the population reads a daily newspaper, is also suggestive of a much higher state of exposure to the news in it than is actually the case. Studies of communities deprived of newspapers in the course of strikes make the point that newspapers fulfill social and psychological functions more often than intellectual or intelligence functions, even when readers express their loss in terms of missing "what is going on in the world."[23] A more accurate impression of the extent of reader-

[20] Cf. surveys by NORC and AIPO, the former quoted in Paul Lazarsfeld and Patricia Kendall, *Radio Listening in America*, New York, Prentice-Hall, 1948, p. 34, the latter in *The Flow of the News*, p. 58, both of which are cited in Theodore Kruglak, *The Foreign Correspondents*, p. 41n.

[21] Cf., e.g., the data of this kind on p. 58 of *The Flow of the News*, and the data showing the low levels of information actually held by readers, on the pages immediately following.

[22] Cf. Martin Kriesberg, "Dark Areas of Ignorance," in Markel, ed., *Public Opinion and Foreign Policy*, p. 60.

[23] Bernard Berelson, "What 'Missing the Newspaper' Means," reprinted from Paul Lazarsfeld and Frank N. Stanton, eds., *Communications Research, 1948-1949*, in Wilbur Schramm, ed., *The Process and Effects of Mass Communications*; Charles F. Cannell and Harry Sharp, "The Impact of the 1955-56 Detroit Newspaper Strike," *Journalism*

ship of international news is suggested by data from a survey in Albany, New York, in 1949.[24] Forty-seven per cent of the respondents read "just the headlines" of the national and international news, 4 per cent did not read even that much, and another 4 per cent read "not much more than headlines." At the other end of the spectrum, 6 per cent claimed to read both kinds of news "very carefully," and another 1 per cent read international news carefully, but not national news. In the middle, 33 per cent picked and chose among items, and "sometimes read carefully, sometimes not." V. O. Key's interpretation of these data is that "Day in and day out the odds are that less than 10 per cent of the adult population could be regarded as careful readers of the political news,"[25] and one would have to knock a few percentage points off even that figure for news of foreign affairs.

Who are these few careful readers? They seem to be the same few people who show up as well-informed on repeated surveys of information on international affairs, the people whom Gabriel Almond called the "elites" and the "attentive public."[26] Readership of foreign affairs news increases with age, education, and economic status; with an increase in these variables, the newspaper is used increasingly for information and decreasingly for entertainment; more men than women read such news; the larger the community (counting suburbs

---

Quarterly, xxxv, No. 1, Winter 1958, pp. 26-35; Penn T. Kimball, "People Without Papers," *Public Opinion Quarterly*, xxiii, No. 2, Fall 1959, pp. 389-98.

[24] Survey Research Center, *Interest, Information, and Attitudes in the Field of World Affairs*, Ann Arbor, Mich., 1949; these data are reproduced in V. O. Key, Jr., *Public Opinion and American Democracy*, as Table 14.5, p. 352.

[25] Key, *op.cit.*, p. 353. He also suggests the importance that should be attached to headlines over national and international news stories, when that is all that half the people read; the suggestion is made via a reference to Percy H. Tannenbaum, "The Effect of Headlines on the Interpretation of News Stories," *Journalism Quarterly*, xxx, No. 2, Spring 1953, pp. 189-97.

[26] *The American People and Foreign Policy.*

as part of metropolitan areas), the higher the interest in and readership of international events. Basically, however, it is educational level and socio-economic status that seem to be the best predictors of newspaper readership of foreign affairs.[27]

The significance of all this is generally missed by newspapermen, many of whom tend to think that the market for foreign affairs news can be—and should be—enlarged by techniques of simplifying the news and making it more attractive,[28] or even by providing more of it.[29] But an individual's exposure to foreign policy communication and his interest in international affairs that directs that exposure are concomitants of attitudes that have deep roots in his psychological orientations and his social setting.[30] And so long as this is the case, the important variables in determining interest and participation in foreign affairs and exposure to information on the subject will be found chiefly in the life patterns of individuals, in the things that are relevant to their perceptions of and orientations to the political universe, and only marginally in such ephemeral things as the way foreign affairs stories are written for the newspapers, the amount of pictorial or human-interest content in them, and so forth.[31] These relevant variables

[27] Cf. Wilbur Schramm and David M. White, "Age, Education, and Economic Status as Factors in Newspaper Reading," reprinted from *Journalism Quarterly*, XXVI, No. 2, June 1949, in Schramm, ed., *Mass Communications*, pp. 438-50; and Hero, *op.cit.*, esp. chap. 4, "Newspapers and World-Affairs Communications," which summarizes much of the literature on this subject. See also Key, *op.cit.*, and Kenneth P. Adler and Davis Bobrow, "Interest and Influence in Foreign Affairs," *Public Opinion Quarterly*, XX, No. 1, Spring 1956, pp. 89-101.

[28] Cf. *The Flow of the News*, pp. 67-83; and Chapter IV, *supra*.

[29] Cf. the remark of Herbert Matthews quoted above: "The failure to provide the news perpetuates the ignorance of the reader, and this ignorance leads to the lack of interest."

[30] Cf. the extensive literature on attitudes and attitude change; esp. M. Brewster Smith, Jerome S. Bruner, and Robert W. White, *Opinions and Personality*, New York, John Wiley and Sons, 1956; and Carl I. Hovland, Irving L. Janis, and Harold H. Kelley, *Communication and Persuasion: Psychological Studies of Opinion Change*, New Haven, Yale University Press, 1953.

[31] Cf. W. Phillips Davison, "On the Effects of Communication," *Public Opinion Quarterly*, XXIII, No. 3, Fall 1959, pp. 343-60.

change slowly, and they are not readily amenable to modification by the stream of information the very exposure to which they in fact regulate. Consequently, the hope that the audience can be expanded significantly by a greatly simplified discussion of foreign affairs is illusory. It is no doubt true that most newspaper readers find foreign affairs news rather complicated and difficult to understand, but it does not necessarily follow that their interest would be stimulated if the material were presented in more simplified ways or more abundantly. It is equally likely that their basic disinterest in the material contributes to their impression of its difficulty. Furthermore, even if the hope were not illusory, even if one could succeed in attracting substantially larger numbers of readers to a discussion of foreign affairs that has been simplified by the use of pictures and one-syllable words, leavened with human interest, and related to everyday life on Main Street, the degree of simplification involved would be so great as to cause some doubt whether there would be any net increase in the capacity of the American people to understand and think through the undeniably complex issues of international relations. In other words, simplification might succeed in drawing a new audience, but to material that is so far from reflecting difficult international political realities as they confront responsible statesmen that it has no politically relevant public opinion uses.

Since the available evidence suggests that the chief market for foreign affairs coverage in the American press is a small policy and opinion elite, and a somewhat larger attentive public whose personal characteristics and interests are much the same as those of the policy and opinion elite, though their roles are not so specialized, it is important to think about foreign affairs coverage in terms of its relevance and usefulness for the professional and personal interests and needs of this audience. This argues for a quantitative and qualitative improvement, an up-grading, of foreign policy news and comment, rather than the down-grading that is implicit in the attempt to attract new people into the audience. What this up-grading would mean for reporters and editors we shall explore further in the next chapter. But two problems immediately arise in connection with such a suggestion, and should be disposed of first: the philosophical problem wrapped up in "the people's right to know," and the practical problem of ensuring the survival of newspapers and even cultivating their prosperity through mass circulation.

Let us consider the latter first. The present endeavors of reporters and editors represent a compromise between the foreign policy interests of a few and the news values or tastes of a mass audience that "ought" to be interested in foreign affairs but presumably has to be seduced into reading about them. The practical effect is that the specialists and the attentive few are thus drawing and depending heavily on material written for a mass market that is relatively indifferent to the effort made on its behalf. This compromise is clearly not to the taste of any of the parties involved. Those who are steady consumers of foreign affairs news are dissatisfied with the daily fare they get in almost all American newspapers, to judge from the comments of foreign policy officials and of Congressmen, from the running criticism of the press in intellectual circles, and from the 8 per cent of the population who would like to see newspapers reduce the amount of local or national news in order to make more space for foreign news.[32] The large majority that rarely or never looks at foreign affairs news is most likely neutral towards its presence, in the sense that it is merely something these people walk around; but their non-readership is itself a good measure of their preference for other kinds of newspaper content.

It is possible to conceive of ways to satisfy the needs or preferences of a small audience for a higher order of foreign policy intelligence without raising the costs of publication, and without changing the character of a newspaper in ways

[32] See fn. 12, *supra*.

that might alienate the larger numbers of non-readers—granting, however, that we do not even know what kind or proportions of material would give offense to people who do not read it.[33] The important obstacle, it would seem, has been thinking about this problem in the context of the customary shape and format of the daily newspaper. But there is no reason why larger amounts and different kinds of foreign affairs content, whatever its sources, need take up more front-page space than at present, or be reflected more often in the dominant headlines. Since it would be meant to serve a specialized audience, it could be handled like other materials that have few customers, like financial news or shipping news (or even materials like comics and sports that have many customers!): whatever was not deemed important by conventional standards could be put in an unobtrusive place without much regard for format, headlines, and the other trappings of "news." It is possible in this way to think of substantially increasing the amount of foreign affairs information in the average newspaper without changing the over-all identity of the newspaper and with only a very marginal increase in the costs of production.

Since such an endeavor would take nothing away from the present exposure of the general public to foreign affairs news, there could be no complaint about it on philosophical grounds that cannot already be leveled at the mass media. Despite the low level of attentiveness to problems of foreign policy and the low priority given them by the public at large, one can justify the general order of importance that the press attaches to a few foreign policy questions on the ground that it is important to pretend that everybody is listening—that acting *as if* foreign

[33] As we pointed out earlier, there is no satisfactory evidence on what makes a paper succeed or fail, so far as the amount of space it devotes to international affairs is concerned. For the argument that "a publisher with the necessary resources and talents who wishes to run a paper with serious international content may make a go of it even in relatively 'unfavorable' communities," see Hero, *op.cit.*, p. 101.

affairs were of widespread public interest has important consequences in the realm of public confidence in the basic actions of government. This particular function, however, can no doubt continue to be served by the present (comparatively small) allocation of front-page foreign affairs news, thus permitting us to think about additional coverage more in terms of the particular needs of particular audiences. In any case, since there is considerable evidence that much of the information on world affairs currently at the disposal of the general public comes to it not directly from the media but at one remove or more, via people who have a greater interest in the subject and expose themselves to mass media discussions of it,[34] any alternative that increases the flow of information and analysis to these primary consumers should result in a subsequent larger flow to *their* secondary audience. Thus the broad political-philosophical purposes of press coverage of foreign affairs can be served by additional news that is directed primarily towards its few direct and heavy readers than to its many marginal scanners.

Further support for this argument stems from the point, made earlier, that the press is itself one of the most important components in the public audience for foreign affairs. From this point of view, greater press responsiveness to foreign policy developments and problems of foreign affairs, even in the form of specialized inside-page coverage of them, would inherently enlarge the scope of interaction between the government and its foreign policy public. Hence, increased coverage and more substantial analysis of more specialized problems as well as of issues already "in the news" would be an important contribution to democratic foreign policy-making even if this material were read only by foreign policy officials and a small group of attentive citizens. At its best, it might narrow the

[34] See Key's summary of the literature on these propositions, *op.cit.*, pp. 359-66; in addition, see Elihu Katz, "The Two-Step Flow of Communication," *Public Opinion Quarterly*, xxi, No. 1, Spring 1957, pp. 61-78.

range within which major miscalculations in policy might be made as a consequence of insufficient exploration of alternatives and their implications within the confines of a bureaucratic structure, and as a consequence of insufficient interchange of value premises and preferences among policy officials and articulate people on the outside. The history of America's China policy after the Second World War should stand as a vivid reminder of the things that can happen when the political interests of outside publics have not been engaged in policy discussion and formulation.

But a problem still confronts us. There are also many historical examples of rigidities introduced into foreign policy when the political interests of outside publics *have* been engaged—for instance, America's China policy after the Korean War. This reminds us that wide public participation is not the only criterion of a good foreign policy, or the automatic guarantee of one.

CHAPTER IX

CONCLUSION

———••——

NO MATTER where one starts in an attempt to explore the significance of the findings in the preceding chapters, one quickly comes back to the massive central issue in the debate among scholars and among political and journalistic practitioners concerning the place of the press in American foreign policy-making. This issue, which we can abbreviate here as the competing demands of diplomacy and democracy on the organization and conduct of foreign affairs reporting, is clearly at the base of many of the attitudes and modes of behavior we have been discussing. The argument between those who attach the highest priorities to the needs of diplomacy for privacy, and those who attach the highest priorities to the needs of democracy for publicity and information, reverberates through modern American history. The issue has never been settled, nor have the lines ever been sharply drawn —and for good reason. From President Wilson's unparalleled articulation of the principle of openness and his simultaneous pursuit of privacy, to President Kennedy's outspoken defense of privacy and his thoroughgoing openness to reporters, we see the chronicle of a political system in pursuit of central values that, in their purest expression, are incompatible.

The priorities placed on privacy by the responsible foreign affairs specialist are upheld by many scholars and by some journalists who focus on the substantive problems of formulating intelligent and effective decisions and actions in foreign affairs, and on the political and administrative problems of managing a foreign policy establishment so that it "speaks with one voice" in support of those decisions and actions. The spokesmen for this set of values regard the press as a disturbing intruder, violating the necessary security of the administrative process and upsetting the delicacy of international relationships. But while the defense of privacy rests on the question, "How can we run a foreign policy if the press is heavily involved and dedicated to early exposure?", the defense of publicity asks, "How can we run a democracy if the press is not so dedicated and involved?" Journalists are supported in this question by scholars, too, and even by foreign policy specialists, sometimes as a matter of principle and sometimes as a matter of policy. Their case for heavy press participation runs in the opposite direction from the defense of privacy; it involves doubts about administrative infallibility in foreign policy, and a deep-seated preference for widespread participation in political decision-making.[1]

These alternative viewpoints run so deep, and are built so firmly into the structure of the American political system, that they have come not only to define much of the relationship between press and government, as we have seen, but also to create further problems for the political system. The official wants the press to serve his interpretation of the government's interests—to publish his version of reality where publication promises a good return, and to refrain from publication whenever the official has any doubts about the wisdom or propriety of disclosure, or even its convenience, since the larger the

[1] The extraordinary events in connection with the blockade of Cuba in the Fall of 1962 clearly illustrate both of these positions. The attitude of the Administration, which imposed an elaborate set of restraints upon the regular channels of information (subsequently celebrated as "news management"), was well expressed by Robert J. Manning, Assistant Secretary of State for Public Affairs: "We are now dealing with question [sic] involving the possible incineration of men. Negotiations are very complicated and very delicate and we must use a great deal of discretion." (*New York Times*, November 2, 1962.) The issues between the Administration and the press were explored by James Reston in his column, "Washington," in the *New York Times*, November 2, 1962, and by Max Frankel, "Kennedy vs. the Press," in the *New York Times*, November 19, 1962. See also the transcript of the President's press conference of November 20, 1962, in the *New York Times*, November 21, 1962.

circle of interest, the greater the number of people who want to share in the policy decision. The press, from his vantage point, should be motivated at every step by the policy maker's sense of the national interest. But the journalist generally believes that the national interest, whatever it may be, is best served by maximum disclosure, by full freedom of information, and he wants to exercise his own judgment, to publish his own interpretation or version of the reality that he thinks is important or newsworthy while it is still fresh and new. No wonder, then, that some people in each of these camps regard the press and the policy-making institutions as "natural enemies."[2] Both the reporter and the official are constantly concerned to find ways to improve relations between the foreign policy agencies and the press, but this usually means that each side wants the kind of understanding and acceptance from the other that would permit it to achieve its own preferences in the way of coverage.[3]

The very confrontation of these viewpoints, however, creates a new reality. Not only are there two institutionally different ways of looking at the role of the press in the foreign policy arena; more importantly, there is a further set of consequences growing out of these opposing attitudes and behaviors. The way the press operates in the foreign policy field—suspicious and skeptical of the motives of officials, slapdash and occasionally inaccurate in its approach to problems, anxious for a good front-page story sometimes even when the consequences of publication are adverse for policy—makes most policy officials distrustful, secretive, defensive, and nervously sensitive to the disruption and damage that a

[2] Cf., e.g., Charles E. Bohlen, quoted in Joseph and Stewart Alsop, *The Reporter's Trade*, p. 18: ". . . 'officials and reporters are natural enemies, because the reporter always wants just what the official should not give him.' " See also Cater's description of the Acheson-Reston exchange of sentiments on Acheson's last day of office as Secretary of State. (*The Fourth Branch of Government*, p. 20.)

[3] For the same contest in the field of military reporting, see Joseph Mathews, *Reporting the Wars*, pp. 204-5.

careless or inaccurate or premature story can leave in its wake. But the way the officials behave, in turn, underpins the reporters' suspicion of official news sources, sharpens their distrust of the self-seekers, and in general throws them back on their own inadequate resources for the bits and pieces that make up the stories they put together on their own. The result is foreign policy coverage that is spasmodic, piecemeal, impressionistic, and oversimplified, sometimes inaccurate or garbled, and generally failing to deal with policy issues until they have become matters of public record. In other words, the prevailing structure of attitudes that reporters and policy makers hold toward each other and toward their respective functions sustains all the other tendencies (which we noted in prior chapters) toward discontinuity and superficiality in the press treatment of foreign affairs.

Furthermore, the operational rules of the reporter's craft— those that define the reporter's main job of impersonally and objectively transmitting an account of the things that are happening day by day—often have the effect of ceding the initiative in the creation of foreign policy news to the foreign policy official, since he is in a good position to say what has been happening on any particular day. On the other hand, the most common attitude of foreign policy officials toward reporters—"We don't seek them out; they come to us with questions"—has the effect of handing the initiative right back to the reporter, who will ask questions stimulated by existing news stories in the absence of any new happenings. One result is the loss of a lot of foreign policy information, since neither side accepts any responsibility for a thorough, comprehensive airing of events and developments; and discontinuity and lack of intellectual structure mark the foreign affairs coverage that does emerge. Another outcome of this process is an enhancement of the impact, on the total pattern of foreign policy coverage, of those few people in government and in the press who are independently active as "in-putters," who do not accept the premise that as individuals they cannot influence the market in foreign policy news.

The partisans of each side in the debate between the claims of democracy and those of diplomacy have the advantage of contesting on only one clearly marked front, and in a lifelong institutional battle. The person who sides with neither is likely to draw the fire of both. Nevertheless, the important (though obvious) conclusion is that, given the commitment both to democratic institutions of policy-making and to national security politics on an international scale, neither point of view can be regarded as "right" to the exclusion of the other. The competition between the two should be seen not as an argument between sense and nonsense, as the participants often put it, but rather as a continuing *political* question with strength on each side that varies from occasion to occasion. The foreign policy institutions have obvious political resources in this encounter, but the press, drawing both on its favored position in American political philosophy and on its practical usefulness to foreign policy officials, is also a political actor of tremendous consequence.

Viewing the relationship between the press and policy officials as a political competition suggests that it might be appropriate to restate the public-policy aspects of the "problem" of the press. The question is not merely how to create for foreign policy officials an information environment in which they can pursue security policies singlemindedly and efficaciously, or how to create for journalists—and thus for the public—ever wider and more timely access to the critical decision-making points in the foreign policy structure. More centrally, the problem is how to influence the terms in which this political competition is waged, so that it loses some of its zero-sum character, its "I win, you lose" flavor. In other words, we should be searching for modes of behavior from the participants that minimize the costs, in terms of one set of these values, of advancing the other set. We are interested both in effective foreign policies *and* in democratic procedures for reaching them, and what we should be asking from the press and from policy officials are attitudes and approaches that increase the area of compatibility between them.

We have been concerned throughout this book with the effects of the existing pattern of press coverage of foreign affairs on the foreign policy-making environment; but it seems clear from this analysis that the press itself is such an important institution in the policy-making network that *any* pattern of press coverage would leave a substantial mark of one kind or another on the participants and thus on the process. If the logic of our inquiry up to this point suggests that we might usefully explore some alternative patterns of foreign affairs reporting, we should do so in the light of our understanding that any different mode of behavior by reporters, editors, or their news sources in the government would have some bearing on the political competition between press and policy makers. And if we are interested in increasing the compatibility of privacy and publicity in foreign policy-making, then we should be sensitive to the impact of possible changes in the nature and production of foreign affairs news on these two values.

What leads us to consider different patterns of foreign affairs coverage? Our reasons lie in our belief that the existing pattern poorly serves the manifest interests of those who share in the formation of foreign policy. Although drawing issues to the forefront of policy attention, the press—in its choice of issues and in its treatment of them—at best contributes only randomly to intelligent policy-making in the democratic context, and at worst is destructive of coherence and planning in the pursuit of foreign policy objectives.

Alternatives to the present state of affairs are not without their problems. The chief difficulty is created by the fact that the work of the press is read by non-governmental and governmental audiences simultaneously, so that the coverage best suited to maximize intelligent participation by opinion elites—which is to say, more systematic, analytical attention to issues in advance of decisions—may for that very reason be likely to impair the flexibility of response and the imaginative exploration of alternatives that we hope for in our foreign policy officials (though such coverage might also be of substantive interest to them). The converse may present no fewer difficulties. Coverage that is useful to the policy maker—that gives him better political information on the issues he must contend with every day and a higher quality of analysis of those issues—would also be useful to the opinion elites and attentive public that represent the democratic process as it operates in foreign affairs. But here, too, the mere process of simultaneous exposure inescapably helps to shape the issues and alternatives in the public eye to which the policy makers must respond, no matter how "prematurely" in terms of considered exploration of alternatives.

Each of these sets of possibilities, however, focuses more centrally on both of the values we seek than does the present course. Since the basic audience for foreign affairs information is the relatively small policy and opinion elites, and a somewhat larger though less active attentive public, a conscious effort to serve the interests of *either* the policy *or* the opinion elites (as we have defined those interests above) would do more to enhance the values of *both* "diplomacy" *and* "democracy" than does the present process of treating foreign affairs largely as a commodity for mass consumption, a process that ostensibly aims to further the value of democracy through publicity but in reality serves the interests neither of intelligent policy-making nor intelligent public participation.

The practical forms that this conscious effort might take contain many elements of controversy—not only because they are so different from the present way of doing things and pose utterly new standards, but also because they cannot be wholly neutral as between the two sets of values that are contending here. What is involved in this search for better political information and analysis of a higher quality?

To begin with, asking for more systematic, more analytical, more theoretical coverage of foreign affairs raises a basic problem in the identification and treatment of news. United States foreign correspondents are distributed around the world in an uneven pattern, concentrated in the major capitals and news transmission centers, and spread out thinly over other areas of the world.[4] When events make the grade as news in one of the less well-covered areas, there is an influx of correspondents and the coverage increases dramatically. If a reporter has been sent to an area at some expense in order to cover "the news," there is at least an implicit understanding between the correspondent and his editors that he will send in a good stream of reports and that they will be published. This news flow lasts until the interest of the journalists is captured by events elsewhere and the reporters move on. The result, particularly in a world of rapid political change, is an apparently random pattern of coverage, where events break into the newspapers with dramatic suddenness and their antecedent conditions get explored only in the midst of the crisis. The issue is kept "in

[4] Figures on the number and distribution of foreign correspondents keep shifting, because the number of correspondents abroad is constantly changing and because different observers use different standards in their classification of reporters abroad. Kruglak, e.g., estimated that in the mid-1950's there were 286 American correspondents working full-time for all the U.S. information media in Western Europe, and that these constituted about 75 per cent of the world-wide force of full-time American correspondents. (*The Foreign Correspondents*, pp. 72ff., 112.) Another account several years later agreed with this number of correspondents in Europe, but put that number at slightly less than half of the world-wide force of full-time American correspondents. (E. G. Burrows, in UMBS series: "The Foreign Correspondent.") For earlier data, see Russell F. Anderson, "News from Nowhere: Our Disappearing Foreign Correspondents," *Saturday Review of Literature*, November 17, 1951, cited in Karl W. Deutsch, "Shifts in the Balance of Communication Flows: A Problem of Measurement in International Relations," *Public Opinion Quarterly*, xx, No. 1, Spring 1956, p. 147.

the news" for a while, but the events themselves generally develop slowly, so the daily account is augmented by considerable recapitulation of preceding developments. The repetitiveness of the accounts thus makes an issue look like an old and familiar friend—yet it is just as quickly forgotten when a new situation draws the spotlight. The disorder in this pattern is magnified by editors, as we noted earlier, when they print only a small part of the uneven, discontinuous coverage that comes to them from the reporters.

To reverse this pattern of coverage would require a different attitude on the part of both reporters and editors toward the writing and publishing of material that is not "news" in the customary, contemporary, meaning of the term. To cite an obvious example, if the processes of political development are significant to American foreign policy when they are dramatic or violent or revolutionary, then they are no less significant in the interstices of those events when the elements of change are taking shape in undramatic, less spectacular form. Typically, however, most news is thought of as discrete, tangible, hard—an event that has happened. Even those who criticize this kind of news accept its basic definition; Kruglak, for example, echoes many reporters when he writes that the "*whys* of these news events are more important than the news itself."[5] But if news is viewed as the flow of information relating to contemporary issues, on the basis of which political opinions take shape and decisions are made, then the "whys" are *an integral part of the news itself* rather than something extra that needs to be justified as equally important or even more important. If there is some policy significance in the information that comes from the press, why must that significance remain implicit as a matter of doctrine—i.e., the worship of objectivity—and as a matter of practice—i.e., the customary separation of reporting and interpretation as two quite distinct enterprises handled generally by different people? Some theory

[5] Kruglak, *op.cit.*, p. 10.

of causal relationships is necessary to any evaluation of the importance or significance of events; if the applicable theories are explicitly cultivated and aired, then the nature of relevant information—i.e., "news"—becomes easier to ascertain.[6]

Reversing the prevailing trends of foreign affairs coverage would call not only for different attitudes toward "news," but also for different modes of distributing correspondents around the world in order to gather it. In an area where United States correspondents are not resident, the newspapers and wire services now have either to depend on foreign nationals for their stories, or to import their own correspondents after a particular event has broken into the headlines. In the latter case, as we observed above, there will be a tendency to "overreport," so long as the correspondents feel they have to provide hard news coverage of front-page quality in order to pay their way. The use of foreign nationals, on the other hand, which is an extensive practice having historical antecedents in the use of foreign journals or foreign news agencies as sources of news,[7] raises questions concerning the criteria of significance that underlie the selection of relevant news. If the news is rigorously objective and "hard," in order to minimize possible biases, then it suffers all the defects that we earlier associated with this conception of news; and if it is more analytical and evaluative, then it becomes important to know what theories are shaping interpretations and selections—i.e., who is drawing the relevant maps of reality. A possible (though expensive)

[6] Walter Lippmann was stating the importance of a substantive theory of international relations when he told a group of Nieman Fellows that "he conceived of his column as an effort to keep contemporary events in such perspective that his readers would have no reason to be surprised when something of importance occurred." (Harry S. Ashmore, "Apostle of Excellence: The View From Afar," in Marquis Childs and James Reston, eds., *Walter Lippmann and His Times*, p. 159.)

[7] Cf. Edward W. Barrett and Penn T. Kimball, "The Role of the Press and Communications," in American Assembly, *The United States and Latin America*, pp. 94-97; Kruglak, *op.cit.*, pp. 19, 25; and J. Mathews, *op.cit.*, p. 47.

way out of this dilemma would be for United States news media to maintain resident American correspondents on a full-time basis in places where they are not presently found—particularly in non-Western regions, but including Western countries away from the "cockpits" of world politics. These would be correspondents who operated in the context of the new attitudes toward news discussed above. Thus they might not feel compelled to manufacture hard news events every day, nor would their editors expect such dispatches. The editors would have at their disposal on a continuing basis a more extensive range of policy-relevant information and analysis; but to make use of these regularly requires much more space than the average, or even the better-than-average, newspaper currently allocates to foreign affairs. This adds force to the recommendation in the preceding chapter of a way to achieve more extensive coverage of foreign policy developments for a small but specialized audience.

For changes of this kind in foreign affairs coverage to take place, new standards of training and competence for foreign affairs correspondents, and for their editors, would be necessary. The burden of these requirements rests most heavily on the prevailing conception of news, and on the related notion that a good reporter of news in any context will be a good reporter in the foreign affairs field. The parallel between the foreign affairs correspondent and the diplomat, which was suggested earlier, merits further attention here, for it affords a wholly different context within which to think about the meaning of being a "good" reporter of foreign affairs.

The reporter and the policy official frequently admire one another's personal qualities and professional competence, yet they are so bound up in the daily struggle with each other that they do not see that the competition between them grows in part out of the very similarity in their functions. The professional Foreign Service Officer says, "The two professions—journalism and diplomacy—are antithetical. Their job is to get news, to find things out." The reporter, too, though he often aspires to be a policy maker, sees a major difference between the two: he demands *expertise* as the major qualification for a diplomat or intelligence man, yet he often asks no more of himself than "experience" in the business of reporting. But the similarity of their function in supplying political intelligence to the foreign policy-making process—often even to the same audiences within that process—is striking, and not without historical counterpart or significance. In the early eighteenth century, for example, diplomatic representatives actually served as active foreign correspondents for newspapers; subsequent experiences and developments have changed the nature of specialization in performing this intelligence task, but not the nature of the task itself.[8] To the extent, then, that the reporter and the diplomat share this same function, it is useful to think about training them in similar ways. This is not to say that the correspondents should be treated like diplomats, but rather that the professional equipment of both groups should be re-examined in the light of the common function to be served.

Much of the emphasis in public discussions of the professional qualifications of both the diplomat and the foreign correspondent has been on such things as foreign-language competence, ability to understand another society and culture and to empathize with its people, and correctness of behavior. Problems that have long troubled the Foreign Service—e.g., how to identify the thin line between staying at a foreign post long enough to learn something and staying there so long as to lose perspective—are familiar in the newspapers' front offices

[8] Cf. Joseph and Stewart Alsop, *op.cit.*, pp. 47-48, where the authors compare their judgments about the future of the French in Indo-China with those of the diplomats, and find theirs superior. Reinhold Niebuhr, however, focusing on the wide public audiences of the journalist-commentator, likens him to the professor rather than to the diplomat. ("The Democratic Elite and American Foreign Policy," in Childs and Reston, eds., *op.cit.*, p. 174.)

and in the literature of journalism.[9] These are real problems, to be sure, and useful qualities and skills, but they do not tackle the central issues involved in the selection and analysis of political data for political audiences. What seems to be required, in addition to these tools of the trade, is more explicit training in theories and modes of analysis of international relations and foreign policy—the kind of intellectual equipment that not only provides substantive criteria for differentiating degrees of foreign policy relevance and significance in events, but also suggests hypotheses that might be tested among the data available to reporters wherever they might be. The reporters may not recognize the need in terms of substantive or theoretical competence, but this is surely what is meant in statements like this: "There's a great deluge of facts. The problem is to get space for people who understand these cultures, who have some more profound concept of what this whole struggle of the world is about, and all its ethnical and cultural and religious as well as military and political aspects."[10]

Competence of this kind would help to free the correspondent from the tyranny of headlines, from the obligation to report foreign affairs within the context of the prevailing market for hard news of wide and immediate appeal, and thus from his helplessness vis-à-vis an official who knows the rules of the reporter's trade well enough to use them for essentially self-seeking purposes. Such competence would also provide the correspondent with some counterweights to the unavoidable biases or constraints that develop from the reporter's need to be trustworthy in the eyes of officials, and his need to establish and maintain close associations with good sources within the foreign policy establishment. All in all, it would enable him

[9] Cf., e.g., Robert Desmond, *The Press and World Affairs*, pp. 42-47. Desmond's discussion of the correspondent resembles Harold Nicolson's treatments of the diplomat.

[10] Eric Sevareid, in UMBS series: "The Foreign Correspondent."

to serve the major market for foreign affairs news with policy-relevant information of more long-run significance.

This position could be achieved only after comparable changes in the outlook of all those associated with the production of news—of officials who have access to information, and also of editors and publishers who have the final responsibility for the shape of news in the newspaper and thus for the going market for "news." Just as the correspondent requires some theoretical competence to differentiate the relevance of data independently of what may be in the headlines, so do editors need comparable criteria to inform their "play" of the news independently of recommendations based on mass-consumption standards.[11]

But a trained competence is only one of the attributes that does—and will increasingly—distinguish the can-openers from the gourmet cooks among the foreign affairs correspondents and commentators. In this field, as in every other, it is the bright and able people who do the best work and who can assimilate the best training. It is all the more important, then, as far as future recruiting is concerned, to establish the political significance of foreign affairs reporting, and to treat it at least on a par with the Foreign Service as a career for promising young people. We do not expect our reporters in the Foreign Service to serve their apprenticeship in police courts or sports palaces; why should we continue to rely on such a system of apprenticeship for our newspaper reporters?

Because our interest in this book has focused on the press, we have been concerned chiefly with possible modifications in the practices of journalists. Were reporters and editors to act in accordance with the new understandings suggested above,

[11] "Looking back, we have the impression that the importance of Marshall's speech [on aid to Europe, at Harvard, in 1947] was grasped immediately and that decisive action quickly followed. Actually the implications of the Harvard speech went largely unrecognized. Only the *Washington Post* gave it prominent front page coverage." (Holsey Handyside, "The European Recovery Program: A Case Study," p. 12.)

the policy official might find in the press something approaching a public version of the private flow of political intelligence. This should improve the information on which he can act, as well as diminish the distractions that mass-media standards introduce. To the extent that it does the latter, it might even increase rather than reduce the policy alternatives that are open to him. But the policy maker is a source of news as well as a consumer of it, and he can exercise some influence on the public-information environment within which he makes his decisions. What might we ask of him in such an altered environment?

One might hope that in a situation where reporters were professionally as interested in the developmental aspects of international political relations as in the hard news aspects of current events, the official might find more grounds for cooperation with reporters. For if policy officials could help to narrow the gap between their own definitions of developing situations and those that prevail among interested groups on the outside, they might have less reason to fear that public "intrusion" in the policy-making process would be disturbing in its impact.[12] We may grant the principle, for example, that governments at times must lie to save themselves, but the principle is not controlling unless we can agree on the definition of the situation—that is, on the nature and magnitude of the dangers that a particular government faces. Fortunately, however, these are not the circumstances that most commonly confront us. Information is power in the foreign policy sense,

[12] But the fear can never be completely done away with. For one thing, officials will continue to disagree among themselves, as well as with "outsiders," on the definition of developing situations; and for another, the very *fact* of reporting, independently of the content, may be a disturbing intrusion for the official because it affects the importance accorded to issues. Cf. Ben H. Bagdikian, "Washington Letter: The Morning Line," *Columbia Journalism Review*, I, No. 3, Fall 1962, p. 28: "For what the newspaper story does, especially on foreign affairs, is to take the initiative away from the specialists and force a decision by politicians, or at least by men who must take politics into account."

as Assistant Secretary of Defense Arthur Sylvester has argued, and one may also grant the necessity for governments to manipulate it on occasion as they would other instruments of national power. But precisely because information is power, one can expect that others in a democratic system will demand access to it. And since foreign policy officials in a democratic society also need the power that comes from public acquiescence in and support of the choices they make, they may be expected to have an interest in finding new and viable ways to accommodate themselves to those demands.

INDEX